BODY AND CAUSE IN HOBBES:
Natural and Political

BODY AND CAUSE IN HOBBES:
Natural and Political

by
Martin A. Bertman

Longwood Academic
Wakefield, New Hampshire

© 1991 by Martin A. Bertman

All rights reserved—no part of this book may be reproduced in any form without permission in writing from the publisher, except by a reviewer who wishes to quote brief passages in connection with a review in a magazine or newspaper.

Published in 1991 by Longwood Academic, a division of Hollowbrook Communications, Inc., Stoneham Road, Wakefield, New Hampshire 03872-0757, U.S.A.

Printed in the United States on acid-free paper.

Library of Congress Cataloging in Publication Data:

Bertman, Martin A.
    Body and cause in Hobbes: natural and political / by Martin A. Bertman.
       p. cm.
    Includes bibliographical references (p.) and index.
    ISBN 0-89341-636-3 (cloth)
     1. Hobbes, Thomas, 1588-1679. 2. Causation—History—17th century. 3. Political science—Philosophy—History—17th century. I. Title.
B1247.B46   1991
122'.092—dc20   91-12806
                                                                         CIP

To the memory of Bernard Willms, 1931-91.

He would have provided a sharply witty Latin phrase for this occasion; that is remembered within the larger sentiments of our friendship.

TABLE OF CONTENTS

Preface viii

Part I: Agnostic Metaphysics

Chapter 1. Body and Body in Motion 3

Chapter 2. The Order of the Sciences 17

Chapter 3. Nominalism and Protagorean Humanism, with the appendix, "On Identity" 27

Chapter 4. Heidegger on Hobbes' Nominalism 47

Chapter 5. Action and Reference 73

Chapter 6. Causality and Inner Design Metaphysics ... 99

Part II: Political Science

Chapter 7. Unsociable Man and his Virtues 113

Chapter 8. Equity as Justice and Charity 145

Chapter 9. The Character and Use of Civil Law 163

Chapter 10. Hobbes and Xenophon's *Tyrannicus* 183

Afterword. Hobbes, Kant, and Hegel as Political Theorists 197

Notes 211

Index of Proper Names 219

PREFACE

I will not assert that to be a great philosophy it is necessary to have something of a system, where concepts are both clear and distinct in themselves, and correlated to other concepts, perhaps allowing aristocratic primacy for a few and assuring hierarchical schematization for the system through deduction. Insight, or what Thomas Hobbes called "quick wit," can, like a good joke or aphorism, provide therapy, a clarified vision. Heraclitus does this; so, sometimes, does "wisdom literature" such as the "Pirke Abboth" of the Jewish *Mishna*. Nietzsche recognized the power of aphorism and called for a science of interpretation (*auslegung*) for a person to grow in consciousness towards his (own) deepest insights. In a certain sense, those who have a commitment through belief have often grown in the "fullness" of that belief by wrapping it in agreeable knowledge.

But whether it is the cognitive opacity of a root belief or the primary concept that commands in its system, there is advantage in attaching such principles to the greatest vastness of reach. This has the advantage of explanatory unity. In the instance of a belief, however, the unity may be simply psychological; even paranoic madness shows the unity of a guiding principle by way of a forced misinterpretation or spurious explanation. In a more amiable spirit, many great philosophers have been attracted to the benefits of systematic explanation, because the unity it offers has something of a public credential. It is a unity that seeks a security from idiosyncratic, indefensible principles and the error of unjustified conceptual alignments.

Thomas Hobbes is certainly such a philosopher. His political sense of individuality guarded by community—that is, by the State—has an analog in his view of science as a human interest which is publicly expressed through mutually agreed language whose definitions allow for deductive explanation. Nevertheless, it is obvious that in order to move from the generality of this depiction, it is necessary to examine Hobbes' fundamental concepts in their particularity. The present book begins by examining Hobbes' view of body and causality, and continues with an analysis of certain political and legal issues enriched by the previous examination. The basal concepts, in cooperation with the derivative—though methodologically crucial—concepts of purpose and science will provide for the particular range and limits of Hobbes' thinking, and be valuable in understanding his "civil science." Indeed, Hobbes defines philosophy itself as depending on these concepts: "*Philosophy* is such knowledge of effects and appearances, as we acquire by true ratiocination from the knowledge we have of their causes or generations: And again, of such causes or generations as may be from knowing first their effects." (*EW*, I, 4) And again, "Method, therefore, in the study of philosophy is the shortest way of finding out effects by their known causes, or of causes by their known effects." (*EW*, I, 66)

Hobbes' conception of both "true ratiocination" and cause, developed in the midst of the inventiveness and discoveries of the "new science" of the seventeenth century, is paradigmatically different from the scholastic Aristotelian orientation of previous centuries. This is certainly true of the theological Aristotelianism centered in Paris, but it is also true of the "scientific" School of Padua, where Galileo taught and Harvey, Hobbes' friend and benefactor, studied; according to Hobbes, Galileo and Harvey are the only inventors of new sciences since Euclid. Hobbes himself claims to be the inventor of the science of civil philosophy or political science, as well as of the science of dioptics. Indeed, complications in interpreting Hobbes result because the concept of purpose, which is the hallmark of Aristotelian science and philosophy, is necessary to his political doctrine, whereas explanations based on final or purposive causes are denied by Hobbes in his philosophy of nature. This seems to create a methodological schism in his thought.

As Homer spoke of Odysseus, his hero of the quest, as "a man of many devices," so one may speak of Hobbes. Hobbes, as we shall see, tries to avoid making man so special that, in the last resort, his differences from other natural creatures amount to treating him as supernatural. Consequently, despite his politics demanding purposive explanations of human action, that high road is provisional and, on a deeper level of physical explanation, it collapses into a nature understood without reference to final causes.

The tension in Hobbes between his political philosophy and his natural philosophy, putatively not contradicting each other, is clearly seen when Hobbes tries to hold the proposition that though the will wills purposively in man (and in other animals), it is determined by causal chains, which denies to it any fundamental additional principle of action other than the efficient causality which applies to nature. This means that the internal operation of deliberation or calculating interest is reducible to a view of all of nature, including man, as explainable in terms of *external motions*. This of course brings forward the question of moral responsibility.

Seemingly, moral responsibility is ultimately reducible to matter in motion and determined—like the motion of billiard balls or a toothache—by an externally oriented method where the pain and pleasure of moral music becomes the mathematics of motion. Like Pythagoras' great discovery that music can be explained publicly by mathematics, it seems that Hobbes' moral world with its "hidden inwardness" of conscience can be explained by treating man as a machine. This explanation seems the reductive one which keeps man a natural creature and not a supernatural one.

In their discussions on the nature of the human will, Bishop Bramhall pressed our "monster of Malmsbury" about the existence of God, and in fact Hobbes' natural philosophy seems to have no place for God. To this, Hobbes' strong response is to separate belief from knowledge: he argues that the way in which Bramhall understands God—as an object of belief and, indeed, a being without body—can hardly be subsumed under the laws of cause and effect. Yet, our man of many devices has a speculative argument whereby God can reasonably be considered as first cause, since the natural system demands in principle an explanation from outside it of the world as a complex of causes. God seems to provide the initial efficiency for the natural order, i.e., its creation. This speculation adds difficulties. If God is responsible for the natural order, then God seems responsible for the actions that men call immoral.

Though the mechanistic orientation of the new science, with its triumphs, posed a challenge to rethink man, the world, and God, in classical times there had already been a debate that contained some noteworthy similarities. On one side in this debate was Aristotle's understanding of reason and cause[1]; on the other side were the Stoics and, to some lesser extent, the Skeptics. This ancient debate reminds us that the notion of cause did not always focus on the explanation of events, a connotation habitually held after Hume. The four causes or, perhaps better, factors (*aitia*) of Aristotle—the efficient, material, formal, and final—provide a descriptive explanation of the existential quality of things, including how a thing can be what it is, by the final or purposive cause.[2] The ontological force of this expalantion obviously has a linkage to the rationality of the natural order; Sextus Empiricus spoke of cause quite differently when he limited the notion to the active or efficient cause (*energetikon aition*): "the cause is that because of which in virtue of its being active the effect comes about." (*Ph.* III, 14) The Stoic view (especially that of Chrysippus) makes the same point even more clearly. Seneca says: "The Stoics take the view that there is just one cause, that which does something (*facit*)." (*Ep.* LXV, 4) Further, Seneca provides insight into how the Stoics argued against using the notion of cause for Aristotle's four factors or for Plato's five, even undercutting the material cause. Seneca says, "That something is a necessary condition does not mean that it is a cause." (*ibid.*)

It is in this sort of explanation, limited to description of action considered as the movement of a thing or an event, that Hobbes relies upon when he supposes that the world system was caused by God. There is no need to give any further reason or value for this. In fact, since for Hobbes nothing else can be predicated of God, a non-material entity, God's rationality or His goodness cannot even be assumed except as a belief. The names that are predicated of God, Hobbes tells us, are merely for the sake of honoring Him; they do not (from nature) explain anything. But if, indeed, Hobbes reduces moral considerations to physical motions, he must relegate all values merely to a perspective of human beings (and other animals) which, for a more fundamental understanding, has the neutral value of merely happening. The distance between one's humanity and this possibility of a person's deepest understanding grows out over what one is tempted to call an abyss. The proud may be humbled by this God, but there is no sharing of values with Him. This sort of God doesn't ask his reluctant and immature prophet Jonah whether he would want the Creator of the World to destroy Nineveh, a city with a multitude of persons and many cows (*behemoth*).[3] Perhaps, in the end, the most interesting question is how Hobbes understands man in relation to values. This question cannot be answered without understanding how Hobbes discusses reason and cause in relation to nature and to human nature.

This book weaves new and recently published materials into a pattern for understanding and questioning Hobbes. Some of the material herein was written for other occasions, and I ask the reader's forbearance in regard to any stylistic shifts, repetitions, and unsmooth transitions. Material that has previously appeared has come from articles in *Hobbes Studies,* the Hobbes issue of *History of European Ideas, Thomas Hobbes: De Metaphysique a la Politique,* and *Hobbes Oggi.*

PART I:
Agnostic Metaphysics

CHAPTER ONE

Body and Body in Motion

The chapter in Hobbes' writing which immediately precedes his discussion of body, and the initial chapter of Part II of *De Corpore,* subtitled "The First Grounds of Philosophy," provide a thought-experiment that seems meant to be a literary parallel to Descartes' striking *fabula* at the beginning of his *Meditations*—and to oppose the conclusions Descartes had drawn there. Hobbes had already criticized the *Meditations* when it was circulated by Mersenne before publication, and his criticism is available to us along with Descartes' reply to Hobbes.

Hobbes begins by "feigning" the annihilation of the world with the exception of someone "to consider as the subject of philosophy, or at all to reason upon; or what to give names unto for ratiocination's sake" (*EW,* I, 7, 91) With this, Hobbes proposes a similar therapeutic physical isolation with an initial atmosphere of solipsism by holding to the rule that he would doubt anything that he cannot know with certainty. This certainty must be so firm that it cannot be overturned by the most outrageous probability invented by the imagination. Hobbes doesn't go the route of provisional solipsism based on doubt; he merely interrogates the memory of his feigned isolated human being. Yet, Descartes' objection to the reliability of memory to provide knowledge is not in force against Hobbes. He can readily agree with Descartes on the common observation that memory is unreliable in any particular instance to provide a certain recollection of a past event. But however wrong the particular recollection, it will contain such concepts as space, time, and body, which must be considered the "counters" of our thinking. And it is precisely that which Hobbes wishes to discover. With such a discovery, and the definitions that result from it, Hobbes does not promise a certainty free from skepticism, but rather the concepts necessary for thinking. This is in line with Hobbes' objection to Descartes' approach that it remerchandises old skeptical quibbles. Instead, the argument about the actual existence of the memory is avoided to get to a categorical structure of the human mind. It is not the individual—i.e., Descartes—thinking, it is any man, and this provides at the outset the anthropological emphasis that one finds also in Aristotle, before Hobbes, and in Kant, after him. Hobbes comments on his privative thought-experiment:

> Now things may be considered, that is, brought into account, either as internal accidents of *our* [my italics] mind, in which manner we consider them when the question is about some faculty of the mind; or as species of external things, not as really existing, but appearing only to exist, or to have a being without us. And in this manner we are now considering them. (*EW*, I, 7, 92)

Perhaps it may still be asked how Hobbes could respond to any persistent Cartesian who points out that any concept so arrived at could be doubted as applying to any world; on the rule of strict certainty, it is doubtable that such a world is there or ever has been there. To this, I believe Hobbes would reply as Wittgenstein did about solipsism—that such a doctrine or quibble is maintainable but silly, since it would mean such a disorientation of our life in the world that nothing would make any sense.

For Hobbes the concept of body is so basic that without it nothing makes any sense; it is so fundamental that it orients the rest of our conceptual apparatus—concepts like space, time, number, part, whole, etc. But by Hobbes' definition of "body," body exists independent of ourselves. Ingeniously, Hobbes substitutes the notion of body for Descartes' notion of God as the perfect being in which is contained the necessity of the existence of that being. For Descartes, the existence of the Perfect Being implies the existence of the world. In Hobbes, the concept of body provides directly for the existence of the world, that is, of an existence external to ourselves. We must think that the world exists or at least existed, if we think. With Ockhamite parsimony (and with a play on the future words of La Mettrie to the King), Hobbes might have said to Descartes, "Sir, God is a certainty with which the world can do without." In that we have provided Hobbes with a joke, it is well to point out that the thought-experiment provided by Hobbes himself is a bit of a joke. Its punch-line is that we conceive of a man existing without a world, including his own body; it is a philosophic jest that exposes itself as such just by the philosophic point it provides.

If we take this as a piece of comedic subtlety in Hobbes, can we not, by considering the matter yet further, find a tragic subtlety also? We have seen that we must consider body to exist independent of ourselves; nevertheless, we cannot consider any particular body without its most common accidents of motion and magnitude, and accidents are exactly the result of the body acting upon us. Before Kant, Hobbes made of a body a *ding an sich*, a thing-in-itself which is disclosed by our nature and not by its own. The Protagorean "man the measure" wins out here, and it is the limits of being man that is the essence of the tragic. Indeed, Descartes shows his Platonism by his ontological argument for the existence of God. He argues that the existence of God is known with the greatest degree of certitude; His existence is even more certain than that of our own existence, since it is forced upon us by the *lumen naturalis*, the light of nature, through a recognition of our limitations. Descartes argues that the existence of a Perfect Being is contained positively in the idea of perfection. Brandt's depiction of Descartes as "a philosopher of extension," ignoring his theological idea, misses what is deepest in Descartes; and by the same token, his characterization of Hobbes as "a philosopher of motion," rather than of body, misses what is deepest in Hobbes.

Because for Hobbes extension or magnitude is so invariably conceived when body is considered—except if we feign for the sake of mathematical calculation that a body is two-dimensional like a point or a line—it is Hobbes rather than Descartes who is better called the philosopher of extension. And since the central thesis of the atomists is that matter cannot be destroyed, it can be seen from Hobbes' own words how he can be considered as one of their party:

> . . . though we may imagine something to rise where before was nothing, and nothing be there where before was something, yet we cannot comprehend in our mind how this may possibly be done in nature. And therefore philosophers, who tie themselves to natural reason, suppose that a body can neither be generated nor destroyed, but only that it might appear otherwise than it did to us, that is, under different *species,* and consequently be called by other and other names; so that which is now called man, may at another time have the name of not-man; but that which is once called body, can never be called not-body. But it is manifest, that all other accidents besides magnitude or extension may be generated or destroyed; . . . and therefore bodies, and the accidents under which they appear diversely, have this difference, that bodies are things and not generated; accidents are generated, and not things. (*EW,* I, 8, 116-7)

For Hobbes, then, extension is "the essence of body" (*ibid.,* 117), since that which is called the essence of something is "that accident for which we give a certain name to any body, or the accident which denominates its subject." (*ibid.*)

The intimacy of the accident of magnitude or extension to the concept of body poses difficulties. It gives a privileged status to extension that may be epistemological or ontological or both, and it is the choice among these possibilities that is the difficulty.

Consider how Hobbes speaks of extension as real space in contrast to imaginary space:

> The extension of a body, is the same thing with the magnitude of it, or that which some call real space. But this magnitude does not depend upon cogitation, as imaginary space doth; for this is an effect of our imagination, but magnitude is the cause of it; this is an accident of mind, that of a body existing out of the mind. (*EW*, I, 8, 105)

We have seen that body for Hobbes is a substance and magnitude is an accident. As substance, which has already been brought forward with the Kantian phrase *ding an sich*, it must exist. Such a positing of a substratum is also in the philosophies of Aristotle and Locke. And to such a positing, there has always been a philosophical reaction because of a residual unrationalizable aspect in such a positing. The substratum seems necessary to its proponents to explain how accidents, which involve the nature of our own minds, are caused by an existent independent of us. The problem is obvious: the positing, however deeply intuitive or *a priori*, is merely an epistemic strategy, and what is posited has only this to warrant it ontologically. Hobbes does not do less, though he doesn't develop a metaphysics from this positing.

Attend to how Hobbes treats imaginary space. It is a useful epistemic device, he says of physics: "That space, by which word I here understand imaginary space, which is coincident with the magnitude of any body is called the *place* of the body; and the body itself is called the *thing placed*." (*ibid*.) "Motion is the continual relinquishing of one place, and acquiring of another." (*EW*, I, 8, 109) "That is, it is said to be at rest, which, during any time, is in one place; and that to be moved. . . [which] was formerly in another place than that which it is now in." (*ibid*., 110) All this talk about place allows for the mathematics of physics, since as an imaginary construct it can be treated as a point which is occupied by a body and the change of place can be treated as a line: it is graphic through the invention of Descartes' co-ordinates or geometric in Galileo.

But, then, is real space or extension Hobbes' "ghost in the machine"? A thoroughgoing methodological nominalism would consider it so, but Hobbes does not. Yet, that it is an accident of body allows for an *epoche*, that is, a suspension of considering it ontologically for the sake of some imaginative manipulation. But that it is the *essential* accident of body brings the imaginative treatment, e.g. in the science of physics, seemingly to depend on the more fundamental conceptualization of philosophy, with the one piece of privileged knowledge (and the one piece of knowledge not properly belonging to either science or philosophy) the ontologically posited body. So, we see the ontological-epistemic nexus in Hobbes' thought to be body, and again recall that it has a much similar function in his thought as the concept of God had for Descartes.

There are difficulties for Hobbes which must be discussed more clearly because of the intimacy of extension or real space and body. Because of this intimacy, it is impossible for the mind not to consider that a body does not have extension when considered ontologically and, therefore, that real space or extension does not travel with the body when it is moved, that is, fills a place. But this seems to take body to be a rigidly determined entity. This doesn't seem to leave a conceptual place for *conatus*, the theory that assumes that bodies are constantly moving internally. There seems to be a gap between the fundamental positing of body and the consideration of bodies in motion.

I believe that Hobbes does not consider the rigidity of a body as an epistemological device, but that he treats the concept of conatus as such. It is extension, not motion, that is for Hobbes the essence of body, though we have already quoted Hobbes to the effect that both are the most common accidents of body. Indeed, upon giving that characterization, he continues with a methodological *apercu, viz.,* "This place therefore most properly belongs to the elements of geometry." (*EW*, I, 15, 203). He then defines 'endeavour' or 'conatus': "I define endeavour to be motion made in less space and time than can be given; that is, less than can be determined or assigned by exposition of number; this is motion made through the length of a point, and in an instant of time." (*ibid.*, 206) Obviously, conatus is not treated as ontologically fundamental. Its benefit is as a device that allows for flexibility in mathematical treatment of motion, so any particular motion can be further considered as refinable or divisible and so to be a container of other motions, and so infinitely allowing body as quantity, time, and motion to be divided. So it seems from Hobbes' explanation of the concept:

> For the explaining of the above definition it must be remembered, that by a point is not to be understood that which has no quantity, or which cannot by any means be divided; for there is no such thing in nature; but that, whose quantity is not at all considered, that is, whereof neither quantity nor any part is computed in demonstration; so the point is not to be taken for an indivisible, but for an undivided thing; as also an instant is taken for an undivided, and not for an indivisible time. (*ibid.*)

The evidence seems to allow us to take conatus as a pragmatic epistemological device. But how are we then to take the expression "in nature" in Hobbes' explanation? Is nature itself a construction, an epistemological device? If not, and if we return to an ontological perspective, we not only inherit Zeno's paradox, but we cannot make sense of identification when we consider body to be equivalent to appearances or phenomenal bodies. Of the ontological body we cannot say it is one or many, we cannot say it is a whole and therefore made of parts, we cannot say it is the same as us or different from us. Here we seem to have Parmenides revisited. Unless, that is, we take the positive aspect of its definition, *viz.*, "coincident or coextended with some part of space" to mean that real space is disclosed in its characteristics by the imaginary space of mathematical physics. The difficulty is that real body, or body as it exists aside from our grasp of it, initiates a work or action to cause phenomenal bodies. One the one hand, we can in no way understand this action. On the other hand, because of this action, through not being able to conceive of it except by the accident of real space or extension, we depict body in terms of accidents—mental classifications—that Kant called categories of the understanding. We seem to be put in the uncomfortable position of having an opaque ontological entity, body, whose actual existence is implied by a construction, phenomenal nature, which we realize is merely the human perspective and, therefore, inadequate to escape the imagination, an epistemic selfishness.

Since it is necessary that motion involves the relinquishing of space, as place, and that a body when moved "keeps always the same magnitude (or extension or real space) both when it is at rest and when it is moved; but when it is moved, it does not keep the same place" (*EW*, I, 8, 105), we see the tension in Hobbes' ontological and constructive considerations. Is motion to be considered to be part of Hobbes' construction or part of his ontology? Gary Herbert comments, "Descartes built his theory on the doctrine that body and extension are identical, but fails to draw the conclusion obvious to Hobbes, that space is thereby made phantasmal, that is, subjective."[1] What I have shown is that body and extension are not identical for Hobbes, from the consideration that one is substance and the other an accident; yet, this accident is the essence of body. As such, it is to be considered as coextensive with body so that when once this connection is made, body has the properties of an object, inhabiting a place, and capable of being moved by another body contiguous to it. Therefore it is open to the numerous operations of the imagination, e.g., division. Body as object and its extension are taken to be identical, except when considering the other accidents which characterize objective bodies. Thus there is an identity in the consideration of matter but not in the consideration of form. But it is precisely, one must suppose, this lack of identity with the form, and also the process for attaining some sort of form, that provides a cogent reason for Hobbes to identify body as substance with its essential essence, extension. For it is the substance that—aside from extension, its essential accident—allows other accidents to result in the form of (phenomenal) bodies.

Surely it is not fortuitous that the penultimate topical division of the *De Corpore* chapter "Of Body and Accident" turns to Aristotle's notion of first matter, *materia prima*. The comment seems to warrant what I have concluded to be Hobbes' position:

> And as for that matter which is common to all things, and which philosophers, following Aristotle, usually call *materia prima*, that is, first matter, it is not any body distinct from all other bodies, nor is it one of them. What then is it? A mere name; yet a name which is not of vain use; for it signifies a conception of body without the consideration of any form or other accident except magnitude or extension, and an aptness to receive form and other accident. So that whenever we have use of the name *body in general*, if we use that of *materia prima*, we do well. (*EW*, I, 8, 118)

Thomas Spragens, in *The Politics of Motion: The World of Thomas Hobbes*, writes, "In Hobbes's world the Aristotelian configuration of purposeful, finite movements had disappeared entirely. In their stead remained a homogeneous swarm of incoherent, aimless perpetuations of momentum that had no capacity for growth, for fulfillment, or for rest."[2] Quoting this passage, Jeffrey Barnouw writes, "Hobbes did indeed strip the natural world of Aristotelian teleology, and this had a profound effect on his conception of the character of human goals and desire, but he resolutely affirmed that purpose had its origin and place in human life, and that purposes could be understood therefore not as established from the beginning in the objective structure of nature but precisely as emerging from human experience and open to change within experience."[3] In another article, written a year or two before, Barnouw begins by saying, "Purpose is a kind of cause for Hobbes, but not in the same way it is for Aristotle, because Hobbes takes final causes, where they are really causes, to have their effect as efficient causes. This conceptual 'reduction' of purpose to efficient causality is sometimes seen as a denial of purpose, as if Hobbes was carrying over into human psychology the banishment of final causes from nature that was a prominent feature of the 'new science' of the seventeenth century, in order to frame a strictly mechanistic model of mind."[4]

What I have tried to do in this book is to stress that ultimately the successfulness of Hobbes' thought must be judged on his ability to reconcile the lack of purpose or teleology in nature with its central place in the understanding of human action. Even Hobbes' theology, which espouses the doctrine of mortalism[5]—the need for a person to be resurrected in the body to be alive—tilts toward a naturalistic view of man in order not to be in opposition to reason. Purpose in man is a perspectival and, therefore, epistemically useful fiction which, in the end, must give way to the non-purposive method of physics, i.e., the most general treatment of the motions of natural things. Spragens' emphasis on the latter, therefore, can be seen to be an attempt to grasp Hobbes' deepest thought on the human condition. In his conversations with Bramhall, Hobbes himself seems to have to wished to keep the discussion private because it involved matters too harsh for public consumption. He says:

> A wooden top that is lashed by the boys, and runs about sometimes to one wall, sometimes to another, sometimes spinning, sometimes hitting men on the shins, if it were sensible of its own motion, would think that it proceeds from its own will, unless it felt what lashed it. And is a man any wiser, when he runs to one place for a benefice, to another for a bargain. . . and seeth not what are the lashings that cause his will? (*EW*, V, 53)

Those lashings are of course our desires, which can be called our purposes. There is competition among our desires.

Led by ingenuity, a person attempts to satisfy them all. When he cannot satisfy them all, a person must satisfy the strongest force, which may be a single desire or some group of them. A preference for perhaps satisfying desires B+C+D over desire A, even when A is preferred in itself to either B or C or D, shows that the preference or value is based on the force made by their accumulated motions, as Hobbes sometimes speaks of it. Such a calculation of desires and aversions is the basis of the concept of purpose, yet this does not offer us more than a description of how we choose, i.e., an efficient causal analysis. It does not provide us with what we ought to choose, where "ought" is considered either in terms of best interest or of a moral consideration. Now, indeed, for many philosophers and for Hobbes also in his own way—as we shall see—the ought of interest and the ought of morality converge. Nevertheless, the matter at hand makes for the observation that Hobbes, unlike Aristotle, does not ultimately provide final causes to explain the choice; he does not propose that man is a certain sort of creature in a rational order, so that his fulfillment as the sort of species-being that he is requires this choice (and context) rather than that choice. Instead, Hobbes simply asserts a perspectival basis for purpose in human choice and the lack of an "art for obtaining all desires." Of course, Hobbes has a point in that there is a limit to our inventive *virtu* in taming circumstance. (The Hobbesian analysis of the origin of the State makes that clear.) Further, Hobbes does allow that one can err by miscalculating the consequences of one's choice, either through a lack of knowledge or through bad technique. Yet, unlike Aristotle, for Hobbes *no desire is faulted for itself,* though the consequences of acting on some desires seem inevitably to lead man to a future where he is harmed (e.g., smoking). To recognize this, to reason rightly, does provide for policy or the organization of activity in a purposive way, even though there is nothing intrinsically bad in any desire. Even death, to which men (usually) have the chief aversion and fear, can be taken circumstantially. For Hobbes' naturalism, though death is a boundary condition for having any desire, a life with great pain can make death a good. So, also, Hobbes can say that lying and treachery in war are to be accounted virtues. By Hobbes' emphasis on circumstance, he shows himself to be of the party of common sense and, also, of the opportunist opponents of the Platonic tradition.

I will later elaborate upon Hobbes' similarities with the sophists. But, as I have conducted the argument here, I think Barnouw is mistaken in maintaining that Hobbes does not have "a strictly mechanistic model of man," since I think I have shown, even in the brief and incomplete remarks above, that Hobbes reduces purpose to the mechanisms of calculation or reason, a quantitative calculation, and the motions of desire. And this means Hobbes offers a strict mechanism despite, as Barnouw points out, Hobbes' using "purpose" and "goal" to explain some human actions from the perspective of consciousness. What is misleading, as Hobbes suggested in his analogy of human action to the spinning of a top, is the element of human consciousness. Unaware of the mechanism of his decisions, a person has the proud illusion that the will wills itself rather than that the will is an epiphenomenon of the human mechanism. Purpose taken without further ado is an error of such pride.

Many Hobbes scholars have accepted the judgment of Frithiof Brandt in his classic book, *Thomas Hobbes' Mechanical Conception of Nature* (1927) when he emphasizes Hobbes' attention to motion. Brandt writes, "when Hobbes has been, and still is, called a materialist, this is in a certain sense misleading. The concept of matter plays an exceedingly small part and has a constant tendency to disappear. Hobbes should more correctly be called a motionalist, if we may be permitted to coin a word. He is the philosopher of motion as Descartes is the philosopher of extension."[6] Spragens seems to accept this judgment, as evidenced by his book's title, *The Politics of Motion*; so does J.W.N. Watkins in *Hobbes' System of Ideas*. Also, recently the articles of Barnouw and Gary Herbert's *Thomas Hobbes: The Unity of Scientific and Moral Wisdom*—to mention particularly interesting discussions—have emphasized that Hobbes' concept of conatus or endeavor, which influenced Leibniz and seems conceptually felicitous with the calculus, qualified or even opposed Hobbes' mechanism. Herbert writes, with the imperceptible motions of body or conatus in mind: "Brandt's observation, which is surely correct, becomes more difficult to understand if it is simply incorporated into the traditional view of Hobbes' natural philosophy, and taken to reflect a rigorous mechanics. Mechanics makes no provision for the generation of bodies from pure motion. The individuated world of things could not be accounted for exclusively by mechanics. . . For Hobbes, motion is not merely mechanical (though it may be discussed mechanically). The smallest and most fundamental of motions, *conatus,* is an endeavor. It is the nature of this smallest of motions to oppose and resist other motions."[7]

I think these scholars have understood Hobbes wrongly on the subject of the relationship of matter (or better, of body) to motion. They have given much attention to the concept of *conatus* and, in their enthusiasm for it, they have mislaid Hobbes' own emphasis on body. For Hobbes, motion cannot be considered without body, but body can be considered without motion. Motion is an accident of body—"Motion and magnitude are the most common accidents of all bodies" (*EW,* I, 15, 203)—and "an accident is that faculty of any body, by which it works in us a conception of itself." (*EW,* I, 8, 103) The human mind has the working concept of motionless body, but it cannot have the notion of bodiless motion. Of course, the concept of conatus, of the constant motion of every body (including those that are for certain purposes called bodies at rest) is a hypothesis introduced to provide a theoretical correction of our sense experience (and our *illusion* of a self moving moral will). The fundamentality of the concept of body is not undercut by this. For Hobbes, body, unlike the accidents of motion or magnitude, does not depend on "a working on us." Indeed, it provides the structural occasion for that working, and so it must be considered external to ourselves and independent of us—*viz.,* Hobbes' definition: "a body is that, which having no dependence upon thought, is coincident or coextended with some part of space." (*EW,* I, 8, 102)

We know from ordinary sense experience that, at least sometimes, bodies can be experienced as being at rest. Hobbes' theory of their essential or constant motion is actually testimony to the sophistication of Hobbes' thought rather than a contradiction in it. To assume it is a contradiction involves a conflation of Hobbes' levels of explanation. When we turn to a focussed discussion of Hobbes' nominalism as the underpinning for his theory of science, it will be apparent that multi-leveled discourse is, for the most part, practical and practicable. It should be noted as well that conatus provides a necessary mechanistic concept (*pace* the above-named scholars) for a physical theory of human decisions which considers desires as either competing or cooperative physical forces—that is, as additions or subtractions in the conscious process of deliberation leading to choice. The will is the last of the internal motions before the external motion of acting. The physical description of human physiology complements the awareness of introspection, the method which Hobbes uses for discovering the psychological basis of his science of politics. The appetites located by introspection are brought squarely under a mechanistic perspective (just as motion in general, at the level of basic concepts, or the grounds of philosophy, is better explained in terms of pushes and pulls) by conatus, *viz.*, "for where there is an appetite, the entire cause of appetite has preceded; and consequently the act of appetite could not choose to follow." (*EW*, I, 25, 409) Just so, Hobbes provides the following physical theory of human and animal action:[8]

> Wherefore (from the initial sensitivity of the embryo in the womb) appetite and aversion are the first endeavours of animal motion. Consequent to this first endeavour, is the impulsion into the nerves and retraction again of animal spirits, of which it is necessary there be some receptacle or place near the origin of the nerves; and this motion or endeavour (*conatus*) is followed by a swelling and relaxation of the muscles; and lastly, these are followed by contraction and extension of the limbs, which is animal motion. (*EW*, I, 25, 408)

CHAPTER TWO

The Order of the Sciences

In the *Iliad,* Zeus boasts that if he were atop Mount Olympus and all the other gods were below, attached to him by a golden cord, they would not be able to pull him down, but he would be able to pull them up. The fundamental principle of an intellectual system should stand in something of this relationship to subordinate principles. Hobbes suggests that his project is systematic when he provides the order of things to be demonstrated. After giving two properties of demonstration, *viz.*, rules according to proper syllogisms and having the first premises of all syllogisms arrived at from first definitions, he gives this order:

> ... that after definitions, he that teaches or demonstrates any thing, proceed in the same method by which he found it out; namely, that in the first place those things be demonstrated, which immediately succeed to universal definitions (in which is contained that part of philosophy which is called *philosophia prima*). Next, those things which may be demonstrated by simple motion (in which geometry consists). After geometry, such things as may be taught or shewed by manifest actions, that is, by thrusting from, or pulling towards. And after these, the motion or mutation of the invisible parts of things, and the doctrine of sense and imaginations, and of the internal passions, especially those of men, in which are comprehended the grounds of civil duties. or civil philosophy.

> And that this method ougnt to be kept in all sorts of philosophy, is evident from hence, that such things as I have said are to be taught last, cannot be demonstrated, till such as are propounded to be first treated of, be fully understood. (*EW*, I, 6, 87-88)

These remarks were presented nearly a decade after the publication of *De Cive*, the book in which Hobbes claimed he had founded a science of politics based on the natural facts of the human passions, derived through introspection, and checked by the experience of human behavior. He tells us he wrote the last part of his system before the first because he hoped that it would ameliorate strife in his country by teaching his fellow citizens their political duties. Despite this motive, why are these duties justified by a science when that science is presented independently of what he later claims is necessary for it to be "fully understood"?

Hobbes completed his system by publishing the second of the three parts after over twenty-five years had elapsed; *De Homine* appeared in 1658. In its Dedication, Hobbes again comments on the character of the topics of his system:

> Having completed this section, *De Homine*, I have finally fulfilled my promise. For you now possess the prime elements of my philosophy in all its divisions and subdivisions. Moreover, it happens that the two parts whereof this section consists are very dissimilar. One is very difficult, the other very easy; one consists of demonstrations, the other of experience. One can be understood by few, the other by all. They are therefore somewhat abruptly conjoined; but this was necessary, granted the method of my work as a whole. For man is not just a *natural* body, but also a part of the state, or (as I put it) of the body *politic*; for that reason he had to be considered as both man and citizen, that is, the first principles of physics had to be conjoined to those of politics, the most difficult with the easiest. (*H*, "Dedication")

The State is an artifacted entity, but it has its ground in human nature. The natural carries through into human fabrications, though there is a somewhat epistemologically different treatment of each. But here our difficulty arises again. Can the purpose which is implicit in any fabrication be reduced to more fundamental natural principles where purposiveness is unpacked as mere efficient causality? This assumption is seemingly necessary for the first of the above quotes: the "fully understood" of political action here demands—intellectually, though not practically—more than the admitted necessary grounding in the human nature located by introspection. If it is demonstrated fully, it must have a link through physics to geometry, and ultimately to *philosophia prima.*

This linkage is obscure, as Hobbes seems to recognize in *De Homine* when he says, "They [the physiological and physical theories underpinning experience with direct observation of oneself and others] are therefore somewhat abruptly conjoined; but this was necessary, granted the method of my work as a whole." Is the demonstrative linkage that would make the knowledge full a heuristic ideal, one to which Hobbes still holds, but one which he himself has not achieved?

Further, considering Hobbes' discussion of the nature of science, there seem to be problems in the order and relation of the sciences for a "full knowledge" of human action. For he makes a distinction between those sciences like geometry and civil philosophy, "because we make these ourselves," and sciences like natural philosophy or physics, chemistry, physiology, etc., whose basis in experience means that they are hypothetically constructed from observed effects.

> The science of every subject is derived from a pre-cognition of the causes, generation, and construction of the same; and consequently where the causes are known, there is a place for demonstration, but not where the causes are to seek for. Geometry therefore is demonstratable, for the lines and figures from which we reason are

> drawn and described by ourselves; and civil philosophy is demonstratable, because we make the commonwealth ourselves. But because natural bodies we know not the construction, but seek it from effects, there lies no demonstration of what the causes be we seek for but only what they may be. (*L*, pp. 23-4)

From the above, it is clear that the order of demonstration considered for full knowledge is not one where there seems a plausible method to proceed directly from one science to another. This seems to be attested to by the variance of the degree of certainty between the sciences that proceed from cause to effect and those that proceed from effect to cause.

The motion of natural bodies—physical things—must remain conjectural in terms of the uncertainty of the epistemic justification. When Hobbes deals with the cause of the tides and the refraction of light in *De Corpore,* what Watkins calls his "second-order interests," and what we would call scientific problems in the modern sense, he can only provide possible causes. He is obviously aware of this epistemic divagation, but he emphasizes that his physical reasons or hypotheses are probable and clear.

The relationship of the explanation of particular phenomena to the basic conceptions of *philosophia prima* therefore seems more like a layering of knowledges than a deductive chain. The more fundamental and certain term of body, in concert with its essential accident, extension, and the other accidents that are basic to man's conceptualization of physical reality—place, number, whole, part, and especially motion—are the *revetements* of both particular physical explanations and of geometry. However, this merely means that geometry and physics and physiology and civil philosophy (or political science) cannot provide a concept that is absurd or in contradiction to those of *philosophia prima.* It does not mean the specifying, basic concepts of the sciences are derivable from *philosophia prima.*

But why does Hobbes give an order to these sciences? Does geometry precede physics because of its generality, its application to any possible world? But, then, what of its being made by ourselves? It is not apparent to me that Hobbes takes a strong, clear, and consistent view of the nature of the relation of the basic concepts of first philosophy and those of geometry in ontological terms—unless it is that the only term that has ontological authenticity, body, has had an ontological transfer to it of essential accident, extension, or magnitude. The other accidents of first philosophy are necessary, as I showed in the previous chapter, to characterize the motion of bodies and, consequently, they are necessary for any causal explanation in a science: geometry, physics, politics, etc. The basic terms of first philosophy, however, are qualified by the terms of the particular science, so in geometry circles, squares, etc., are considered from a certain point of view. They are constructed from the limitations placed on such basic geometric terms as point and line. This is done by definition. Of course, the proper credential of definitions demands that the terms of a definition do not contradict or are of a different conceptual order. Consider Hobbes' statement of the character of a circle:

> How the knowledge of any effect may be gotten from the knowledge of the generation thereof, may easily be understood by the example of a circle: for if there be set before us a plane figure, having as near as may be, the figure of a circle, we cannot possibly perceive by sense whether it be a true circle or no; than which, nevertheless, nothing is more easy to be known to him that knows first the generation of the propounded figure. For let it be known that the figure was made by the circumduction of a body where of one end remained unmoved, and we may reason thus; a body carried about, retaining always the same length, applies itself first to one radius, then to another, and successively to all; and, therefore, the same length, from the same point, toucheth the circumference in every part thereof, which is as much to say, as all the radii are equal. . . . he who knows that a circle has the property above declared, will easily know whether a body carried about will generate a circle or no. (*EW*, I, i, 6)

The definition of a point, for example, which should precede the above construction of a circle, does not have any ontological warrant. The process Hobbes gives for constructing a circle is a physical one, in the sense that reason considers it a physical process; but it may be a physical process that cannot in fact be carried out. The geometrical circle, created in thought, may never have been created by the motion of a physical thing. But because many physical things present themselves to our senses as circular, it is useful to treat them geometrically, by definition, as circles. Hobbes' enthusiasm for Galileo's mathematical physics is obviously the basis for geometry preceding physics on his list of the order of the sciences. Indeed, at the end of *De Corpore* he separates the last part, dealing with physics, from the earlier three parts of the text which deal with logic, the first grounds of philosophy (or the basic concepts of mind), and the proportions of motions and magnitude (or motion considered geometrically). He says,

> In the first, second, and third parts, where the principles of ratiocination consist in our own understanding, that is to say in the legitimate use of words as we ourselves constitute, all the theorems, if I be not deceived are rightly demonstrated. The fourth part (the natural sciences) depends on hypotheses; which unless we know them to be true, it is impossible for us to demonstrate their causes, which I have here explicated, are the true causes of the things whose productions I have derived from them. Nevertheless, seeing I have assumed no hypotheses, which is [sic] not both possible and easy to be comprehended; and seeing also that I have reasoned aright from those assumptions, I have withal demonstrated that they may be the true causes. (*EW*, I, 30, 531)

Despite Hobbes' use of the word 'demonstration', it seems the order he provides from *philosophia prima* to civil philosophy is a system of organization rather than a system of deduction—

but perhaps not quite, since that organization involves the refinement of a basic and more general concept of the ordered sciences as the order proceeds downward. It is tempting to say that this "motion" from science to science involves both discursive and metaphoric qualities, since there is an intellectual structure but one that at every science introduces something new. So the concept of motion in terms of the artifice of the State is not simply apart from one's understanding of body in motion in first philosophy, geometry, physics, and physiology; yet, it presents something new. When Hobbes says, for example, that money is the life's blood of the State or that the sovereign is an artificial God, or when he treats the State as an individual, Hobbes' metaphors express or imply the connection and also the difference between his concepts of the science of politics and other sciences.

Various commentators viewing Hobbes' understanding of the relationship of the sciences tend toward one or another aspect of sameness or of difference. The first quotation to follow is from Alan Ryan; the second is from Noel Malcolm.

> Hobbes believed as firmly as one could that behaviour, whether of animate or inanimate matter, was ultimately to be explained in terms of particular motion: the laws governing the motions of discrete material particules were the ultimate laws of nature, and in this sense psychology must be rooted in physiology and physiology in physics, while the social sciences, especially the terminology of statecraft, must be rooted in psychology.[1] (Ryan)

> But the resort to "experience," i.e., introspection, which Hobbes makes use of when setting out the basis of his political theory, surely produces a quite different kind of truth from the truths which might be derived from the physiology of the brain and the nervous system. And this objection is not merely a special point about the peculiarity of introspection. If we attempted to follow Hobbes' "method" through, ascending from one level of knowledge to the next, we would find that each new level required the introduction of concepts which were simply

> not contained in the subject-matter of the previous level. Physics will give us the concepts of "motion toward" and "motion away from"; but only psychology will provide the concepts of "desire" and "fear".[2] (Malcolm)

As Malcolm points out, Ryan uses the word "rooted" in the passage quoted above, and this organic metaphor seems to me to fudge a determined mechanistic view of the seldom-held, grand sort, where everything can be reduced to a fundamental idea of matter and motion. It is my position that this indeed is Hobbes' maxim or conclusion, and perhaps even his heuristic ideal, in that its spirit guides scientific work. However, in terms of what Hobbes offers as his method, it strikes me that Ryan is quite justified in using the non-reductivist word "rooted" in preference to Hobbes' own word "demonstration."

Interestingly, Malcolm's stress on the newness of concepts, even when they are presented under the same name as those in another science, has a similarity to the Aristotelian understanding of the relation of one science to another. In Aristotle each ontologically superior level of existence has something new which cannot be reduced to the previous level. The specific difference of matter (*hyle*), that which essentially specifies its ontology, is extension; the specific difference of vegetative things is life; the specific difference of animals is motion from an inner principle; and the specific difference of man is rationality. Of course, this ontological ascendancy can speculatively be continued (as it was, in fact, by many medieval Aristotelians) and applied to angels, in their ranks, and to God. In each case, except perhaps for supernatural beings, the specific differences of lower ontological levels are contained (but not *as* specific differences) necessarily as accidents in the individuals of a higher order. So man is defined by his rationality, but a man must necessarily have extension, life, and animal motion. Nonetheless, reduction for the Aristotelian here is impossible, both ontologically and conceptually, for that just destroys the existence or the explanation of the higher being.

From this, it is easy to realize that those who, like Hobbes, hold a reductivist position stand in great opposition to those who, from Plato onward, have been guided by a maxim of the ontological gradation of being. Therefore, Hobbes' use of "new" concepts in his sciences cannot be taken in terms of "the friends of Plato." I think the similarity relates to something else in his method which is quite un-Platonic, *viz.*, his nominalism. It is his nominalistic theory of language, a primary tool of his science—the consequence of one affirmation to another, where the terms of these are defined—that helps one to better understand how Hobbes develops his sciences without recourse, as in Aristotle, to a method which is dependent on ontology, much less ontological grading. I have emphasized that the only ontologically developed concept for Hobbes is body. We may say that its presence, both by intellectual rootedness and by metaphor, is felt in everything, and especially in the natural sciences. But, taking into cognizance the intuitively given accidents of *philosophia prima*, whose complement is necessary for understanding body in motion, Hobbes does not give a method which exemplifies an ontology. His nominalism provides unity by characterizing what he means by a science, and his mechanistic materialism is in partnership with his nominalism and provides the reductive viewpoint.

CHAPTER THREE

Nominalism and Protagorean Humanism

Hobbes' materialism is rooted in the unique ontological credential he gives to the concept of body. The essential accident of body, magnitude or extension, and the other accidents discussed in *philosophia prima* are the archangels, so to speak, for organizing further accidents that arise from sense experience, e.g., hot, dense, loud, long, etc. All accidents cannot be defined directly; Hobbes, in principle, is not able to present what accidents are in themselves, and defines them by what he calls "circumlocution." Since the causal nature of accidents are opaque, there cannot be any reason given for them except the deeply intuitive assumption of body somehow causing them. On the surface, accidents arising from sense can be defined by animal motion.

> For whenever the action of the object reacheth the body of the sentient, that action is by some nerve propagated to the brain; and if the nerve leading thither be so hurt or obstructed, that the motion can be propagated no further, no sense follows. (*EW*, I, 25, 392)

These phantasms or acts of sense are, therefore, definable in terms of relating our conception of them to some observed physical process. Yet, Hobbes speaks of accidents, including both the accidents arising from sense and those accidents which allow us to organize. He characterizes them, however, mysteriously:

> But most men will have it be said that an accident is something, namely some part of a natural thing, when, indeed, it is no part of the same. To satisfy these men, as well as may be, they answer best that define an accident to be the manner by which any body is conceived; which is all one as if they should say, an accident is that faculty of any body, by which it works in us a conception of itself. Which definition, though it is not an answer to the question propounded [of what an accident is]. (*EW*, I, 8, 103)

What seems implied by Hobbes' agnosticism about the nature of accidents and of the nature of body as the substratum for these accidents, is that the body-mind problem and other problems of traditional metaphysics are incapable of being answered in principle. Man has no window to any reality other than that which he finds in himself. Nature is brought forward in a Protagorean manner; we speak of it by the measure of its effect on ourselves.

But science proceeds, in its organization of human experience, to present definitions, which involve "the apt imposing of names." (*Lev.* 5) This also involves the employment of nominal categories, so the above discussion of accident in *De Corpore* continues:

> ... For if concerning the name of a body, that is, concerning a concrete name, it be asked, what is it? the answer must be made by definition; for the question is concerning the signification of the name. But if it be asked concerning an abstract name, what is it? the cause is demanded why a thing appears so. As if it be asked, what is hard? The answer will be, hard is that, where of no part gives place, but when the whole gives place. But if it be demanded, what is hardness? a cause must be shewn why a part does not give place, except the whole give place. Wherefore, I define an accident to be the manner of our conception of body. (*EW*, I, 8, 103-4)

The importance of naming for human beings is enormous: "By the advantage of names it is that we are capable of science, which beasts for the want of them, are not, nor man without the use of them." (*Elements,* I, v, 2) So that though Hobbes considers reason natural to man, he says, "if you will be a philosopher in good earnest, let your person move upon the deep of your own cogitations and experience; those things that lie in confusion must be set asunder, distinguished, and every one stamped with its own name and order; that is to say, your method must resemble that of creation." (*EW,* I, 2, 14)

Because of their usefulness to the enterprise of ordering our thoughts, and therefore of science, it is universal names which must be discussed particularly. Especially, in that this discussion is the plausible entrance into estimating the character of Hobbes' nominalism. Consistent with his materialist ontology, Hobbes does not think the world contains any universals or real essences; consequently, it is obvious that he stands in opposition to the Platonic realist tradition. Instead, he finds universals to be merely a matter of language, i.e., the position of nominalism.

As Watkins puts it, the use of a universal name is "a sort of pluralized version of a proper name."[1] This means that a number of specific individuals are grouped together and treated as an individual. Hobbes calls this process, using scholastic terminology, "the second intention." The second intention treats classification obviously when it employs such terms as 'class', 'novel', and 'species'. But it also does so when it speaks of 'dog', 'man', etc., that is to say, the species of dog, man, etc. We cannot, of course, see 'dog', the universal; it is an abstraction from the particular dogs we see. The name Hobbes employs for matters of direct (possible) experience is the phrase "first intention." Not only does the world not contain universals or real essences, but the mind does not contain any universal ideas, in that we must imagine a particular dog and we obviously cannot imagine the class.

> . . . this name universal is never the name of anything

existent in nature, nor any idea or phantasm formed in the mind, but always the name of some word or name; so that when a living creature, a stone, a spirit, or any other thing that is said to be universal, but only that these words, living creature, stone, etc. are universal names, that is, names common to many things; and the conceptions answering them in our mind, are the images and phantasms of several living creatures, or other things. And, therefore, for the understanding of the extent of an universal name, we need no other faculty but that of our imagination by which we remember that such names bring sometimes one thing, sometimes another, into our mind. (*EW*, I, 2, 20)

Now, I think Hobbes is wrong to claim no other faculty than imagination to be the basis of universal names, since the images before the mind which are to be taken for the collective are taken from the perspective of so standing and just that is not part of the imagination. It seems to rely on our capacity to reason. But reason for Hobbes is limited to addition and subtraction, as in the process of going from whole to part—analysis or, to use his term (the popular one of such discussions) "resolution"—and the process of going from parts to whole—synthesis or, to use his term, "composition."[3]

George Berkeley, like Hobbes, also argues that universals or general ideas are represented by an image of a particular. He would concur with Hobbes that it is an error to say that "the idea of anything is universal; as if there could be in the mind an image of a man, which is not the image of some particular man, but a man simply, which is impossible; for every idea is one, and of one thing." (*EW*, I, 5, 61) Also, Berkeley agrees that there are universals or general ideas. He speaks about the representation involved in having a particular image stand for the general idea:

> I do not deny that there are general ideas, but only that there are abstract general ideas; . . . [a] particular line

becomes general, by being made a sign, so that the name
line, which taken absolutely is particular, by being a sign
is made general. And as the former owes its generality,
not to its being the sign of an abstract or general, but of
all particular right lines that may possibly exist; so the
latter must be thought to derive its generality from the
same cause, namely, the various particular lines which
it indifferently denotes.[3]

Though Berkeley seems in agreement with Hobbes about the significative function of mental images in relation to universals, there is a subtle difference which results from the direction taken by the two thinkers.

Whereas Berkeley uses this analysis of universals within his brand of idealism, Hobbes' nominalism moves outward to bridge the gap between the idea and the description of the world. Brandt insightfully suggests this: "Berkeley includes the general in the particular, Hobbes lets the particular disappear in 'the names'."[4] It does not seem inapt to say that Hobbes considers language to work upon chaotic images or image possibilities in the mind in order to relate some of them to one or another conceptual-linguistic system. And that process, it must be stressed, can only adequately succeed in a cooperative social dimension. Indeed, the implicit or explicit agreements among persons in language use are for Hobbes not simply a matter of ordering the images in any particular person's mind, but rather they are generally a reflection of the interest of a group of language users:

> . . . names have their constitution, not from the species
> of things but from the will and consent of men. And hence
> it comes to pass that men pronounce falsely, by their own
> negligence, in departing from such appellations of things
> as are agreed upon. . . . (*EW*, I, 5, 56)

From this, we see that Hobbes has taken a step to separate

science, as an outgrowth of language, from metaphysics. As Ernst Cassirer puts it,

> Hobbes. . . had definitely withdrawn the philosophy of language from the sphere of metaphysics. Since names are signs for concepts and not signs for objects themselves, the whole question as to whether they designate the matter and the form of things, or something composed of the two, could be set aside as empty metaphysics.[5]

Cassirer's emphasis on the neutrality of language in Hobbes' ontology is a conclusion further shored up by Hobbes' emphasis on the social and voluntaristic aspects of language. Yet, this does not mean that there is no relationship between language and general human experience, something which would be very foolish to hold. After all, Hobbes thinks the interests of men are fundamentally similar; otherwise, introspection would not be an appropriate method for "reading all men in oneself." Also, as we have seen, the concepts of *philosophia prima* and the faculty of calculation are in all persons. These considerations suggest that the choices of organizing experience through language are not arbitrary. Consequently, Watkins' agreement with Leibniz that Hobbes is a "supernominalist" is misleading.[6] Hobbes eschews ontology as the standard for language, unlike Plato in the *Cratylus*. But the organization of the natural sciences for the explanation of phenomena is rooted in concepts that justify, if not depend upon, Hobbes' materialist ontology. Whatever the aspect of phenomena which is organized by a natural science, for Hobbes it is only the material framework that is in concert with experience and avoids meaninglessness and absurdity.

Even more important than the creation of sciences, language offers the possibility of political cooperation. This is more basic than the sciences, both because it provides the only possible environment that produces science and because the peace that cooperation brings, and the many advantages for living, is the most fundamental human interest. Its opposite, war, violently endangers life itself. Without language, "the most profitable invention. . ., [there is] neither commonwealth, nor society, nor contract, nor peace, no more than amongst lions, bears, and wolves." (*Lev.*, 4, 100)

But as language yields many goods, so, contrariwise, the abuse of language endangers civility and other benefits. Hobbes provides four categories of advantages and correlated abuses. First, as men provide themselves with the sciences and arts by means of the proper signification of names, by misuse or the improper signification of names "they deceive themselves." It is not only that improper use can be a tool to mislead others, therefore, but that it can cause disorder in one's own thinking. For Hobbes, harmful political and religious doctrines result from such an abuse. They suggest themselves as knowledge though they rest on error, and give values on this false ground. While the first emphasizes self-deception, the second and third abuses involve the deception of others and the fourth, the use of language to aggrieve others. Here are Hobbes' own words:

> Social uses of speech are these: first, to register, what by cogitation, we find to be the cause of anything, present or past; and what we find things present or past may produce, or effect: which in sum, is acquiring of arts. Secondly, to show to others that knowledge which we have attained; which is, to counsel, and teach one another. Thirdly, to make known to others our wills, and purposes, that we may have the mutual help of one another. Fourthly, to please and delight ourselves, and others, by playing with our words, for pleasure or ornament, innocently. To these uses, there are also four correspondent abuses. First, when men register their thoughts wrong, by the inconstancy of the signification of their words; by which they register for their conceptions, that which they never conceived; and so deceive themselves. Secondly, when they use words metaphorically; that is, in other sense than those they are ordained for; and thereby deceive others. Thirdly, when by words they

declare that to be their will, which is not; Fourthly, when they use them to grieve one another. (*Lev.*, 4, 101-2)

This makes the point that for Hobbes language can be considered politically in a number of ways. But this has been somewhat of a digression, and I would like to focus again on the relation of language to the doctrine that names are not signs of things, but of thoughts. Hobbes says, "*Nomina. . . signa sunt conceptum, manifestum est ea non esse signa ipsarum rerum.*" (*EW*, I, 2, 17) Let us add another important Hobbesian nominalist doctrine: that truth consists in what is said, not in a thing—"*Veritas enim in dicto, non in re constitut.*" (*EW*, I, 3, 35) This brings forth Hobbes' understanding of scientific propositions: "The words 'true', 'truth', and 'true proposition' have the same force." (*ibid.*)

Hobbes sees the development of science through propositions, and it is not the existence of truth in the things they refer to but in them that is hallmark of his nominalism. Fundamental for any science are primary propositions which are "nothing other than definitions, and these alone are the principles of demonstration, namely, truths established by the decision of speakers and hearers, and therefore indemonstrable." (*EW*, I, 3, 37) It is here that the particular interest of a science is put forth simultaneously with the boundaries of its intellectual enterprise, e.g., the choice to consider lines in two dimensions or in three dimensions orients the following propositions to be those of plane or solid geometry. Consider an experience such as a man falling overboard from a ship. We may generate many scientific truths from this event. If we consider the matter from the viewpoint of physics, we deal with the man as a mere body of a certain weight, falling a certain distance in a certain time. If we deal with the man from the viewpoint of physiology, we treat such things as what happens to the heart and lungs when a person falls such a distance. When we deal with the man's psychology, we may discuss the conditions of a suicide. With each science we choose certain primary propositions that express our interest and which are the boundaries of its perspective.

In each case the language we use develops its particular perspective. It is improper to ask which of the sciences really gives the truth. Truth is not a matter of "really" or "the real" for Hobbes; it is caught within the limits of a particular science—or, rather, it is caught within propositions considered within a framework. Though ordinary human experience is not a science, it also provides a "loose" framework, so that one can ask from a "commonsensical" perspective if it is true that the man fell overboard. Here one seeks confirmation of a fact, by prudence, in mostly observational terms. Yet, though Hobbes does not discuss this particularly, there may be something like basic propositions here as well, certainly less open to deduction, more oriented to a looser criterion of evidence, and much mixed with prudence. For Hobbes prudence is the only knowledge that exists aside from scientific knowledge, and, unlike science, it is not deductively organized. In this last case it seems that we have considered the use of "true" in the prudential realm; indeed, it is worth noting that its feature of correspondence is less amenable to nominalism.

Hobbes always makes clear the main thrust of his doctrine. Hobbes emphasizes his nominalist approach to science. The Aristotelian *tou dioti*, the WHY of things for science, rests on the organization of the *tou oti*, the bare fact of our conceptions. In the natural sciences, dealing with the objects of phenomenal experiences as the causal source of our conceptions, the progress of science is oriented by sense experience. Hobbes' nominalism, therefore, does not mean that "saving the appearances" has no place in the physical sciences. On the contrary, his interest in explaining the cause of phenomena make the appearances crucial to the truth of their propositions. That is important to remember, because Hobbes cannot be faulted as a reactionary in regard to the development of modern science, as perhaps those imply who call him a "supernominalist." Granted that the sciences we invent ourselves—e.g., geometry and political science—need an analysis similar to the nature of games, where the rules that govern the game are similar to primary propositions; nevertheless, the sciences that deal with natural objects are certainly not "windowless monads." So Hobbes says: "The first principles of scientific knowledge of all things are the phantasms of sense-experience and imagination. We indeed *naturally* know what they are, but to know why they are, or from what causes they originate, is the work of *ratiocination.*" (*EW,* VII, 1)

Let us go deeper into Hobbes' understanding about these propositions, these building blocks of science. Hobbes says, "A proposition in speech consists of two copulated names by which the one who is speaking signifies that he conceives the name which occurs second to be the name of the same thing as the name which occurs first." (*EW,* I, 3, 30) To this Hobbes adds, "the names certainly arouse in the mind the thought of one and the same thing. But the copulation induces the thought of the cause on account of which those names are imposed on that thing." (*ibid.*, 31)

We must keep in mind that a name for Hobbes need not be a single word. It can be a number of words—for example, both the proper name "Scott" and a definite description of the person to whom the proper name refers. For example, "the author of *Waverley*" is a name. For the proposition "Scott is the author of *Waverley*" we have the form "A is B," so that the copula separates two names, no matter how many words each name contains. This is also the case with propositions that use negation, such as the statement "Moliere is not the author of *Waverley.*" For Hobbes, the word 'not' is treated as part of the name which presents itself after the copula. Just as negation, so also quantifiers like 'some,' 'all,' and 'each.' They are treated as part of the name. This treatment of quantifiers and operators is inefficient from the viewpoint of modern symbolic logic, but Hobbes makes an important philosophical point by his formulation. He emphasizes his nominalism by asserting that these terms, which are fundamental for computation or reasoning, have no direct referential function in themselves; they merely help organize a body of knowledge.

Especially important for his holding a semantic theory of truth, truth by the definition of names, is the organizing work of the copula. This can be clearly seen by considering the copula's connective function in scientific propositions which are either universal or hypothetical. It connects by asserting an attribution of a subject—its "attributive reference" in the phrase of Donnellan.[7] Hobbes asserts that "the gross error of the metaphysicians" is to consider nominal essences, the definitions of names, to be real essences, that is, to reify names or to give them an ontological character. An example of the kind of error Hobbes wishes to avoid is taking a particular individual human being to exemplify the rational form of man. The ontology of the idea has a force on the individual to fulfill his character: this is final causality.

Both the nominalist and empirical aspects of Hobbes' thought work against an interpretation in terms of Platonic or of Aristotelian realism. Locke is the philosopher more commonly associated with an empirical opposition to realism, but there are historical reasons for this. Perhaps Locke's political doctrine seemed more congenial to most persons than that of Hobbes. Nevertheless, Locke's understanding of general words moves in the same path as that of Hobbes. Locke writes,

> What kind of signification do general words have? For, as it is evident they do not signify barely one particular thing; for then they would not be general terms, but proper names, so on the other side, they do not signify a plurality; for 'man' and 'men' would then signify the same. . . That then which general terms signify is a sort of things; and each of them does that, by being a sign of an abstract idea of the mind; to which idea, as things existing are found to agree, so they come to be ranked under that name, or, which is all one, be of that sort.[8]

This is obviously in broad agreement with Hobbes. Though it is noteworthy that Hobbes' nominalism would refine and extend Locke's ranking of things under the general idea, Hobbes also deals with general ideas in the "game" terms of geometry and political science. Hobbes seems to have this consideration in mind when he says that a general word or, in his own terminology, an abstract name, "denotes the cause of a concrete name, not the thing itself," though he employs the word 'cause' here with this understanding: "for though understanding is the cause of understanding, speech is not the cause of speech." (*EW,* I, 3, 43) For Hobbes, language maps both empirical and artifacted things by describing the connection between their properties.

What propositions capture are the descriptions of the properties of the things in which we are interested, whether they arise through our own invention or arise as the phantasms of sense-experience. Indeed, the copula provides the proposition with a way to present properties, but it does not refer to the status of the existence of those properties. Russell provides a much-respected recent comment, noting the possibility of confusing the syncategorematic function of the copula with a reference to existence. Russell says, "The proposition 'Socrates is a man' is no doubt *equivalent* to 'Socrates is human,' but it is not the same proposition. The 'is' of 'Socrates is human' expresses the relationship of subject to predicate; the 'is' of 'Socrates is a man' expresses identity. It is a disgrace to the human race that it has chosen to employ the same word for these two entirely different ideas."[9]

Existential propositions, taken to assert existence rather than to provide classification, are not scientific propositions for Hobbes. The knowledge they provide is rather, as mentioned above, one of prudence—prudence because such propositions assert a contingency, a fact, and provide no definitional necessity *qua* existence. Existence cannot be derived from the meaning of words; even the use of 'body' for first philosophy can be negated by the thought of the destruction of the world. There is no intrinsic impossibility that no thing exists. Unlike Anselm and Descartes, whose discussion of the ontological argument holds that the idea of God or perfection involves the necessary existence of God, Hobbes' ontological elevation of body only means that we conceive of body as having magnitude or as existing in a certain way outside of thought; it does not mean it must necessarily exist because of our conception of it. If we take "Scott is the author of *Waverley*" as a contingent proposition, which it usually is, for Hobbes this cannot be a proposition of science. And, of course, it would be rather strange to take this proposition as providing us with a definition or scientific classification since, though most unlikely, it might in fact turn out to be that Moliere is the author of *Waverley.* The evidence of contingent propositions is developed in the arena of prudence. In this arena it is prudent to reject certain definitions or conclusions of science because they not well map our sense-experience; nevertheless, science has something of an epistemological immunity from this. Because science is classificatory for Hobbes, it may turn out to be unhelpful in explaining the world but nevertheless be a science. The *scientia* or knowledge is the result of definitions, useful or not. Therefore, the primary definitions of a science are what Kripke calls "rigid designators"[10] or what Putnam calls "indexical terms."[11] Their stipulative quality is the most decisive fact in their employment. It is from this nominalist viewpoint that Hobbes asserts their certitude and truth: " 'Man is a rational, animal being' remains true even though it is not [actually] necessary for either man or animal to exist in eternity." (*EW*, I, 2) Though such propositions arise from experience, they cannot be overturned by experience, for as Hobbes often says, experience provides nothing with certainty.

This may strike one as an odd conclusion. Man not only creates truth by the act of definition, but also, in a sense, creates eternity. Of course, remembering Russell, the eternity spoken of here is not an existential condition; it is outside of existence in the sense that it occupies an intellectual space. Like body, which is necessarily qualified by the accident of extension, the definitions that we create have provided certain subjects with the eternal nominal necessity of certain properties, thus providing science with certain knowledge.

This closed, formal system approach to knowledge in the sciences has certainly found opponents in modern times. For though it provides a firmness for deduction or demonstration which is in line with the ideal language programs of such modern thinkers as Tarski and Carnap, it has the disadvantage of being somewhat unresponsive to paradigmatic reformulations. Also, it is not in concert with the tentativity of ingathering new facts that qualify, if not overturn, the conceptual arsenal of a science. Obviously, from his understanding of the hypothetical nature of the natural sciences, and the possible nature of reformulating concepts to explain or save the phenomena, Hobbes is not oblivious to this. But for him there seem to exist, in principle, uncomfortably numerous eternal sciences. Some seem to differ because of one fundamental change and its implications, e.g., how the parallel postulate is treated in various geometries. From this viewpoint the physical paradigms of Newton and Einstein are not the history of one science, for they are two sciences, but they are the history of an ongoing attempt to understand the motions underlying phenomena.

In order to avoid the trivial proliferation of formal systems as sciences, Hobbes suggests *prudence* in dealing with abstractions. With a similar caution, Spinoza remarks on the difference between existing and concepts: "any natural thing whatever can be just as well conceived, whether it exists or does not exist. As then the beginning of the existence of a natural thing cannot be inferred by its definition, so neither can its continuing existence."[12]

If certain truth comes with classification, it is the authority to classify that seems very important indeed, especially in the creation of a legal system. Hobbes says, "To make a law is to make a cause of justice, and to necessitate justice." (*EW,* IV, 253) Indeed, Hobbes is in agreement with the conventionalist viewpoint of the sophist when he says, "It is not wisdom but authority that makes a law." (*Dialogue,* 55) With this he takes issue with the Platonic viewpoint that distinguishes real rulers—those that are fit to rule a State—from conventional rulers, namely, those that are in control of the State apparatus. Hobbes' similarity to the sophists also exists in his diremption of truth and goodness.[13] The worth of a person is conventional in the sense that it asserts the convenience or circumstance of need: "The value or worth of a man is as of all other things his price." (*Lev.* X, 51)

It must not be lost on us that Hobbes' conventionalism, his circumstantialism, his perspectivism, which fit so well with nominalism, are a humanism. He is in the tradition of the sophist Protagoras, who takes man as the measure of truth and values. Indeed, thereby his position confronts another humanism: the tradition of Plato, that grounds truth and goodness in the structure of being, where man has his natural place which he can discover but which he doesn't invent. This is the humanism of *homo naturans,* not of *homo faber.*

In Plato's dialogue, Protagoras presents a mythos of the origin of society which, like Hobbes later, presents man as weak and endangered in his first nature. It is only by later gifts, *techne* or art by Prometheus and *dike* or justice by Zeus, a second nature, that he can preserve himself in society. This charming story is suggestive of Hobbes' doctrine; he takes the gifts to be man's artificial control of circumstance through the certain creation of truth and the social good by the civil laws.

The struggle between a Platonic and a Protagorean humanism is to be seen as well between Descartes and Hobbes. In the *Cratylus,* Plato had proposed the thesis that language is based on nature; that is, beneath the historical shifts and inventions is an ontological imperative in the rationality of language. Cartesian linguistics, in the private capacity of the *cogito,* by the *lumen naturalis,* finds certain ideas like God's existence; this is the metaphysical ground for the essential structure of language and science. The certainty here is natural and not artificial or conventional. Such a doctrine can ground a notion like the "rights of man" of the French Revolution; and, certainly, in spirit, it opposes Hobbes' doctrine that each sovereign is the measure of all the citizen's civic obligations. With Platonic or Cartesian humanism a universal and natural sense of justice is fundamental; with Protagorean or Hobbesian humanism a conventional sense of justice, established through contract with one's countrymen, is fundamental.

The debate continues in the twentieth century. There is an obvious linkage between Chomsky's politics and his Cartesian linguistics. Depth grammar can be called the natural essence of each surface or ordinary language; it is the logical frame that normatively binds each particular historical language. This structure or rationality is in human beings innately; if such a depth structure is also taken for the moral order, one can conclude that here too men understand their surface or historical condition from the privacy of innerness. The normative standard, the way to avoid moral and political absurdity, is not of the surface but of the depth, just as one avoids the absurdity or impossibility of doing just anything with syntax.

Wittgenstein is a man of the surface; it is very hard to live on the surface: it takes much discipline not to seek values in a reified profundity. This is a Zen attitude. In a qualified, but broad sense, Wittgenstein has inherited Protagoras' part in the debate: "rules," he says, "without institutions, hang in the air." "Auf den *privaten* Uebergang von dem Geschehenen zum Wort koennte ich keine Regeln anwenden. Hier hingen die Regeln wirklich in der Luft; da die Institution ihrer Anwendung fehlt."[14] Whatever subtlety Wittgenstein's position has, its explicit force is to support the conventional. Anthony Kenney, a close student of both Descartes and Wittgenstein, writes: "If Descartes' innovation was to identify the mental and the private, Wittgenstein's contribution was to separate the two. Since Wittgenstein, we tend to equate the mental with what is peculiar to language users: and if Wittgenstein's arguments are valid, language cannot be private."[15]

It is not at all far afield to substitute Hobbes for Wittgenstein in the above quotation. Men may employ sensible tokens or marks, Hobbes tells us, but "unless the tokens which he may have invented for himself be common to others also, his scientific knowledge will perish with him." (*EW*, I, 2) Those tokens must be made into signs upon which men agree, like names, so that cooperative tasks, like the natural sciences, may take place. Hobbes' surface is not only a straightforward taking on of the obligation of obeying the sovereign's will, but also, like that of Wittgenstein and Protagoras, his psychology is not ontological. Though considering human nature, it does not hope to establish its fundamental norm metaphysically. His humanism has it that the agreements between men, explicit or tacit, create the *Lebenswelt*; thereby, men express their desires by an act of will. If one grants the factor of circumstance involved in this, the question of whether nothing else is necessary to achieve justice is at the heart of the debate.

APPENDIX: ON IDENTITY

In the chapter "Identity and Difference" in *De Corpore*, Hobbes discusses individuation in a nominalist manner: "Wherefore the beginning of *individuation* is not always to be taken either from matter alone, or from form alone. But we must consider by what name anything is called, when we inquire concerning the identity of it." (*EW*, I, 11, 137) Even the identity of a person must therefore become the public judgment of him, since names are the result, in an overwhelming consideration, of cooperative elections, some institutionalized and some not. Hobbes' treatment of personal identity eschews the metaphysical by way of the political, much incorporated in naming. The problem is not how the child and the man can be the same individual despite the difference of their bodies, or how a person with amnesia can be the same person he was before the amnesia. It is to present the matter of identity of the person, or any object or objects, in terms of interest. Hobbes treats the identity of a person, a man's individuation, in terms of motion. He says, "from the same beginning of motion, thus, as long as that motion remains, it will be the same individual thing; as that man will always be the same, whose actions and thoughts proceed from the same beginning of motion, namely, that which was in his generation." (*ibid.*)

In this passage the choice that Hobbes provides is characteristically oriented toward the material. Nevertheless, the identity, for example, of a person in a legal decision may provide other considerations. For instance, even upon granting for some legal interest that a man before and after his amnesia can be considered in terms of the same generation, the man before the amnesia and the man after can be treated as two identities. For Hobbes, this is perfectly legitimate. Hobbes' own suggestion of generation for personal identity reflects not a logical necessity, but his own interest in having a materialist framework to guide us in a general understanding of the world.

When Kant discusses personhood as a paralogism of transcendental psychology, he considers that we have to assume unity, that there exists an *entia per se*, because there is no way to provide an indefeasible connotation of "person." He does not want to treat a human being as what the scholastics called *entia per alio* or what Chisholm[16] gives as its equivalent, "ontological parasites"—entities that do not exist in their own right, but only appear because of something else. Yet, for Kant, the I, the world, and God provide only the "schema of a regulative concept," that is, as things-in-themselves. Therefore the I or soul, Kant says, should be treated as a single principle and

> ... viewed *as if* it were a real being; indeed, it is attainable in no other way. The psychological itself can signify nothing other than the schema of a regulative concept. For were I to inquire whether *the soul in itself* is of a spiritual nature, the question would have no meaning. In employing such a concept I not only abstract from corporeal nature, but from nature in general, that is, from all predicates of any possible experience, and therefore from all conditions requisite for thinking any object for such a concept; yet only related to an object can the concept be said to have a meaning. (A684/B712)

Of course, Hobbes doesn't have the Kantian machinery with its transcendental considerations. For him, the empirical self is considered from the viewpoint of a materialist ontology. But that ontology is itself rooted in *entia per alio*, since Hobbes recognizes that accidents or phenomena are necessary to the human perspective. Body, the only posited noumenon or thing-in-itself, stands in a primitive relation to the description of the phenomenal world, and is itself only posited as a principle in terms of the basic accidents of a mechanist description. It stands opaquely as an *ens per se*, behind its essential attributes of magnitude and all the other accidents of *philosophia prima*. But individuation involves the classification of matters in terms of interest. For Hobbes, London Bridge is a legal individual, and it would remain such even if its parts were replaced with others, as happened in the classic example of the ship of Theseus, which Hobbes discusses. The empirical reality is its function, perhaps related to a certain location, which provides the interest for classification. Therefore, with a nominalism that can attach itself to physical characteristics—and often does, because of human interests—Hobbes fixes the subject by a name.

Naming creates a unity, one that has a context provided by an interest. And this must be considered from Hobbes' understanding of action. The unity involved in action is the man, yet the physical process occuring within the individual's body is expressed in terms of physical movements stimulated by some outer object, either as something to be desired or something to be averted. Yet this process of the person's body is treated as the motions of individuals, e.g., heart, brain, the circulation of the blood, etc. It is as if the individual is considered as a world, which upon further investigation turns out to be composed of individuals.

> As, in sense, that which is really within us. . . is only motion, caused by the action of external objects. . . so, when the action of the same object is continued from the eyes, ears, or some other organs to the heart, the real affects there is nothing but motion, or endeavour; which consisteth in appetite or aversion, to or from the moving object. (*Lev.*, p. 33)

For Hobbes, the relationship of the various organs and parts of the human body is expressed mechanically as the cause/effect relationship of one upon the other. These are the ways such terms of consciousness as introspection, deliberation, anger, wanting, etc., are to be described physically. But this reduction of psychology to physiology involves an analysis where the unity of the person is reduced to the units involved in the physiological process. In a sense this is an inwardness; the inner man is the physiological components of his body. But the mechanical analysis of those physiological units involves, once again, action from without, in a causal chain. Time is involved, but we have already seen Hobbes has a difficulty, because he would prefer to treat cause as a classificatory consideration and, therefore, as not temporal—or rather, as action having the cause and effect simultaneous. Perhaps this results from having one understanding of cause as a term of explanation and another understanding of it as a description of physical processes. Michael Frede has noticed that the Stoics, who opposed final and formal cause, had the same difficulty as Hobbes. He writes that when "the Stoics conceive of the cause in the narrowest sense in such a way that it recaptures the explanatory force, causes seem to lose owing to their restriction to active causes. Nevertheless, it is important to realize that the shift in the notion of a cause threatens the simple and straightforward conceptual link between cause and explanation."[17]

The physiological analysis of a human being destroys the unity of the psychological subject, much as nature is a unit in relation to God, but that unity is destroyed when we speak of the events in nature. Each natural science creates different units by its names which, in a causal analysis, have a relationship to outer individuals of its analytic level. While nominalism provides a certain initial flexibility for method to follow its interest, it tends to provide an atmosphere where metaphysics cannot find an opening. Further, when the mechanical method of explanation is employed with it, as in Hobbes, individuation is likewise provisional as an expression of interest that considers any individual in process with its circumstances or environment. Consequently, no motion can be attributed to the individual itself, except perhaps as a residue of—a postulate of—other outward motions. Is this not the mysterious *conatus*?

CHAPTER FOUR
Heidegger on Hobbes' Nominalism

Die Grundprobleme der Phaenomenologie, published in 1975, is fundamentally Heidegger's summer lectures at Marburg of 1927. Coming soon after *Sein und Zeit*, these lectures attempt to locate phenomenology as ontological science. Interestingly, Thomas Hobbes' *Computatio sive logica*,[1] the first part of *De Corpore*, is discussed in over a dozen printed pages in terms of Heidegger's assertion of and reaction to Hobbes' doctrine about being and truth. Heidegger does this in a section of his book entitled "Arguments in the History of Logic," the specific sub-section of which is "The being of the copula in the horizon of whatness (*essentia*) in Thomas Hobbes."

Despite his ultimate lack of sympathy for Hobbes' position—he maintains that even Hobbes must retreat from his own doctrine in order to avoid absurdity—, Heidegger nevertheless has high praise for Hobbes, saying, "this extreme nominalistic formulation of the problem is carried through with insurpassable clarity in which—quite apart from the question of its tenability—philosophical power is always manifest." (p. 194)[2] Heidegger apparently agrees with Leibniz' view of Hobbes as a "super-nominalist" and Heidegger's criticism of Hobbes is a direct result of his understanding of the limits of the nominalist position.

Though I have the scruple that Heidegger's discussion of Hobbes is but a fragment of his intention to explain and defend phenomenology as an ontological science, my intention is not to engage Heidegger's essential programmatic interest, except when it is necessary to explain his reaction to Hobbes. My limited intention, then, is to evaluate Heidegger's view of Hobbes.

* * *

Heidegger initiates his Hobbes discussion by defining nominalism: "Nominalism is the view of logical problems which in the interpretation of thought and knowledge starts from the thinking expressed in assertion and indeed from assertion as it manifests itself as a spoken verbal complex, words and names." (p. 183) He continues, "All the problems that arise regarding the proposition and thus also the problem of truth and the question of the copula, are oriented by nominalism toward the context of words. . . in ancient logic one form of nominalism was already widespread, that of the sophists. . . " (*ibid.*)

There is little to quarrel with in Heidegger's text-bookish characterization of nominalism, except that it seems unnecessary to have emphasized the "spoken" (even if one is not sympathetic to Derrida's positional reaction to Heidegger on written versus spoken). What excited my attention was the casual *apercu* Heidegger makes that locates Hobbes in the sophistic tradition. (He also mentions the English Franciscans, especially Ockham, as nominalists with some influence on Luther.) Before reading Heidegger, I had already come to the same conclusion, though the Hobbes literature (notably Leo Strauss) when placing Hobbes' reaction to Plato and Aristotle emphasizes his materialist turn through the lineage of Epicurus. Now, such intellectual genealogies are inevitably the less fully satisfactory the greater the putatively epigonic thinker—consider the difficulties in saying Aristotle is a Platonist or, even, Plotinus is a Platonist. Nevertheless, such a classification opens a certain interpretive viewpoint, which if it meets resistance in the important matter of what is original, it yet provides a frame that focuses attention and releases one's imagination to a new scoping of the thinker's intellectual complexity. In unknowing agreement with Heidegger, I had hoped to accomplish this by classifying Hobbes in the tradition of the humanism of Protagoras, and opposing it to Platonic humanism, though this not only takes a liberty, on some level, with Plato and Protagoras, but, as my teacher P.O. Kristeller would emphasize, with an historically bounded phenomenon: humanism.

These comments relate to Heidegger's discussion of Hobbes in two ways. Heidegger's appropriation of Hobbes' nominalism as sophist allows him to respond to its limits in the manner whereby Plato showed the logical untenability of similar sophist positions, (e.g., Plato's arguments against conventionalism and 'man the measure' in his *Protagoras, Gorgias,* and *Philebus*). But if Heidegger accepts Plato's logic against the sophists, he does not accept Plato's ontology, which speaks to how Heidegger stands in relation to Hobbes' language determination of truth. This second aspect of his Hobbes critique rests on Heidegger's intention to offer a 'science of ontology'. Sciences *per se* do not need proper names or past positions (even those of Plato, Protagoras, or Hobbes); sciences need only 'arguments'. If it is assumed that Heidegger agrees and, it is recalled, that his intention is to present Hobbes for the sake of the larger project, ontological science, then his historical classifications and the limits of his discussion of Hobbes must be seen in that light. Heidegger's Hobbes critique is a rhetoric that prepares for, but is not, science or philosophy; this explains its selectivity of topic and text.

But now on my own account, I note my disagreement with Heidegger that Hobbes is reduced to silence by Plato's arguments against the sophists. At least, I will show that Heidegger's specific arguments against Hobbes are either frail or simply wrong. Further, though attending more to Hobbes' materialist assumptions than to his nominalism, which Hobbes coordinates with the former as the proper method, I will present Hobbes' reaction to Descartes for the sake of suggesting his response to the Platonic position. I am therefore more impressed by the actual worth of Hobbes than is Heidegger because I am more sympathetic to sophist and materialist positions. Also, whatever excuse can be made for Heidegger as a reader of Hobbes' and other thinkers' doctrines—say, from the viewpoint of his own original intentions—I will show Heidegger's reading of Hobbes to be irresponsibly partial and therefore misleading.

What I can make clear I will make clear; yet because I respect Heidegger's philosophical intuitions, though it is obvious to me that he has not based his view of Hobbes on proper evidence, I am not ready to say he is entirely wrong.

* * *

Heidegger's approach to Hobbes as a nominalist logician leads him to concentrate on Chapter Three of *De Corpore*, where propositions are discussed. It is here that the copula, the connective between the subject and the predicate of a proposition, is asserted to have an instrumental function and not an ontological meaning. For Heidegger, Hobbes thereby "remains on the horizon of *essentia*" and does not illuminate or reach *existentia*. The crucial assertion of Hobbes' discussion of the proposition is this: "The words 'true', 'truth' and 'true proposition' have the same force. For truth consists in what is said and not a thing." (*Co.*, III, 7) According to Heidegger, therefore, Hobbes offers "a pure sequence of words" (p. 192) and, like all nominalists, he errs because "He is necessarily compelled to relate his verbal sequence to some *res*, but without interpreting in further detail this specific reference of names to things and the condition for the possibility of this capacity for reference, the signative character of names." (*ibid.*) Consequently, in summarizing his evaluation of Hobbes, Heidegger concludes, "Subjected to the constraint of the phenomena involved in the interpretation of the assertion as a sequence of words, Hobbes more and more surrenders his own initial appraoch. This is characteristic of all nominalism" because "beyond the purely verbal sequence there emerges a manifold that belongs to assertion in general: identifying reference of names to things, apprehension of the whatness of the thing in this identifying reference, the thought of the cause for the identifying referability." (*ibid.*)

What Heidegger misses is that for Hobbes psychology is the road to ontology. He overly flattens Hobbes' thought by not considering the psychological basis of "Names are not signs of things but of thoughts." (*Co.*, II, 5) Not only does Heidegger not discuss the *De Corpore* beyond the *Computatio sive logica* but, of this first part of the book, he almost exclusively attends to Chapter Three. Thereby, Heidegger does not properly consider Hobbes' comments on reason in Chapter One, "On Philosophy," and Chapter Two, "On Words," which prepare the reader for Chapter Three. Also, as one might assume that the early chapters prepare the context to discuss the logic of the proposition, one might assume that those that come after it discuss the implications of Chapter Three. Chapter Four discusses the syllogism; Chapter Five, "Erroneousness, Falsity and Fallacies," is important for Hobbes' understanding of truth; and Chapter Six, "On Method," the final chapter of the *Computatio*, elaborates on the *res* of definitions or primary scientific propositions.

Without belaboring the material, I will present what Heidegger overlooked in Hobbes' exposition. This will prepare my argument against some specific technical points that Heidegger raises against Hobbes' treatment of the proposition; it will also provide a more adequate basis to appreciate the power of Hobbes' thought. First, the psychological basis of Hobbes' discussion is suggested in Chapter One when he equates philosophy to natural reason. Hobbes says that it "is innate in every man." (*Co.*, p. 173) Though Hobbes more narrowly defines philosophy as cultivated by method, it is important to note his anthropomorphic and egalitarian view of mind. Further, the proper definition of philosophy, for Hobbes, emphasizes the knowledge of phenomena on the basis of cause and effect: "Philosophy is the knowledge acquired through correct reasoning, of effects or phenomena from the conception of their causes or generations, and also of the generations which exist from the knowledge of their effects." (*ibid.*)

Since no qualitative distinction is made between philosophy and science by this definition, on its surface at least, it appears, despite Heidegger, to allow for the knowledge of things. It is indeed emphasized by Hobbes that calculation or reasoning is of the properties of things, that is, "of the effects of phenomena or powers of bodies which distinguish one body from another."

(*Co.*, p. 180) The hesitancy expressed by the phrase "on the surface at least" signals that though Hobbes has a robust understanding of things, allowing a physics without skeptical umbrage, and indeed one grounded in the senses (as is shown by the following quotes from his discussion of physics in *De Corpore*), nevertheless, Hobbes' psychology of perception is not a naive realism. It offers a sophisticated doctrine of knowledge in which constructive rationality presents the world perspectively. Heidegger's remark that Hobbes is forced to deal with things despite a nominalist method that disallows the going from words to things is made as a claim from Heidegger's examination of the method. But my claim is not only that Heidegger's examination of Hobbes' method is inadequate, but that one reason it is inadequate is that Hobbes' psychology of perception, scientific constructivism, and nominalism are balanced and interrelated parts of his whole philosophy. Heidegger, after focussing on Hobbes' discussion of the copula, simply ignores that discussion as embedded in a complex of interrelated theories. In order to make this omission plausible, Heidegger claims that Hobbes, or the nominalist, cannot in principle reach the *res* of the world since language is made the ultimate and even sole standard for knowledge. From Heidegger's viewpoint the following quotes from Part IV of *De Corpore* are beside the point. But I think not. Despite Heidegger's silence about such material and the theories they imply, I see them as a proposal of how nominalism arises from and serves an empirical materialism. Consider, then, the following:

> Of all the phenomena or appearances which are near us, the most admirable is apparition itself (*to phainesthai*); namely, that some natural bodies have in themselves the pattern almost of all things, and others of none at all. So that appearances by the principle by which we know all things, we must acknowledge sense to be the principle by which we know those principles and that all the knowledge we have is derived from it. And as for the

> causes of sense, we cannot begin our search of them from any other phenomenon than that of sense itself. (*EW*, I, 389)

> [Knowledge of things] depends not on such we ourselves make and pronounce in general terms, as definitions; but such, as being placed in the things themselves by the Author of Nature, are by us observed in them; and we make use of them in single and particular and not universal propositions. Nor do they impose upon us any necessity of constituting theorems; their use being only, though not without such propositions that have already been demonstrated (e.g., the nature of time, space, accident), to show us the possibility of some production or generation. (*ibid.*, 388)

But if Heidegger ignores such material from the later parts of the *De Corpore* (and also, say, the discussion of psychology at the beginning of the *Leviathan*) on the basis of the nominalism of the *Computatio*, it seems even more inappropriately odd for him to have overlooked material in Chapter Two of the *Computatio* where Hobbes speaks *against* having his position reduced to a nominalism whose standard for knowledge is words alone. For in that location, Hobbes discusses and gives an example of "reasoning in silent thought without words." (*Co.*, p. 177) Hobbes explicitly denies the fundamental orientation to words against Heidegger's claim, to the extent that the basis of words is in reason which, for Hobbes, is a calculation arising from sense experience, as we have seen in the above quote. Indeed, Hobbes clearly states that this "internal reasoning of the mind works without words." (*ibid.*, p. 179)

What may have confused Heidegger—indeed, it has not been clearly accounted for by many Hobbes scholars either, William Sacksteder[3] being a notable exception—is the constructive aspect of Hobbes' theory of science in relation to his empirical materialism. As indicated in the second quote above, the universal propositions of science are not to be confused with the single and particular propositions of empirical observation.

The physical sciences, those that reason from effect or phenomena to their probable cause, construct theories that are hostage both to the quantity and conditions of experience and to the ingenuity of interpreting the particular experiences actually had. The definitions of such sciences, though universal and regulative, are consequently revisable when the singular and particular propositions, reflecting experience, clash with the *als ob* universal definitions which are the current theoretical projection from experience. In physics it is not the words or propositions that ultimately guide progress in knowledge; rather, it is experience. Science is the scaffold and mnemonic of experience. However, in sciences such as mathematics and the one Hobbes claims to have originated, civil philosophy, where the cause is in ourselves and, therefore, where the effects are of the motions we ourselves initiate, Hobbes' views are more original and complex in terms of experience and construction. It is here that Hobbes claims certainty for our knowledge. This can mislead one to think, as apparently Heidegger did, that this is the vapid certainty of existentially unguided stipulative definitions. Even math objects are neither the result of mere stipulation nor separated from an origin in sense-experience.

Hobbes takes a determinately un-Platonic view of mathematics, i.e., geometry. As quoted in a previous chapter, he speaks of the generation or cause of a circle where a string held at a central point would produce the circle when being moved around this center. This construction, whether or not any particular circle is produced by it or by some other method, explains the most important property of this object—that its peripheral boundary is equidistant from its center at every point. The construction of mathematical objects from actual or possibly experienced motions provides certainty, because it expresses the properties of the construction of a class of motions *from our own causing of the construction*. The properties are contained in the subject, and that is precisely what Hobbes understands by a scientific, universal proposition. It is one where the copula transparently asserts the predicate to belong to the subject of the proposition. I say "transparently" because the copula does not express the existence of anything outside of ourselves; it is part of the grammar of concepts, namely, their conjunctive coordination. Therefore, to express what is true about circles, or the truth of circles, or true propositions about circles, there need not be even one circle in the world.[4] It is, however, apt to say that if a motion of a certain sort was caused, under such and such conditions, a circle would appear. Truth therefore is of words and not things, since the propositional truth is neutral to facts in the world. "True" is not the opposite of "false" but of "impossible."

Civil philosophy also has the certainty of the cause in ourselves;[5] yet more obviously than mathematics, it is constructed because of an anticipation of some benefit to ourselves. Hobbes' stress has a Protagorean tone: "the goal or scope of philosophy is that we might be able to use previously observed effects for our benefit..." (*Co.,* p. 183), to which he adds, reminding us of Bacon, "Knowledge is for the sake of power. A theorem is for the sake of problems, i.e., for the art of construction. Finally, all speculation is instituted for the sake of some action or work." (*ibid.*) These remarks caution one not to lose sight of the perspectival element in Hobbes' thought. But one must proceed with double caution here, for though Hobbes often remarks that it is the particular position of an individual that determines interest, he is very far from being a crude relativist, since human beings—"man the measure" of good and bad[6]—have certain overriding common interests resulting from a similar nature. Whereas an interest in mathematics may result from curiosity and the enjoyment of intellectual work, heightened and particularly fostered in some men through cultivation, the interest in civil philosophy, as a solution to the problem of maintaining one's existence and living in prosperity and pleasure with others, is a universal demand. Civil philosophy, yielding knowledge of the State, does not satisfy merely an impulse, like curiosity, which can be variously cultivated and satisfied; rather, the State is for Hobbes' supposing a desire structure which, on the most fundamental level, before cultivation or conventions and social positions—and persisting after these—is the same in all men as is their rational capacity, in its broad degree, which must deal with the desires which may harm others. This is summed up in the formula that man is not social by nature. Hobbes comments on the value of science or philosophy and especially civil philosophy:

> Are not the minds of all men of the same kind, are not the faculties of the mind the same? What, therefore, do the ones have which the others lack except philosophy? Philosophy, therefore, is the cause of these advantages. The utility of moral and civil philosophy is to be valued not so much for their comforts, which we have from the knowledge of them, but for the calamities that we have from ignorance of them. All calamities which human industry can avoid arise from war, especially from civil war, for from this comes massacres, loneliness, and shortages of all things. (*Co.*, p. 185)

The psychology is mechanistically modelled and behaviorist in orientation, but emphasizes a fundamental structure; it is evidenced by experience of others and introspection. Aside from the question of its appropriateness, Hobbes obviously intends it as the basis of his civil philosophy. To justify the construction of the State and to explain its necessary character are part of reasoning to contain anti-social behavior. Those desires which lead to violent death and to physical and psychological misery, especially in a condition or war or the condition of nature, are frustrated by fear of the mentioned probable consequences. Thereby, reason and experience foster life, prosperity, and peace by opposing opportunism. To discuss how the construction of the State does this practical task need not detain us here. What is to be considered is Hobbes' concern for the human *res*, despite Heidegger. Both the psychological ground of the State and the form it necessarily follows are testimony to this. Against Heidegger, the very science Hobbes claims to have founded arises out of, and is a response to, the human *res* by providing the greatest usefulness through addressing the conflict among the strongest human desires. Heidegger's claim that Hobbes' nominalism does not in principle allow this attacks what Hobbes considered his great achievement.

To what has already been said, it is useful to add some further doctrines for the sake of arguing that Hobbes' nominalism can go beyond language to the *res*. Let us consider science from the nominalist perspective. For Hobbes, science or philosophy proceeds through the definition of names and the consequent assertion in propositions. This is grounded in experience of the motion of things; that is, the concepts man has assume the *res* of the world. For this purpose, marks provide an aid to the individual's memory and signs provide that and disclose our considerations to others: "it is necessary for the acquisition of philosophy that there be some signs (sensible tokens) by which what has been contrived by some might be disclosed and made known to others." (*Co.*, p. 195) The functions of mark (*nota*) and of sign (*signa*) are performed by name (*nomina*); "names perform both jobs. But they perform the function of marks before that of signs." (*Co.*, p. 197) The scientific use of names involves a clearly constructed organization that is purposive or perspectival. Names, in any case, make for communication and therefore imply an existential mutuality. This, it must be emphasized, is not directly related to things: "Since, as has been defined, names ordered in speech are signs of conceptions, it is obvious that they are not signs of things themselves." (*Co.*, p. 201) They are related in the apt science, in physics not grammar, indirectly by assumption.

What may have confused Heidegger is that the "existential mutuality" need not be directly related to natural motions or, more precisely, to those natural motions that are outside ourselves. The construction of the State involves legal definitions, e.g., of "murder," "property," "marriage," etc., which are artificial. Yet, the artifice of a legal system is the instrument of peace, that is, of dealing with harmful human desires, and thereby it deals with the natural order by invention. It necessarily, if indirectly, reaches the *res*.

Nature also presents indirect constructions through phantasms or secondary qualities. Perceptions of color, for example, are the result of motions external to one's body and to one's organic motions: "For light and colour, heat and sound, and other qualities which are commonly called sensible are not objects but phantasms in the sentient." (*EW*, I, 392) One may speak of, say, the color blue in objective terms, but one can also speak of a bridge as a legal person or the sovereign (an artificial person) using object language. Of course, it should be remembered that, aside from their physical presence as sensible tokens, legal names are not objects; they are concepts devised purposively. So, "murder" relates to the order of judgment about a natural event whose referential word is "died." In parallel, the language of physics for secondary quality events is "phantasm," though in a more everyday language our perspective is objective and evaluative, as in tests for color blindness. Hobbes, as always, is flexible: "But since every name has a relation to some *nominatum*, and if that *nominatum* is not always a thing existing in nature, it is still acceptable for the sake of learning to call a nominatum a thing, as if it were the same, whether the thing really exists or is invented." (*Co.*, p. 203) If from this arises an impression of opposition between the artificial and the natural, or some aspect of nature and another, this contrast—e.g., the state of nature and civil society—is nevertheless to emphasize that the basis of all human action is in man himself, and man is a natural being. What he invents, just as what the world presents to him, depends on his desires and capacities.

Further, the basing of speech on conceptions rather than on things allows Hobbes to contrast absurd speech with truth or true propositions. Absurd speech is "where no series of conceptions in the mind correspond to a series of names." (*Co.*, p. 223) Here what goes wrong is different from an error where, "in the proper sense," there is "a departure from things." (*Co.*, p. 271).[7] But as Hobbes explains, "even if 'true' is sometimes contrasted with 'apparent' or 'fiction', it should be referred to the truth of a proposition." (*Co.*, pp. 234-5) By this we see Hobbes' intent to save appearance and invention from an ontological standard along Platonic lines. Nature is known *as man knows it*; there is a gap between man's knowledge of nature and nature itself. But man is inventive. He can transform his relationship to the rest of nature and the individual's relationship to others. It seems that this is what Hobbes means when he says, "For names are not established by the essences of things but according to the will of the man." (*Co.*, p. 271) For man does not find a standard in nature itself aside from himself. Indeed, Hobbes' neutrality in terms of some ontological sense of truth or falsity speaks to his sophist rejection of ideal or essential considerations for objects. A tree or a man is not subjected to an intraspecies comparison under a form for the ideal functioning of that kind of thing. One cannot say this man is truer than that man; instead, each particular is evaluated in terms of the concreteness of the conditions provoking emotions. So Hobbes in the *Leviathan* gives the famous example of sophist wisdom by saying the value of every man is his price.

The sophist tradition can be cited for evaluative neutrality to the "what-is-in-itself" and the achievement of value through orienting man to man conventionally. In concert with this is Hobbes' employment of the word "promise" for the communicative or language context with its association to the fundamentality of promising in his political theory. He says, "But neither things nor imaginations can be said to be false, since they truly are what they are and they do not promise, as signs do, anything that is not present. . . clouds do not promise rain, but we do when we have seen a cloud." (*Co.*, pp. 272-3) However, Hobbes' consideration of science, especially in the final chapter of the *Commutatio*, "On Method," shows this sophist heritage in relation to his materialism. Recalling the discussion of the previous chapter, he states, "We are said to know scientifically (*tou dioti*) some effect when we know what its causes are, in what subject they are, in what subject they introduce the effect and how they do it. . . Therefore, the first principle of scientific knowledge of all things are the phantasma of sense-experience and imagination. We indeed naturally know that they are, but to know why they are, or for what causes they originate, is the work of reasoning, which consists in composition and division or resolution." (*Co.*, p. 289) But, to this basis in human sensing and its derivative in imagination, Hobbes adds that reasoning brings us to a materialist conclusion, i.e., the motion of things. Of universal definitions, the ones fundamental to science, Hobbes says, "there is one universal cause of all of them and that is motion. And the variety of things perceived in sense-experience, such as colors, sounds, odor, and so on, have no cause other than motion, concealed partly in the object acting and partly in the object sensing. Thus, although what kind of motion it is cannot be known without reasoning, it is obvious it is a motion of some kind... when, therefore, universals and their causes (which are the first principle of knowledge, *tou dioti*) are known, we first have their definitions (which are nothing other than the explications of their simplest conceptions)." (*Co.*, p. 295). Most important, Hobbes makes clear that the conceptions men have lead necessarily to a materialist view of nature. Materialism is therefore a position that necessarily arises from human psychology. Materialism cannot be proven for Hobbes; it is rather the basic assumption of the things we explicate in science. The principles of universals "cannot be demonstrated, since they are principles; and as they are known by nature they indeed need explication, but not proof." (*Co.*, p. 313)

With this in mind, I briefly turn to Hobbes' response to Descartes' *Meditations* for the sake of sharpening points already made and for seeing the conflict between Hobbes and his more Platonic contemporary. I consider material from Hobbes' *Objections to Descartes' Meditations*,[8] beginning with parts of Objection 2, concerning the nature of the human mind:

> From the fact that I am exercising thought it follows that I am, since that which thinks is not nothing. But, where it is added, this is the mind, the spirit, the understanding, the reason, a doubt arises. For it does not seem good reasoning to say: I am exercising thought, hence I am thought; or, I am using my intellect, hence I am intellect. For in the same way I might say, I am walking, hence I am the walking.
>
> . . . It is quite certain that knowledge of this proposition, I exist, depends upon that other one, I think

... But whence comes our knowledge of this proposition, I think? Certainly from that fact alone, that we can conceive no activity whatsoever apart from that which leaps, of knowing apart from a knower, of a thinking without a thinker. And hence it seems to follow that that which thinks is something corporeal; for, as it appears, the subjects of all activities can be conceived only after a corporeal fashion, or as in material guise...

Hence, since the knowledge of this proposition, I exist, depends on the knowledge of the other, I think, and the knowledge of it on the fact that we cannot separate thought from a matter that thinks, the proper inference seems to be that that which thinks is material rather than immaterial.

Descartes notes in his reply that Hobbes takes substance in the most concrete way, "and does not, like most philosophers (the scholastics) distinguish between material and metaphysical or spiritual substances." This is so. It is also correct, as Descartes notes, that the property of extension is directly applicable to material things but not to mental things. Hobbes opposes Cartesian dualism by treating mental things as properties of the physical. As we have seen above, this takes the principle of matter and motion as being the fundamental explanation of natural things, and most natural to mind. For explaining the world, mental predicates or properties are consequently attributed to a proper subject or substance *which can only be physical.*

In Objection 4, Hobbes begins by distinguishing imagination from reason, which allows one to conclude that something exists; then he proposes a nominalism, but connects it to a psychological theory with a materialist turn.

There is a great difference between imagining, i.e., having some idea, and conceiving with the mind, i.e., inferring, as the result of a train of reasoning, that something is, or exists.

> ... But what shall we now say, if reasoning chance to be nothing more than the uniting and stringing together of names or designations by the word is? It will be a consequence of this that reason gives us no conclusion about the nature of things, but only about the terms that designate them, whether, indeed, or not there there is a convention (arbitrarily made about meanings) joining names. If this be so, as is possible, reasoning will depend on names, names on the imagination, and imagination, perchance, as I think, on the motion of the corporeal organs. Thus mind will be nothing but the motions in certain parts of an organic body.

Hobbes' provocative supposition in this objection should be taken less seriously than his own considered words later in *De Corpore*. There, Hobbes is clear, reason is prior to language, and conventions can be called arbitrary in regard to the inventiveness and possible peculiary of some interest, but not arbitrary in the crucial sense that natural science responds to phenomena by a cogent explanation of their probable cause. Descartes quite rightly, however, attacks Hobbes' supposition in Objection 4, and this is also the crux of Heidegger's criticism of nominalism. Thus, Descartes says in reply, "And has not my opponent [Hobbes] condemned himself in talking about conventions arbitrarily made about the meaning of words? For, if he admits that words signify anything, why will he not allow our reasonings to refer to this something that is signified, rather than to words alone?" Though it is quite in character for Hobbes to free reasoning from an ontological determination, in line with his mechanical conception of it as addition and subtraction, this text is troublesome by opposing texts of *De Corpore* in making reason *depend* on names. Yet even here, Hobbes relates names to a natural basis in imagination which is organically or materially determined. Further, Hobbes' emphasis on arbitrary conventions can be seen, in his defense, to speak to a larger character of language than that which merely relates true propositions to existence. It is noteworthy, in this regard, to resort to the first sentence of this objection, which speaks about inference or reasoning leading to the assertion of existence, for this suggests that reasoning can bring us to an understanding of the world. Thereby, Hobbes' unfortunate remark about "arbitrary conventions" is all the less to be taken as opposing his considered argumentation in *De Corpore*.

The last bit of material I will use from the *Objections* is from Objection 14. The point of this objection is to separate essence from existence. In Hobbes' view essence relates to language and not to existence, for by propositions the essence of a thing remains even after it no longer exists. The "is" of the proposition relates to "the image of the unity of a thing designated by two names." Note again the reference to the underlying imagination: "I see Socrates" and "I see a man" are examples of propositions which may relate to different degrees of perceptual refinement.

> The proposition, man is an animal, will be eternally true, because the names it employs are eternal, but if the human race were to perish there would no longer be a human nature. Whence it is evident that essence as distinguished from existence is nothing else than a union of names by means of the verb is. And thus essence without existence is a fiction of our mind. And it appears that as the image of a man in the mind is to the man, so is essence to existence. . . is, or to be, has underlying it the image of the unity of a thing designated by two names.

In a way, Descartes went even further than Plato in elevating the mental mode over the physical mode of explanation. Descartes' idea of a perfection or God that must necessarily exist (or, at least, that we cannot avoid thinking as existing) does not only exist in a psychological domain, but it closes the existential gap between its own psychological existence and its reference to reality. This is a unique concept, as Anselm had argued against the monk Guanilo. It is not unique by arising without need of proof or by the *lumen naturalis*, for other concepts also so arise, though with lesser force, such as the *cogito ergo sum* and certain mathematical notions like the triangle. But it is unique by its necessarily having existence as a property. Thus reason, for Descartes and the Platonic tradition, is more than mere Hobbesian calculation. It has an ontological weight that presents metaphysics as the ground of the other sciences, since their propositions are, considered in themselves, *als ob*. Metaphysics speaks to the other sciences from its own ontologically credentialed superiority. It conceptualizes nature as either enlarged to a non-material existence or, if leaving nature material, it claims to speak intelligibly of a super-natural dimension with a relation to nature. Hobbes, of course, signals his rejection of this approach by equating philosophy and science. Further, by grounding concepts in the sense-experience and its derivative, imagination, he proceeds along a materialist mode which has a place for human invention, actually fostered by an activist view of man and nature, but one which has no place for a dualism that elevates the mental mode. Since science, for Hobbes, is a construction based on human needs and perspectives, there is an element of will always present in it. By defining names, one commits oneself to organize the world in a particular way, to see a condition or general state of affairs chemically, biologically, psychologically, etc.—just as, for example, your reading this sentence can be considered under various sciences, including English grammar with all its conventions. Indeed, Hobbes divides names into "four genera, namely, bodies, accidents, phantasms, and names themselves" (*Co.*, p. 273) and argues that the copulated names of a proposition must be in the same genus to answer "to the composition of conceptions in the mind." (*Co.*, p. 215) Indeed, Hobbes sees the arising of metaphysical arguments like those of Descartes and the scholastics as a violation of the genus rule for propositions and therefore not relating to any possible concept in the mind. He uses the word "absurdity" for this.

Heidegger's attack against Hobbes, which claims his nominalism cannot arrive at the *res,* takes umbrage at the nominal certitude and eternality of propositional truth that Hobbes champions. The force of the Platonic tradition insinuates itself in opposing this humbling of the concepts of certitude and eternity by Hobbes. It cannot conceptually make the certitude that arises through men's will in naming, and in persuading others of the name's worth—the sophist tradition—cohere with the probability of physical knowledge, for a world considered without metaphysical contemplation or vision. At least this is my supposition, for Heidegger uses Plato's strategy against the sophists when dealing with Hobbes' theory of the proposition—namely, he isolates this aspect of Hobbes from other theories that relate to it. Further, more importantly, by not considering that for Hobbes one function of language is to create reality (e.g., as when the judiciary defines murder) but rather insisting that language is to be properly ruled by reality, Heidegger reduces Hobbes' greater methodological scope for language—signaled in finding truth a matter of language—to arbitrariness, as Plato similarly reduced "man the measure" to anomic relativism. This does not do justice to Hobbes' view that reason, working in the natural sciences, is governed by fundamental concepts of motion that disclose existence, as when through such propositions about motion one makes a prediction of an eclipse or the tides.

But Heidegger has a position of his own which is the crucial background for his treatment of Hobbes' nominalism. His assertion against treating truth as a matter of language should consider Heidegger's own view:

> ... while truth belongs in a certain way to things, it is not present among things themselves as another extant entity like them. And on the opposite side, truth is not in the understanding if understanding is thought of as a process within an extant physical object. It thus will emerge that truth neither is present among things nor does it occur in a subject, but lies—taken almost literally—in the middle "between" things and the dasein. (p. 214)

This is Heidegger's preliminary statement (for which, he

believes, he is indebted to a proper understanding of Aristotle). To bring us closer to his view, he introduces several further notions. Emphasizing his debt to both Plato and Aristotle, he sees truth as an "unveiling." But this can only be accomplished by Dasein, that is, a being whose own truth, which is a self-recognition, arises in the processes of unveiling the existence of extant things, just because the process of unveiling puts the Dasein in a certain relation to what is unveiled: "Being-true means unveiling. We include in this the mode of uncovering as well as that of disclosure, the unveiling of the being whose being is not the Dasein and the unveiling of the being that we ourselves are." (p. 216) This relation is to be taken along the phenomenological lines of intention as a structure, and further, a structure that ultimately, as in the later Husserl, is seen to be transcendent. So Heidegger says, "To the Dasein as *unveiling* there belongs essentially something *unveiled* in its *unveiledness,* some entity to which the unveiling relates in conformity to an intentional structure. There belongs to unveiling, as to every other intentional comportment, an *understanding of the being* of that to which this comportment relates as such." (p. 217) "The phenomenon of truth is interconnected with the basic structure of the Dasein, its *transcendence.*" (p. 218)

Perhaps Heidegger is as much indebted to Kierkegaard's understanding of the individual as a relation relating himself to himself when relating himself to the eternal[9] (as transcendence) as he is indebted to the notion of intention in the phenomenological tradition. In any case, it is inapt here to pursue Heidegger's position; rather, with this preparation, I turn to Heidegger's own view of the copula in assertion, in the penultimate section of Chapter Four, "The Thesis of Logic." He titles this sub-section "Unveiledness of whatness and actualness in the 'is' of assertion. The existential mode of being of truth and the prevention of subjectivistic misinterpretations." Afterwards, I will return to the earlier Hobbes discussion of Chapter Four, where Heidegger provides a "test" for Hobbes' understanding of the copula.

Consequent to having called truth a phenomenon which is interconnected with the basic structure of *Dasein* (p. 218),

Heidegger says:

> We are now in a position to focus more sharply on the problem of the "is" in the proposition. Here the "is" can mean (1) the *extantness* of a being, existentia, (2) the *whatness* of something extant, essentia, or (3) both together. In the proposition "A is," "is" asserts being, for example being extant. "A is B" can mean that B is predicated of A as a determination of A's being-such, where it remains undetermined whether A is or is not actually extant. But "A is B" can also signify that A is extant and that B is a determination extant in A, so that the existentia and essentia of a being can be intended simultaneously in the proposition "A is B." In addition, "is" signifies *being-true*. Assertion as unveiling intends the extant entity in its *unveiled*, its *true* being-such. (*ibid.*)

Since Heidegger considers Hobbes to remain "on the horizon of essentia," when turning to the "test" of Hobbes' use of the copula, it is (1) the extantness of a being and (3) the extantness of a being and its whatness which he deems incapable of being expressed in Hobbes' nominalism. Heidegger even takes Hobbes to be unable to deal with the remaining category of the use of the "is" in propositions: (2) "the whatness or essentia of something extant." That Heidegger adds "of something extant" already prepares an argument against Hobbes in that he takes him to be unable to move from words to existence. For Heidegger nothing is immune from being, that is, from the process of unveiling that establishes the Dasein in its being; and the last sentence of the above quote directs us to the intention to establish Dasein's unveiling character as a principle of ontological science. The remainder of this sub-section, instead of pursuing the complexities of the three distinctions on the uses of the copula, shows instead an eager interest in ontological science. Consider the following characterization of what Heidegger calls "assertions" (which, I take it, include propositions but are larger in scope, since body language, winks, stares, etc., can assert):

> The extant entity is itself true in a certain way, not as intrinsically extant, but as uncovered in the assertion. Uncoveredness is not itself extant in the extant entity, but instead the extant entity is encountered with the world of a Dasein, which world is disclosed for the existent Dasein. Viewed more closely, assertion, as communicative-determinative exhibition, is a mode in which Dasein *appropriates* for itself the uncovered being as uncovered . . . There is truth—unveiling and unveiledness—only when and as long as Dasein exists. . . Truth belongs to the ontological constitution of Dasein itself. . . grounded in *Dasein's transcendence.* (pp. 219-222)

In the chapter's last sub-section, Heidegger provides the direction of his intentions, *viz.*, to investigate the priority of Dasein for the problems of ontology both for the sake of "the question of the being of beings and the question of the different regions of being." (p. 224) But this investigation, which he calls "fundamental ontology," is "preparatory because it aims only to establish the foundation for a radical ontology." (*ibid.*) Radical ontology, he says, is the vitally active aspect of philosophy since Parmenides.

Faced with this "grand narrative" with its many knotty words, one might look to Hobbes, or to some other philosopher, to provide the service that Alexander provided to the Gordian knot. Others will say audacity does not count in philosophy and that one must really untangle the tangled. I myself am tempted by both procedures. But here I am saved from my warring inclinations by the Hobbes focus of this work. Before continuing, then, with Heidegger's treatment of Hobbes on the copula, I offer only this single critical question: If the Dasein is the ground of ontology and a necessary condition for truth, how can what Heidegger calls transcendence be separated from Dasein? Or again, how is radical ontology possible? It is perhaps Heidegger's eventual abandonment of a science of ontology that implicitly answers my question.

In order to show that Hobbes' nominalist position on truth, being a matter of names and not of things, cannot deal with even a "trivial proposition," Heidegger offers "to test our understanding of this entire contexture." (p. 203) The two propositions for the test are "The sky is blue" and "The sun is."

Of the proposition "The sky is blue" Heidegger says, "Hobbes interprets this proposition in conformity with his theory by taking the two words 'sky' and 'blue' to be referring to one and the same *res*... because in this something, in which subject and predicate names are identically related, the whatness gets expressed." (*ibid.*) First, there seems to be a confusion in Heidegger's specific critical intention, since by speaking of the whatness of this proposition he seems to have in mind a scientific proposition where the predicate is essentially related to the subject—the sort of proposition he classified as a type two use of the copula. However, "The sky is blue" is a contingent proposition. If Heidegger is aware that he is referring to a contingent proposition, then his use of "whatness" must refer simply to a particular state of affairs. Skies are not always blue, for example, before a storm. That the sky is occasionally blue refers to a possibility for the sort of thing sky is. Consequently, if the reason for this possibility was propositionally expressed, e.g., "when chemical composition x is present, the sky is blue," it would be a scientific proposition about the chemical essence of sky. Only then, on Hobbes' view, would we have a nominal designation, i.e., a proposition that is capable of scientific deduction. Hobbes' example of such a scientific proposition is "Man is an animal." His example of a contingent proposition, "All crows are black," shows that the universal quantifier does not guarantee the sort of certitude that definition has. On the contrary, it signals that one merely has a generalization arising from the inferential string of propositions "This crow is black," "That crow is black," "Yet another crow is black," etc. Another piece of slipshodness by Heidegger is the expression "identically related," for it supposes that subject and predicate both relate to some other thing; but, for Hobbes, who does not hypostatize being or speak as if it is radically beneath phenomena, the predicate is a property of a subject. Being is not a super-subject, nor would Hobbes speak of the transcendence of Dasein as being in truth. For Hobbes truth is through names and not in things because truth is a methodological consideration and not an ontological one. Thereby, Hobbes' view that names refer to concepts in the mind need not overthrow the certainty of truth by a skepticism about the ground of those conceptions. Indeed, we have seen that for Hobbes, the color blue results from the motion of an external thing and our own organic motions. In this sense blue is misleadingly imputed as a property of the sky; more properly, some necessary but not sufficient motion of the sky causes man to see it as blue. As I already mentioned, a science that goes from effect to cause is inferential and merely probable; therefore such scientific propositions are certain in the sense of their logic but not in the sense of their predictive power. It is the latter aspect of Hobbes' theory that tempts a criticism of his use of truth, for "truth" is a word commonly used for a theory that succeeds in prediction, as opposed to a false theory that does not succeed. But isn't this also a methodological matter rather than an ontological one, at least in the proper meaning of the word "ontology" as the logic of being? If our own concepts provide the material for the definitions of names organized by a science, how are we able to penetrate to an ontology except by the products of the physical sciences themselves? Since, for Hobbes, reason only organizes what is experienced directly by sense or indirectly by memory, it appears that the sole opening to an ontology beyond science is unavailable, i.e., except as we have discussed the basal meaning of body.

"The sun is," Heidegger's other test proposition, is also one he believes "Hobbes is simply unable to interpret." (*ibid.*) Again Heidegger bases his claim on nominalism's supposed inability to go beyond words to existence; Hobbes, thereby, in principle, cannot assert the existential fact of the "extantness of a thing." Yet, as we have seen, this is just what contingent propositions do. Such propositions commonsensically disregard skepticism and assume existence, so that the above is a short version of something like the following proposition, which is usually unnecessarily fussy: "The sun is an object with now present physical properties x, y, z, etc." Consider: Hobbes says "Socrates is a man" is an eternal truth; in his limited sense of "eternal" the names of subject and predicate are essentially combinatory. But "Socrates is alive" does not necessarily refer to "Socrates"; it is not necessarily a property of Socrates, whereas the name "man" is so by definition. It is a fixed designation that, on the one hand, allows for an orderly, if inferential, epistemic relation to contingent propositions and, on the other hand, is a *revetement* against anomic skepticism (and relativism), against how-do-you-really-know questions such as "How do you know Socrates is a man and not a robot?" or "How do you know that after the death of his body Socrates is not alive in the Isles of the Blest?"

Is Heidegger's attack on Hobbes as unable to speak of existential facts reducible to a skeptical quibble? Though Hobbes' principle that names are signs of conceptions and not of things speaks against a naive realism, it should not be made prey to skepticism either. Existence, for Hobbes, is a concept that may inferentially refer to objects outside the concepts in one's mind, because of the persistence of sense experience. It makes no sense to deny the existence of things outside the mind, as one sees in the persistent action of reason in organizing our relation to the world. Hobbes' point is that the world does not make sense without materialist assumptions, nor do we ourselves. If we did, emotions would be deracinated, as they are sometimes imagined to be in some pale, supernatural existence. This line of argument suggests the reason for Hobbes' impatience with the skepticism of Descartes' *First Meditation*.

Reason does not close the gap between truth and the world for Hobbes. In that Heidegger is quite correct. Hobbes states his position with great clarity in *Leviathan:*

> No discourse whatever, can End in Absolute knowledge of fact, past, or to come. For, as for the knowledge of

> Fact, it is originally, Sense; and ever after, Memory. And for the knowledge of Consequence, which I have said before is called Science, it is not Absolute, but Conditionall. No man can know by Discourse, that this, or that, is, has been, or will be; which is to know absolutely: but only, that if This be, That is; if This has been, That has been; if This shall be, That shall be: which is to know conditionally; and that not the consequence of one thing to another, but of one name of a thing, to another name of the same thing. (*Lev.*, VIII, p. 131)

It is this conditional knowledge that is "required in a philosopher." (*ibid.*, p. 147) But, then, is the relationship of names to one another, itself, not related to existence? "Everything is either substance or accident."[10] Therefore, the names that referentially connect a substance with its accidents in the necessary propositions of science persist despite the Heideggerian interrogation about *existentia*. To summarize, I have argued that the scientific conjunction of names in the physical sciences, not being what man himself causes,[11] is also a matter of epistemology and not ontology. It is assumptive and therefore has the character of a construction. Of course, skepticism is possible concerning the existential reference of scientific propositions. But this seems the wrong attitude or perspective, just because we desire: that is, we live, we reason, we name.. Skepticism is beside the point of the natural construction of humanity, which is *gratia nostri,* for ourselves, and *gratia aliorum,* for others, both a mark and a sign of striving.

CHAPTER FIVE

Action and Reference

Machamer and Sakellariadis in "The Unity of Hobbes's Philosophy" write cogently:

> We have claimed that the only way to achieve a viable understanding of Hobbes' philosophy is look at the structure of his system as a whole. The unsatisfactory traditional interpretations arise out of an insistence that the relation of the different levels of Hobbes' system can be understood in terms of the levels themselves, without regard to Hobbes'. . . . theories of cause, language and so forth. Our proposal is to show that only if one takes into account Hobbes' theory of philosophy and language, especially his version of nominalism, can we get an adequate account of what Hobbes is trying to say. . . . It is this nominalist theory of meaning that provides Hobbes with the bridge between the levels of philosophy. It functions to unify his system into reasonably coherent causal structure.[1]

If, then, unity is achieved in a broad sense by the presuppositions of a mechanist natural philosophy and by a nominalist theory of language, it is worthwhile to attend to those areas in Hobbes' philosophy that show strain and stress despite these unifying aspects. With this consideration, I turn to the complexity of reference in Hobbes' description of action for one and another scientific or contextual perspective, a complexity which contains underlying conceptual difficulties in his understanding of reality.

Since, for Hobbes, the sciences are of our own creation or construction of causal theories about the phenomena presented to us through the senses, by nature, there arises the question of the existence of a God who created this Nature. It is the shifts of meaning and reference in orienting creator and created that cause so much difficulty. The important themes in considering Hobbes' philosophy in a unified mode are the relationships of the conceptual contexts orienting natural man, political man, and God.

Hobbes is deservedly known as a clever writer. Perhaps all of Hobbes' writings, including those on the above themes, are fashioned by him for particular purposes. And it is not always clear how his employment of some "level of discourse" stands to his most fundamental considerations of the nature of reality when those specific texts are to be considered as coherent in relation to each other. Of course, as Machamer and Sakellariadis suggest, the general structure provided by the grounding concepts of first philosophy is always to be consulted as a resource when a consideration arises that seems to endanger the consistency of Hobbes' thinking. This is not to be forgotten when we focus on the word "action" as it refers to the domains of natural man, political man, and God. We must see if bridges exist in Hobbes' thought to organize one reality or whether, in the end, Hobbes merely provides perspectives of reality which stand in a puzzling and problematic relationship to one another. Like water out of a puzzle-jug, it may be that meaning only comes forth when some of the exit-ways are blocked.

As agents, natural man, political man, and God seem to stand in relation to the same motion of the physical world. It is plausible to begin by asking how this is possible. Granting a mechanist explanation of agency, can attributing action to a subject mean anything else than the ultimate reductive explanation of action in terms of bodies in motion? But if this is so, how can the same physical state of affairs refer to the action of many agents, e.g., man and God? The answer involves the consideration that neither God nor the sovereign—the political ruler—are bodies in the same sense as natural man. It is then possible that such words as "responsibility," "justice," "will," and "authority" shift in their meaning when used in regard to one or the other agents. How are they referentially linked in the shift of meaning, and how not? The character of unity in Hobbes' philosophy depends on the answer to this question.

Let us begin with natural man by quoting again the striking simile about action that appears in Hobbes' discussion with Bramhall. In *Questions concerning Liberty, Necessity, and Chance,* Hobbes says:

> A wooden top that is lashed by the boys, and runs about sometimes to one wall, sometimes to another, sometimes spinning, sometimes hitting men on the shins, if it were sensible of its own motion, would think it proceeds from its own will, unless it felt what lashed it... And is a man any wiser, when he runs to one place for a benefice, to another for a bargain... and seeth not what are the lashings that cause his will? (*EW* V, 55)

This text offers the same assumption of a mechanist orientation as the more famous passage which opens *Leviathan, viz.,* "For seeing life is but a motion of limbs, the beginning whereof is in some principle part within; why may we not say that all *automata* have an artificial life?" (*Lev.,* 81) I take it that the interrogative form of both texts is Hobbes' careful consideration of the hypothetical nature of all physical explanations, though the remarks remind one of the viewpoint of his definitions of the concepts of first philosophy.

Yet it is important to emphasize that the cognitive status of the mechanist approach to nature is not certain in principle, and therefore neither is its assumption that all events, including the action of human beings, are necessarily determined. Nevertheless, this is over and above the assumption that the first text brings to mind: that being moved to act from without is at odds with a psychological inclination, *viz.*, that when unimpeded in fulfilling his desire, a person is not only free to act, but is absolutely free, or a self-agent. To think that one could have done something else rather than that which one did—the counterfactual—is to accept the illusion that the will can be dislocated from nature's causal chains. That consciousness, then, which we call "the will" is reducible to motions of our physical self; if not, we face the inexplicable situation of a will which escapes the natural order. In a mechanical explanation, *per hypotheses,* everything occurs just as it does because of all of the physical conditions—what Hobbes calls the "entire cause" and nothing else—since "An entire cause is always sufficient to produce its effect." (*EW*, I, 9, 122) The cause of an action is the result of the movement of one body against another, and no cause can occur by a solitary individual body: "no body can produce an act within itself" (*Anti-White,* ch. 27); otherwise the act would exist before it was produced, which is absurd. Indeed, when the necessary physical conditions exist as the cause, the effect occurs "at the same instant." Here is Hobbes' definition of cause:

> A cause simply, or an entire cause, is the aggregate of all the accidents both of the agents how many soever they be, and of the patient, put together which when they are all supposed to be present, it cannot be understood but that the effect is produced at the same instant; and if any one of them be wanting, it cannot be understood but that the effect is not produced. (*EW*, I, 3, 121-2)

From the physical perspective, man is no exception, that is, human beings are undifferentiated parts of nature in terms of causality. This leads Hobbes to the conclusion that man is free to do if he will, but not free to will. The first use of "free" refers to the power to act: "he is free to do a thing that he may do it if he hath the will to do it, and may forbear if he hath the will to forbear." (*EW*, V, 38) In the second use of "free" the phrase "not being free to will" refers to the absurdity or impossibility of the will willing or determining itself. A mechanist orientation cannot properly allow that an effect (always, in the end, understood as movement) can occur without external agency. Since everything that occurs is the effect of something else, this means that mechanism is committed to the universal externalization of causes, not from its effect—since, according to Hobbes, that happens simultaneously—but from anything that is considered a subject or individual body. So if the will is not considered to be reduced to body in motion, it is not to be understood. And, since it is not the will that acts but the man—note the motion shifts from within the human body to produce an intention to the consideration of the body as a single individual, conventionalizing the matter—his causality or power is taken in relation to some object outside of the aggregate of motions called a person's body. For Hobbes, the will cannot be understood aside from these considerations and, therefore, he takes Bishop Bramhall's view that the will is not physical to be an empty concept, making "will" an insignificant word.

But man, unlike God, is a natural being. If we add a consideration of God as a self-moving agent, the difficulty is increased. Not only do we have the concept of self-movement but, in God, we have a being that is not material. God is not to be considered to be moved from outside Himself, and God is not to be considered to be instantiated by body in motion. Consequently, even when God is conjectured to be outside the world or the natural order—understood to be mechanical—the result is a referential opaqueness. It is the emptiness of the *je ne sais quoi*. The specialness involved in speaking about God is clear to Hobbes: "Nor is wisdom in God, a logical examination of the means by the end, it is in men but an incomprehensible attribute given to an incomprehensible nature, for to honor him." (*ibid.*, 212) Hobbes seems to hold that the use of cause in relationship to God is insignificant; it cannot be considered as providing an explanation, since there is nothing, in principle, that can be known of God as an agent. Yet there is, apparently, an exception to this for Hobbes. Without knowing how such an event could occur, there is a reasonable sense in speaking of God as First Cause.

It will be helpful to consider, for a moment, the rather paradoxical situation that confronts us at this point. On the one hand, as we have seen, the mechanist explains the production of physical states by the efficiency of external forces. Every condition of either the subject or its environment, of effect or cause, can be explained by the motion of bodies. Hobbes says, "because nothing can be moved that is not itself moved, it is untruly said that either the will *or anything else* is moved by itself." (*ibid.*, 313) Yet to hold this sort of explanation means that nothing can ever be explained fully. For each explanation is provisional in principle, though it may have a pragmatic or interest-satisfaction which halts us from pressing further. In principle, it can always be asked: "What is the cause of the cause of the previous explanation?"—that is, "What is the physical condition that produced the physical condition that was previously unpacked in terms of cause and effect?" Any particular action, then—no matter the level of its explanation in physical terms—is open to a further explanatory demand to seek a more inclusive and expanded "outside."

Consequently, physical explanations for Hobbes are not "full" physical explanations. Unlike explanations in geometry or civil philosophy, which are built up from stipulated definitions of primitive terms, so that explanation is the mere demonstration of their implications, explanations in the physical sciences have no point of rest except conventionally stipulated boundaries. The basic terms of physics are container concepts, instruments for organizing that which is open-ended in principle. In the other, non-empirical sciences, the basic definitions organize and *prescribe* the certainty of the explanation. These allow for fullness and completeness, much like the condition created by the rules of a game such as chess. Physical explanations in search of a full explanation, *per impossible,* become an infinite regress or an infinite expansion of causal conditions. Therefore, Hobbes' "entire cause" is epistemologically unsustainable; it can only be taken pragmatically. That Hobbes speaks about "causal chains" does not help, for it is not clear how a causal chain could end in a full physical explanation.

Perhaps Aristotle's view that the world is eternal—that efficient causality is infinite—implicitly recognizes this condition. Whereas Aristotle employed final and formal causes for explanation, he unmechanistically asserted a rational condition, one of value and quality, to explain this situation. Hobbes' resource for an explanation eschewing final and formal causality is desire. This is the basis of halting explanation based on pragmatic satisfaction. A human perspective organizes what is offered as real: "the end of knowledge is power. . . and, lastly, the scope of all speculation is the performing of some action, or thing to be done." (*EW*, I, 1, 7)

Thomas Aquinas, whose Aristotelian orientation was reformed by his commitments to Christian doctrine, found an infinite regress of efficient causes intolerable. The creator God—outside of the natural order, but its origin—becomes Thomas' fixed point for physical explanation. Thereby, metaphysics (what Aristotle called theology) is the well-taken, full explanation which mere physics cannot in principle provide. God is taken as First Cause, at the price of an explanatory shift of disciplines. Of course, Hobbes would not do this, since not only does he eschew final causality (which makes the shift somewhat more graceful), but he does not have a metaphysics or rational theology, since his *philosophia prima* is not a science, but rather a grounding of terms used in all sciences. The implication of a materialist ontology contained in his *philosophia prima* is only the explicit definition of those basic terms which express considerations concerning bodies in motion. And, as we have seen, to consider the First Cause or God as a final cause is intellectually abhorrent to the mechanist perspective. The question thus arises: how is it possible, granted their very different orientations, for Thomas and for Hobbes, in some sense, to speak of a First Cause?

In our discussion of how Hobbes considered God to be the First Cause, it was noted that each cause of a physical state, which for Hobbes is simultaneous with its effect, can only be understood by being itself caused by yet another cause or state of affairs prior to it. But we can ask: "In what way prior?"

It is certainly logically prior, as part of what we would offer as an explanation, but how can it be temporally prior? Since any particular state of affairs presents the simultaneous cause and effect, it would seem that there is no way to say that any aspect of a causal chain is an occurrence before or after another. God, then, as First Cause, has an agency that is simultaneous with all natural events. And man's understanding of nature in terms of before and after is an illusion, a limitation of his perspective. But how this illusion arises is puzzling, since it could only arise if we took seriously those accidents of body which are precisely the assumed framework for understanding nature. Are the limits of what Bergson calls the *esprit mechanique* occurring here—an inability to explain motion except by articially cut frames of reference?

If the notion of simultaneity is held tenaciously, then a rather Spinozistic view arises. God and the world are not separated. The mystery we noted about the ontology of body is not quite dissipated, but it can either be taken as God or as one of His modes. Yet such a position hardly seems to be Hobbes, even an esoteric Hobbes. We worked back to this conclusion by a consideration of what for Hobbes is something less primary than body—cause or the motion of bodies. But they are an accident, something that arises in the human mind. Hobbes, unlike Spinoza, has no ontological argument available that allows him to consider the human mind to be capable of some substantial harmony with God (what Spinoza calls "scientia intuitiva").

Perhaps this train of thought misleadingly takes "First Cause" too seriously. Though there is a quandary that arises from the implication of simultaneity—the undifferentiated temporality of cause and effect—we might leave this as a problem between Hobbes' method of explanation (which includes the nominalist aspect of choosing the perspective or science, each of which is based on definitions of its basic concepts) and the implications of this method for an ontological speculation, which Hobbes would surely disallow. It is the ontological treatment, in generosity to Hobbes, that cautions us to consider "First Cause" in some specifically limited way. I think that this is the case, and it will be seen when considering

Hobbes' claim that God's agency is attested to by the causal origin of the world.

The concept of God as First Cause has certain difficulties. In conceiving God as a factor external to nature, it provides a sort of explanation for nature's origin, but at the price of the *je ne sais quoi*. Of course, it is a pious option to seek an explanation in the supernatural or, simply, to leave explanation aside for the sake of faith.[2] Faced with the difficulty of being, the Thomistic recourse to the argument from First Cause, whose opaque agency is dogmatically asserted, is no less reasonable than the mechanistic explanation, if one can use "reasonable" for these conceptually tainted contexts.

Interestingly, Hobbes is like Thomas in introducing a lower grade, rational argument based on analogy when faced with this problem. Analogy seems the only plausible explanation for Hobbes' emphasis that God's attributes cannot be known[3] and yet that causality of the world demands the assertion that God is its cause. In a word, the First Cause argument is taken analogically rather than logically. This involves a peculiar sort of referencing—the having of a subject without known attributes, but yet with a known agency. The weight of "known" in "known agency" is the burden.

The relation of creator to created, especially in the case of God to the world, when taken by analogy, is clearly expressed by Kant. Kant is especially interesting in relation to Hobbes since he, unlike Thomas, shares a broadly similar view of natural explanation. Further, in considering nature Kant posits an opaque *ding-an-sich* which doesn't have the natural attributes we can know and use for explaining the physical world. In the *Critique of Pure Reason*, Kant states that the objects of regulative ideas are to be regarded as ". . . analoga of real things, not as in themselves real things" which, he explains, means that "What we then think is a something of which, as it is in itself, we have no concept whatsoever, but which we nonetheless represent to ourselves as standing to the sum of appearances in a relation (*Verhaltnis*) analogous to that in which appearance stands to one another." (A 674, B 702) Kant draws the theological implication, seeing the idea of God as "a self-subsistent, original, creative reason" which is "the single, highest, and all-sufficient ground of the sum of all appearances." (A 672, B 700)

It is likely that Kant epistemologically upgraded cognitive access to God in the *Third Critique*'s view of teleology, but the above texts give a most suggestive clarification of Hobbes. Hobbes' assertion of God's paternity of the world is neither a metaphor nor a proof. It is rather a ground that is natural for the mind on the basis of its general understanding of the world. If its intuitive force is not proposed to be as strong as Descartes' *lumen naturalis* for his ontological argument for the existence of God, nevertheless, I believe Hobbes offers it seriously as a natural road to knowing God's presence through his efficacy. Perhaps this conclusion is parataxic with the *mythos* of God teaching Job to consider Him as the creator of Behemoth and Leviathan "to humble the proud."

I will dwell on this matter a moment longer, because the pertinent texts in Hobbes are difficult and obscure, not so much in themselves but when they are considered together. There are texts that suggest that Hobbes rejects any rational explanation of God's relation to the natural world: "*actus simplicissimus* [God] signifieth nothing." (*EW*, V, 343) And since he argues that revealed religions should not be believed in opposition to the natural intellect, it is hard to know where this slippery slope ends in a feidism. For example, Hobbes argues for the doctrine of mortalism—that the Bible does not sanction disembodied souls, but rather teaches that life comes with the body resurrected at some future time. Does this mean he understands this revealed teaching not in opposition to nature? Of course for a materialist, life must be attached to body, and so mortalism is in this way plausible; but is such an occurrence plausible in terms of experience? Obviously not. One is therefore left in some doubt about the cash value of Hobbes' naturalistic principle for interpreting revealed religion, even if it does act as a brake in terms of a criterion of the possible, though not of the likely.

Some other difficulties. In *Leviathan* Hobbes writes:

> When we say anything is infinite, we signify only, that we are not able to conceive the ends, and bounds of the things named; having no conception of the thing, but of our own inability. And therefore the name of God is used, not to make us conceive him, for he is incomprehensible; and his greatness and power is inconceivable; but that we may honor him. (*Lev.*, 99)

Despite the explicitness of this text, other texts—by implication or, at least, by plausible interpretation—use "infinite" in the sense of "complete." That moves Hobbes closer to Spinoza's *Deus sive natura*, i.e., the following biblical paraphrase, "there is nothing without God, who is *infinite,* in whom are *all things,* and in whom *we live, move, and have our being.*" (*EW*, V, 302) If the Spinoza interpretation is held, then the infinite regress difficulty of causality is modified by the identification of nature with God, and the problem of agency becomes the problem of the relation of the parts to the whole.[4] Reference of God to the world would here not depend on analogy, but rather on logical modality, so this possibility speaks against the mechanist thesis. Yet the textual weight seems to tip the scales in favor of taking God as outside the world and, therefore, as a subject whose (mechanist) causality is understood analogically.

> By the word *God* we understand the world's cause. But in saying that the *world is God* they say *that it has no cause,* that is as much as *there is no God.* In like manner, they who maintain the world not to be created but eternal. (*Ci.*, XV, 14)

A last text on the subject will show Hobbes' recognition of the difficulty of the issue. Also it suggests that such locutions as "God in which all things move" relate to taking each causal instance to be a change in nature as a whole.

> For there is hardly any one action, how causal soever it seem, to the causing whereof concur not whatsoever *in rerum natura*. Which because it is a great paradox, and depends on many antecedent speculations, I do not press in this place. (*EW*, V, 302)

I intended with the above discussion of God to set in place one of the most important factors in Hobbes' understanding of agency. I take it as the outcome of this discussion, especially in pointing out that analogy explains not God but His effects as we understand them. Here there is usually no need to separate God and nature or the sum of the world, since any cognitive reference to the Creator is perspicuous through his creation. There is therefore no understanding of God's intentions except as one speculatively constructs them through nature. But the fact that Hobbes that holds there are no final purposes in nature demands a modesty and caution in such suppositions, at the least.

My discussion of agency consequently turns to Hobbes' use of natural man and political (or artificial) man. Immediately, it must be noted that for Hobbes the artificial is not outside of nature, as one signifies the supernatural. Indeed, the human capacity to construct an artificial commonwealth is a natural capacity, so that there is no essential opposition between nature and artifice; rather, as part to whole, these are terms which, from certain interests, it is convenient to contrast. With this in mind, I turn to consider natural man and political man so that I can enlarge the scope of the discussion of agency.

It has already been made clear that Hobbes considers man a natural individual, and so necessarily determined. The name "free will" must not refer to man as an uncaused agent or first cause of his action, as Bishop Bramhall would have it. For Hobbes, "free" or "at liberty" in its broadest sense applies to animate and inanimate objects and merely signifies the condition of unimpeded motion; a man is free to leave a room if it is not locked, and water is free to descend if it is not dammed. By a voluntary agent Hobbes means an individual who acts by deliberation, and this limits the concept to some animate individuals. Deliberation is the process of considering the consequence of one's action for achieving one's desires. Indeed, Hobbes almost equates will with appetite or desires, but not quite. He does say, "But no man can determine his will, for will is appetite." (*EW*, V, 34) Because he is a natural individual, man is determined in his character, whether that is expressed in psychological, physiological, or chemical language. It is a presumption for the proper use of any language describing natural man. To equate will with appetite signifies the discourse concerns natural man where the term "appetite" can be elaborated upon either psychologically or physiologically.

I said Hobbes almost makes this equation, but not quite. The "not quite" arises when one has a public or roughly political reference for "will." Consider the following rich text:

> Yet the will and the appetite, though the very same thing, use to be distinguished on certain occasions. For in the public conversations of men, where they are to judge of one another's will, and of the regularity or irregularity of one another's actions, not every appetite, but the last is esteemed in the public judgment of the will: nor every action proceeding from appetite, but that only to which there had preceded or ought to have preceded some deliberation. And this I say is so when one man is judge of another's will but every man in himself knoweth that what he desireth or hath appetite to, the same he hath a will to, though his will may be changed before he hath obtained his desire. (*ibid.*, 93)

Here we are on the way to a totally artificial will as, to use Hobbes' example, the legally created will of a bridge. Of course the sovereign is the most important instance of an artificial will, and it is particularly interesting for us when the sovereign is an individual man or woman. The king's natural will and his "impersonated" or artificial will as a sovereign have a different referential framework, so that the agent of an act may be the particular man who happens to be king, or it may be a formal construction, the sovereign. The sovereign's public judgments—whether the sovereign be composed of one, a few, or all natural persons that make up the commonwealth—have an authority for creating standards. The civil laws or will of the sovereign is created by performative utterances for Hobbes, rather than based on custom. The interpretation of the civil law is not in the hands of the sovereign's delegates, for they are outside of his will; they stand in a third-person relationship to his first-person knowledge of his own desires. The sovereign alone, as the above quote indicates, knows his own will if the sovereign is indeed to be taken paratactically to a natural man that is capable of introspecting and having a "privileged privacy." Indeed, however, as a man deliberates by the "vote" of various of his desires, so also a sovereign is composed of many individuals. Each will of the members of a sovereign can be considered as a desire in the process of deliberation in a procedure resulting in the sovereign's (artificial) will.

Let us catch our breath. What is to be noticed is that the mechanist epistemology, apt for natural man, has now more firmly intertwined itself with nominalism. However, nature as it appears to man—sense experience—is still at the ground of language used for artifice: "There is no conception in a man's mind, which hath not at first, totally, or in parts, been begotten by the organs of sense. The rest are derived from that original." (*Lev.*, 94) The nominalist turn here (as also when speaking of God's attributes) is ingenuous, for it provides a bridge between the natural ground of the State and its obviously artifacted creation of truth by the civil laws, i.e., the sovereign's will.

Since the civil state was constituted in Hobbes' doctrine to restrain gregarious but socially untrustworthy man and to establish peace and prosperity, this ingenious invention is grounded in the character of natural man. The prosthesis for natural man's character—or as John Milton, Hobbes' contemporary might say, "Adam's loss of Paradise"—is the "public judgment" or rational order imposed by the sovereign. In a way, the sovereign's will stands in relation to individual citizens' desires as natural man's will without reason stands to natural man's will with reason. It creates a public context for what is, in fact, good. This is necessary for man's survival and prosperity, as efficacious policy. Otherwise the desires and judgments of men impede one another. The language of public judgment assumes rational coordination.

> Everyman by natural passion, calleth that good which pleaseth him for the present insofar as he can forsee; and in the like manner that which displeaseth him, evil. And therefore he that forseeth the whole way to his preservation must call it good, the contrary, evil. And this is that good and evil, which not every man in passion calleth so, but all men by reason. (*EL* I, 17, 14)

That the sovereign is composed of natural persons who deliberate and act, actually encourages the consideration of how the sovereign is to be understood as an agent, not in its natural composition but in its formal manifestion as a public *persona*. Hobbes himself reminds us that this Latin word means "stage mask": a sign of impersonating nature. "Artificial person" is a phrase which Hobbes uses to stress social organization, "an artificial man created by man who is considered as representing the words and actions of another." (*Lev.*, 217) Another phrase for the sovereign, "mortal God," stresses great power, which is the basis of the sovereign's authority. Such authority qua power can only arise and continue because of the obedience of men. Contrary to the elitist politics of classical tradition, however, Hobbes is determinately egalitarian, so the sovereign's elevated position is not taken as particularly deserved from a natural standpoint. To more sharply bring out the relationship of natural and artificial in terms of the sovereign, I will consider the case when the sovereign is a single individual—he who "when liked is called king and when disliked is called tyrant." Hobbes' doctrine does not formally have it that the nature of sovereignty is changed by the number of persons that compose it; yet, in what I call a prudential or material sense, he himself prefers the sovereignty of a king for centralizing interest and, consequently, for the most reasonable coordination of civic actions.

I will briefly discuss the sovereign under three topics. (1) The king's will is not bound by the foundational contract that created the commonwealth. Thus the king's will is in a certain sense a condition of nature in terms of obedience, just where his subjects' wills are bound by the artifice of the State. (2) How the public will of the king is considered equitable and the problem of the possible inequality of his actual or natural will. (3) How the king's public judgments—e.g., about murder property, marriage—are co-extensively natural and artificial, that is, the relationship of the laws of nature to civil law.

(1) There is a conceptual need for the sovereign's will to remain in the condition of nature, for it is the creator of the artificial standards of civic behavior. This is obvious in the case of the king who "beareth his own natural person" (*Lev.*, 241), but it is equally true of the sovereign composed of more than one natural person. The sovereign must not be a party to the original contract. The natural will of the person(s) composing the sovereign remains after the establishment of the commonwealth, but the public face of the sovereign, its art, depends on the private interest of natural person(s). Without interest there cannot be any motion to the commonwealth. Further, and particularly separating the king from his subjects, is the sovereign's function of creating rules (or that public face) for the subjects to obey. Since he is the criterion of the rules, it is conceptually impossible that he be legally bound to obey them. He is outside the legal sphere; as its creator, he is a "mortal God."

The subject or citizen is (artificially) bound to obey the sovereign's will or civil laws. The subject affirmed just this as a party to the contract of civil establishment, either overtly or tacitly. This obedience relationship is also affirmed in the case of government by conquest. For both sovereign and subject the natural will is necessary for their artificial command-obedience relationship. Preservation and prosperity are the best reasonable chances in the civil condition, and the natural desires for them are therefore continually present. This is the *material* basis and inducement, in nature, for the subject to honor the *formal*, artifacted obligation of obedience.

Therefore civil obedience can be considered from *two* referential standpoints. The first is from the artificial or formal perspective. Here the measure is clear: the sovereign's will is the criterion for obedient acts. He is the last recourse, the only authoritative one, for deciding the meaning or intention of his will as expressed in the civil laws. More clarity and certainty of meaning exist for the civil laws, in principle, than for matters decided by prudence or even in the natural sciences, for the sovereign creates them himself through definition. Of course, this sort of certainty is temporally limited; the sovereign can change a law. The same natural person(s) composing the sovereign can change his mind, or he can be replaced by others who may change the law. Yet, in the ideality of theory, the subject's civil action has a sure guide in the sovereign. Civic action therefore has a terminus, whereas the action of a natural man is not grounded absolutely; as Hobbes puts it, experience teaches nothing with certainty. Consequently—and I wish to stress this point—the second perspective, the material one from natural prudence, has the hazard of a private judgment rather than the certainty of the quintessential public judgment of the sovereign. Whether the commonwealth is *materially* creating peace and, in general, better serving the individual than the condition of nature, with its perils of war, is simply a prudential and private judgment. Therefore, obedience to the civil law is the subject's natural vote of confidence for commonwealth. The *natural meaning* of any act of political obedience is an assertion of the interest of the actor in maintaining civil society, whereas its *artificial* meaning is definitively related to the sovereign's will in a particular of public order.

The attractive sharpness of Hobbes' political doctrine is its either/or quality. Logically, either one acts for civil society by obeying the civil law or acts against it by disobedience. The disadvantage of this, it has been argued, is that aside from delegated responsibility and permitted counsel, the Hobbesian subject has no rational involvement in his civic governance. Especially, by the artificial understanding of civic governance, the citizen is subjected to paternalism, no matter his own capacities: "it is not wisdom but authority that makes the law." (*D*, 55)

(2) Hobbes himself resists the formal conclusion which leaves the sovereign's will unquestioned and obligatory by taking advantage of the actual circumstances, the material condition, of governance. Consider the following: though the judge is formally merely the sovereign's delegate and the sovereign can negate any decision of a judge—for, indeed, those decisions are in his name—nevertheless, this seldom occurs. Though, on the one hand, the judge should take all of the sovereign's laws as equitable, the actual practicable situation of judicial discretion is suggested by Hobbes' remark that judges should have a sense of *natural* equity. Hobbes goes further: the judge ought to provide a decision not in terms of the mere words of a legal statute, but by a supposition of its equitable intention. This endorses a natural rather than an artificial orientation, for to ask how the sovereign considers equity is nearly tantamount to how the asker considers it. Though perhaps it is fairer to speak of it as the evidence of the actual signs of the sovereign's intentions from his past, similarly considered behavior, and the judge's natural prudence. Ingeniously, in this way one has one's cake and eats it as well. The definitional certainty, the artificial reference to the sovereign's will (which of course may not be the actual or natural psychological state of the person or persons composing the sovereign at any particular time) is kept in name; and, in actual fact, the sovereign's indefeasible option directly to express his will can be taken. Nevertheless, the normal practice of rule making and rule interpretations for the State relies on the natural acumen of the sovereign's delegates. Perhaps this bridging of the natural and the artificial, the road between man's socially undependable desires and the need to create and maintain the social order—like bridges made of vines in a jungle—is meant to carry one despite the discomfort of the swing.

The formal and material modes are illustrated by the peculiar condition of the king as both mortal man and "mortal God." Great power is necessary to bring men to obedience, since their natural will or desires cannot be relied upon to establish peace. The king, with his "awesome" power and the subsequent advantages of his position, "seems something of a God to other men." (*Ci*, I) But his natural will is not transformed by his sovereignty. Hobbes rather dogmatically asserts that human nature is always the same—his introspection of himself is generalized as being informative of human nature—though the objects of desire change in terms of circumstance. Indeed, the instrumental use of the commonwealth is to change the objects of desire in order to produce social accommodation.

It is well argued by Hobbes that the king's duty to produce that accommodation is based on such natural laws as gratitude and charity, and that his material self-interest and that duty converge. After all, a healthy and prosperous State makes for a secure and powerful sovereign. Yet, unlike the citizen, whose artificial civil duties are encouraged by the natural threat of the sword, the king's natural duty—he has no other—is a matter of conscience.

Why do not the king's socially unreliable desires make him incapable of fulfilling his duty to the State? Hobbes argues that his position succors his desires, or ought to. For one, though he is in a natural relation to the State in that he has not given up his liberty and become bound by the civil contract to obedience, nevertheless, unlike a person in a condition of nature, he is not oppressed by its conditions. Indeed, the State fulfills the king's vanity—"he is the font of all honors"—and, in a reasonable way, his needs for comfort and possessions. Further, as mentioned, by doing his duty he actually secures and extends these.

> ... considering that the greatest pleasures of sovereign governors proceedeth not from any delight or profit they can expect in the damage or weakening of their subjects, in whose vigour consisteth their own strength and glory.
> (*Lev.*, 238)

This argument of course does not account for the madness or vainglory that sovereigns have actually shown often enough. Perhaps Hobbes offers us here a rational ideal, a piece of protreptic rhetoric.

Alas, the "mortal God" is not the true God, whose needs are immediately satisfied by his power. The mortal God can be maddened by *hubris* and he may desire what for a mortal person is impossible. Hobbes may have been publicly responsible by encouraging kings to their duty by his argument, but he knew it was not a historical consideration. The formal view of sovereignty, that the king always acts equitably, is balanced by Hobbes' commonsense understanding that actual kings often fail in the material sense: they do not act equitably. The *Leviathan* communicates that in an apparent warning to Hobbes' own king: "Negligent government of Princes (as a "natural punishment") causes rebellion; and rebellion with slaughter." (*Lev.*, 407)

Here, then, at the center of Hobbes' politics one sees "duty" and "equity" used in two tracks, with referential distinction of the natural and of the artificial. The strength of the doctrine is in the ingenuity of the intertwining of the *topoi* they refer to. The formal framework, artificially created, provides clarity and certitude, yet it depends on the material condition, on human nature. The artificial arises from interest, from the desires of human nature, and therefore it is an instrument of the natural.

(3) Whenever Hobbes considers the relationship between creator and created, a consideration of action in two tracks emerges. Nowhere is this more obvious than in the sovereign's creation of civil law. The pivot of our present concern, and of Hobbes' legal philosophy, is expressed through the maxim, "The law of nature and the civil law contain each other and are of equal extent." (*Lev.*, 314)

The civil law is constitutive, like a game; it is the rules organizing activity. Each civil society has different civil laws, and these can be changed in a particular civil society just as the rules of baseball have changed in the course of its history.

Since the civil law is the particular expression of a sovereign's will, formally assumed as equitable and to be obeyed by the sovereign's subjects, each civil society is a world of sorts. Yet if one compares the civil laws of one State with another, there is difference and even opposition between them. How can each be equitable if they differ?

The difficulty in answering this question is increased when natural law is considered. Natural law is regulative; that is, it is universally descriptive of human nature. Hobbes assumes that men have the same human nature and must secure a way for their natural desires not to make the lives of others miserable. He says that the "natural laws" are more properly called "theorems of nature," since there is no creator or law-giver of them (unless we consider the matter by belief rather than by reason and make God the law-giver).

These theorems or "qualities that dispose men to peace, and to obedience" (*ibid.*)—justice, gratitude, mutual accommodation, and the avoidance of contumely, pride, and arrogance—are demands against human nature's inclination to resist these laws, theorems, or qualities. It is reason which leads us to desire peace and to see these as means necessary for peace. But the State is also established for the sake of peace. Its constitutive rules made by the sovereign become for Hobbes the presumed concrete expression of nature's regulative wisdom. Different and even opposing laws in different commonwealths— or even in the same commonwealth at different times—are not formally comparable. Different circumstances demand formally opposed laws for the sake of equity.

Let us consider this: to *harm* a man by killing him is a natural act, and the words in this description refer to natural considerations. However, to *injure* a man by murdering him refers to the artificial condition of commonwealth, for not all killing is murder and not all harm is injury or a case for civic judgment. Hobbes clearly emphasizes the difference between the action in nature and the action in law:

> Theft, murder, adultery, and all injuries are forbid by the

laws of nature; but what is to be called *theft*, what *murder*, what *adultery*, what *injury* to a citizen, this is not to be determined by the natural, but by the civil law. (*Ci*, VI, 16)

The sovereign defines the legal terms; this is his will. His will thereby creates the world or individuality of a particular commonwealth. "Murder" and the rest are forbidden by the laws of nature not in this creative sense, but in a general, if vague, understanding that such injustices are against man's greatest interest.

In the above discussion of political man and natural man, there has emerged a similar character of thought as in Hobbes' understanding of physics. His mechanistic conceptualization posited the source of motion of an individual always from the outside. Further, the notion of individuality is perspectival, and constructed it seems, since movement is the principle of an entire system within which the "secondary" individuality of our interest is isolated. So, also, each civil society is a world or individual within which the interest of its components may be focussed upon. Further, looking from inside to an outside for motive power seems to have transitivity: political man's actions must be ultimately explained by the principle of motion in the psychology of natural man; and, in turn, this psychology must be explained by the larger systematic notion of nature which finds its outside, its explanation, in God, who cannot be known in Himself. Thus, opaquely, we come to "the law of nature is all of it divine." (*Ci*, IV, 24)

To grant Hobbes' assumption, the determination of the human will is what it is, as if all of nature, because of God. God is taken as the First Cause that sustains nature entire. Yet, against Bramhall, Hobbes argues that a man's will can be called free even though it is necessarily determined, for a man acts as he wills or desires when there is no outward impediment. That men have a certain character refers to the determination: "the law of nature was written in our heart by the finger of God without our assent." (*EW*, V, 178) That it is proper to educate, to punish, and to counsel does not oppose this determination of the will for Hobbes; rather, it is part of it. It takes the circumstance of the private mind and properly enlarges it by what may be called "public judgments." That the individual is acted upon from without for the sake of a larger or public consideration, or modified and provoked by other desires, does not speak against the freedom of the individual or the determination of the individual.

But as we have seen, the final reference to action in God ends in obscurity. Doesn't this apparent need to have a firm ground from which to move all the rest, added to the obscurity of God as that ground, throw the entire approach into doubt? For Hobbes, "revelation supernatural" provides no intellectual satisfaction for this obscurity, since it involves not only what we know but *what we can possibly know*: "from revelation supernatural, which revelation man may indeed have of many things above, but of nothing against human reason." (*Lev.*, 180)

But this means, granted the obscurity, that when God is spoken of as king or as judge, it is by analogy to human political experience. Yet there is a difference here that makes a difference for the intellectual credential of such speaking. When a man is spoken about as king or judge, the normativity involved does not encounter the metaphysical issue of being the ground of normativity. Hobbes' sovereign is, of course, the ground of the norms of the commonwealth, in that this mortal God imitates the immortal God; yet, at this level of discourse, no metaphysical issue of ultimate creativity presses our considerations.

God as the creator, the First Cause that determines nature, including man, leaves no room, however, for anything that occurs in nature to be bad or evil. This is the mode of God as king: a supremely performative actor. On the other hand, God considered as judge, a normative mode in relation to ourselves, provides a judgment of our actions from the perspective of our own limited and fragmentary vision. We cannot use the first consideration to exonerate ourselves from blameworthiness, and we cannot use the second perspective to justify our every action. By this ultimate issue of Hobbes' philosophy, man stands fragile and stunned. He is bereft of the efficacy of prayer.

> When I say, prayer is not a cause or a means, I take *cause* and *means* in one and the same sense; affirming that God is not moved by anything we do, but has always one and the same eternal purpose, to do the things from eternity he hath foreknown shall be done. (*EW*, V, 220)

This means that the same action, which is our sin but not God's, has a different referential track. Worth and authorship are taken differently. The action when considered as having man as its author may be a sin, but when considered in relation to its metaphysical foundation—the authorship of God—is not only not a sin, but to be called good. Hobbes says:

> Though God be the cause of all motion and of all actions, and therefore unless sin be no motion or action, it must derive a necessity from the first mover: nevertheless it cannot be said that God is the author of sin, because not he that necessitateth an action, but he that command and warrant it, is the author. (*EW*, V, 138-9)

Yet can one agree with Hobbes' separation of the necessitating and the authority for the sin? Is not the very reason that Hobbes provides for necessitating an action the same as the warranting and commanding of the action by God? Either the loss of God's authority or the impotence of man as an agent is reason enough for Bishop Bramhall to consider Hobbes' doctrine monstrous, for either sin is an illusion or man, stunned by God's power, cannot understand His will or His view of good. In this case only the most servile character can exist in relation to God. The latter seems to be expressed by Hobbes when he enjoins men to praise God with words that they cannot possibly understand because they refer to a being outside of nature.

In apparently having "sin" stand paratactically to a particular natural act as "murder" stands to killing a person, Hobbes creates two referential tracks: the normative and the naturally descriptive. But since both his physical theory about nature and his theory about the First Cause, or God, demands the overcoming of this separation, there is a theoretical discomfort in Hobbes' position or positions. In this, Hobbes' philosophy stands in a similar situation as does Kant's, where the determinativity of the mechanistic premises of the *First Critique* relates to the autonomy of value of the *Second Critique*. The debate about whether Kant is conceptually coherent by considering agency from natural determination and also from human freedom is quite pertinent to our thinker of the previous century. Does Hobbes provide a rationally coherent philosophy if a man's or woman's action is grounded in the necessitating causality of God's will, but also, somehow, the man or woman is responsible for so acting?

CHAPTER SIX

Causality and Inner Design Metaphysics

In his *Explanation and Understanding* (1972), the eminent Finnish philosopher Georg Henrik von Wright distinguished two traditions: the Aristotelian and the Galilean. The former focuses on a teleological approach for understanding; the latter, as von Wright puts it, "runs parallel with the advance of the causal mechanistic point of view in man's effort to explain and predict phenomena."[1] Hobbes, who considered his older contemporary Galileo to be the first founder of a new science since Euclid, obviously belongs to the Galilean tradition. I will contrast Hobbes to the Aristotelian tradition, which takes seriously the possibility of metaphysics, that is, that the teleological explains as well as provides an understanding of reality.

In his article on teleology in *The Encyclopedia of Philosophical Sciences* (Part I, 204), Hegel writes:

> The distinction between the End or *final cause,* and the mere *efficient cause* (which is the cause ordinarily so called), is of supreme importance. Causes properly so called belong to the sphere of necessity, blind, and not yet laid bare. . . . The End, on the other hand, is expressly stated as containing the specific character in its own self—the effect, namely, which in the pure causal relation is never free from otherness. . . . By End, however, we must not at once, nor must we merely, think of the form which it has in consciousness as a mode of mere mental

representation. By means of the notion of INNER DESIGN Kant has resuscitated the Idea in general and particularly the idea of life. Aristotle's definition of life virtually implies inner design, and is thus far in advance of the notion of design in modern Teleology which has in view finite and outward design only.

Hegel's remark considers a tradition which excludes Hobbes and most modern, especially empiricist, philosophers between Galileo and Kant. The crucial distinction here turns on whether teleological explanation has an "inner design" which depends on final causality or an external one which depends on efficient causality alone. This difference opens and closes variant possibilities for the ontological description of nature and also human nature. Hobbes' view of causality, both in nature and in the construction of the State, is more clearly understood by his opposition to the metaphysical inner design viewpoint.

But, before turning to Hobbes, I will develop the inner design viewpoint. To do this, instead of locating the discussion in Aristotle, as Hegel suggests, I turn to the magistral Plotinus. His Platonism is less problematic, and, in its doctrinaire format, more clearly confrontational. To start with, Plotinus provides a clear statement of his opposition to explanations merely from efficient causality. Freedom in action, which for Plotinus (as for Kant and for Hegel) is essential to our humanity, cannot be aptly posited, or explained, on the basis of an outer design or external perspective; and so, it cannot be conceptualized by efficient causality. Plotinus says:

> How can a compelling imagination, an appetite drawing us where it will, leave us masters in the ensuing act? Need, inexorably craving satisfaction, is not free in face of that to which it is forced: and how at all can a thing have efficacy of its own when it arises from an external, has an external for its very principle, thence taking its being as it stands? It lives, for the external, lives as it has been

molded; if this is freedom, there is freedom in even the
soulless. (Plotinus, VI, 8)

This statement strikes the same note as Hegel in limiting the power of explaining action by efficient causes on the grounds that such explanations are unable to capture the freedom of the individual. By specifically focusing on the efficacy arising from imagination and appetite, Plotinus might well have in mind his opposition to materialism, conspicuously to the atomic tradition, and especially to the Epicureans. (Cf. Hobbes, *EW*, V, 313: "For I said not, the will is not moved, but we are not moved: for I always avoid attributing motion to anything but body.") In taking pleasure and pain as the basis of action and by reducing this phenomenal experience, it seems, ultimately to matter in motion, Hobbes (as well as Epicurus) is challenged by Plotinus.

In the following quoted material, Plotinus provides a view of action where the rational aspect of the act is timeless. This is self-conscious and reflexive, since man is essentially rational; indeed, because Plotinus also holds that reason controls rather than arises from matter, contemplation is the supreme self-assertive act. Further, freedom is an aspect of a voluntary act involving knowledge and, in the fullest sense, self-unifying knowledge is in the contemplation of the Good. This Good is not conditional, just as our essential nature in its reliance on the Good is not materially conditioned. Consequently, to be free or to actuate our essence means a readiness to prefer the Good to any circumstantial or conditional value: one's biological life, country, children, etc. By acting in time in friendship with the Good, one achieves something of the quality of timeless reality. In Plotinus' own words in the *Enneads*:

> Act, we aver, is timeless. (IV, 1:16)
> Action, thus, is twofold: there is that which occurs in the external, and that which does not. The duality of Action and Passion, suggested by the notion that action

always takes place in the external, is abandoned. (VI, 1:19)

Thought itself need not be an action, for it does not go outward toward its object, but merely attends to it. It is not always an activity; for all Acts need not be definable as activities, for they need not produce an effect: activity belongs to Act only accidentally. (VI, 1:22)

... ignorance is not compatible with real freedom: for the knowledge necessary for a voluntary act cannot be limited to certain particulars but must cover the entire field. Why, for example, should killing be involuntary in the failure to recognize a father and not so in the failure to recognize the wickedness of murder? (VI, 8:1)

Effort is free once it is toward a fully recognized good; the involuntary, precisely motion away from a good. (VI, 6:4)

Virtue and the Intellectual-Principle are sovereign and must be held the sole foundation of our self-disposal and freedom. Virtue does not follow upon occurrences as a saver of the imperiled; at its discretion it sacrifices a man; it may decree the jettison of life, means, children, country even; it looks to its own high aim and not to the safeguarding of anything lower. Thus our freedom of act, our self-disposal, must be referred not to the doing, not to the external thing done but to the inner act, to the Intellection, to virtue's own vision. (VI, 8:16)

Being accompanies the Act in an eternal association: from the two (Being and Act) it forms itself into the Good, self-springing and unspringing. (VI, 8:7)

By considering the Act categorically, and action as something else, that is, as only accidentally belonging to Act, Plotinus offers two ontological schema and, consequently, two frameworks for the explanation of things in time. One is the provisional calculation from experience; here the explanatory are external, finite, and limited. The probabilities of sense experience and the idiosyncratic aspects of personal and cultural values are such. When this sort of explanation is interrogated, Plotinus, like Plato's Socrates, finds it unsatisfactory because of its limited vision of the human condition and, at the least, a tendency to logical incoherence (with a consequent incapacity to generate systematic organization). The other explanatory approach, from eternal principles, proposes to accomplish much of what the first cannot. Plotinus indeed claims finite, contingent-oriented methodologies, e.g., induction from sense experience, point beyond themselves to the Good—that is, to the source and sustaining condition of reality.

It is precisely against such dual ontological schema—and even against the less bold Platonism of Descartes, who did consider the *res extensa* mechanically—that Gilbert Ryle levels the charge of a "ghost in the machine." Ryle, like Hobbes, opposes the inner design explanation. Though their language must be somewhat adjusted, Ryle (at least by implication) and Hobbes consider the will—that aspect of man most like God for Descartes—reducible to phenomenal conditions. Also, the will is assertable of animals as evidenced by their external behavior. What they oppose, as Ryle puts it, is the theory where the workings of the body are motions in space, so that

> the causes of these motions must then be *either* other motions of matter in space *or*, in the privileged case of human beings, thrusts of another kind. In some way which must forever remain a mystery, mental thrusts, which are not movements of matter in space, can cause muscles to contract.[2]

The following quotes from Hobbes show the sharp contrast between his outer design viewpoint and the inner design one of Plotinus:

> For the nature of good and evil follows from the nature of circumstances. (*De Homine*, XI, 4)
> A body is said to work upon or act, that is to say, to do something to another body, when it either generates

> or destroys some accident in it; and the body in which an accident is generated or destroyed is said to suffer, that is, to have something done to it by another body; as when one body putting forwards another body generates some motion in it, it is called the AGENT; and the body in which motion is so generated, is called the PATIENT ... (*EW*, I, Ch. 9)
>
> I conceive that nothing taketh beginning from itself, but from the action of some other immediate agent without itself: and that therefore when a man first hath an appetite or will to something, to which immediately before he hath no appetite or will, the cause of this is not the will itself but something else in his own disposition. (*EW*, V, 372-3)
>
> For will itself is an appetite; and we do not shun something because we will not do it, but because now appetite, then aversion, is generated, by those things desired or shunned, and displeasure necessarily follows from those same objects. (*De Homine*, CI, 1)
>
> Lastly, I hold that the ordinary definition of a free agent, namely, that a free agent is that, which when all things are present to produce the effect, can nevertheless not produce it, implies a contradiction, and is nonsense; being as much as to say, the cause may be sufficient, that is necessary, and yet the effect not follow. (*EW*, V, 385)
>
> ... voluntary presupposes some precedent deliberation, that is to say, some consideration and mediation, of what is likely to follow, both upon the doing and the abstaining from the action deliberated of. (*EW*, IV, 243)

This ensemble of quotes evidences Hobbes' reduction of will to the action of appetites as the spring of behavior: the will and the appetite are for Hobbes the very same thing (see *EW*, V, 93). Further, in contrast to Plotinus, Hobbes' free agent need not be a rational agent, or even a living one. He defines freedom as action without external impediments (cf. *EW*, IV, 273-4). Freedom is merely considered in terms of the equivalent notions of sufficiency and necessity. All things therefore have liberty or freedom for Hobbes, for he takes this to be the very movement or the assertion of capacity of the thing itself. Of Hobbes' position, his contemporary Bishop Bramhall says, "This is brutish liberty, such a liberty as a bird hath to fly when her wings are clipped." (*EW,* V, 40) Clearly, Hobbes' notion of freedom is not only consistent with compulsion, but discusses the same circumstance, though from a different modal perspective. For to say a thing is free or has sufficient power to say it can do what it can do and to say a thing is compelled or necessitated is to say it must do what it does, that is, it has no more power than it has, to do otherwise than it does.

Bramhall notices Hobbes' externalist approach and complains, "It is not inconsistent with true liberty to determine itself, but it is inconsistent with true liberty to be determined by another without itself." (*EW,* V, 32) Unlike the inner design tradition, the use of the word "action" by Hobbes does not demand self-consciousness. Indeed, voluntary action, the action resulting from deliberation or calculation of possible circumstances as action also motivated by desire, is neither more nor less free than the motions of inanimate things. Nevertheless, the particular way that will is reduced to desire is clearly emphasized in Hobbes' understanding of deliberation:

> . . . deliberation is nothing else but so many wills alternatively changed according as a man understandeth or fancieth the good and evil sequels of the thing concerning which he deliberateth whether he shall pursue it. . . So that in deliberation there be many wills, whereof not any is the cause of voluntary action but the last. (*EW,* V, 401-2)

Unlike Plotinus, Hobbes' outer design approach does not use "voluntary" for the process itself of deliberating; by calling the last appetite or consideration of the process leading to an act the will, he places emphasis on the change the individual causes outside himself. Indeed, when pressed by Bramhall that he calls even spontaneous acts deliberate, Hobbes says, "there may be a difference between what may be deliberation and that which shall be construed as deliberation by a judge." (*EW*, V, 350) This avoids a contradiction for Hobbes and it shows us again his inclination to an outward or public credential for names or attributes which are used to describe human action. Further, the process of deliberation, since it must ultimately be explained by matter in motion, the physical processes to which in themselves Hobbes never attaches value, is aside from a consideration of value. Hobbes locates efficient causality in relation to the man and not to the matter in motion from which his individuality arises. In terms of value, the efficient cause is the man, and not his physical condition. Hobbes, unlike Plato in his *Laws* (626d), and consistent with nominalism's referential orientation to individuals, finds it hard to speak of warfare within a man. A man may indeed be mad or foolish, but it is he who acts and not some part of his inner motions; and, he acts always under conditions. Conditions, as they relate to desires, make for pleasure and pain. Since having a desire always demands that an object act on the individual, in this sense a man is neither pleased nor pained by his own self.

In the deliberation to construct a State, outward design also expresses itself in the emphasis on conditions for the welfare of the individual. But since the State is an artificial individual, the notion of cause in reference to it is also artificial. Hobbes says, "To make a law is therefore to make a cause of Justice, and to necessitate justice." (*EW*, IV, 253)

That causality refers to a physical analysis and sometimes to an associated but, nevertheless, different mode—the artifacted—is most important. Hobbes is faced by the conclusion of nature mechanized and ordered by efficient causes, and he like Kant chooses a realm where final causes emerge. But instead of a separate practical reason with free will in an ethical realm (with its ensuing consequence of moving toward the familiar dualism both in the conception of reason and of ontology), Hobbes locates value in desire: in wanting and not wanting. This, however, has the following consequence: desire, like all bodily processes, is ontologically reducible to matter and motion, and suggests that human values are, like secondary qualities, an illusory condition of human perspective: "the variety of things perceived in sense experience, such as color, sounds, odors, and so on, have no cause other than motion, concealed partly in objects acting and in objects sensing." (*EW*, I, Ch. 6) Perhaps this can be put more positively by saying that value exists where nature creates a material condition for complex sensibility; values thus arise from natural forces, but are only present in a particular creature's desires.

For Hobbes, "philosophia prima" merely has an ultimate generality by defining the names involved in the generation of any object whatsoever that might then be investigated by a specific science. Plotinus and the inner design tradition, however, try to separate, at least provisionally, the ontological commitments of science and metaphysics, thereby to allow science to focus on finite, mutable, and temporal material entities while, nevertheless, providing value ultimately for these by metaphysics. Thereby, Plotinus seeks to rescue the "external" and functional explanations of efficient causality from valuelessness by subordinating them to the final causality of essences. For Hobbes, this is absurd. He writes:

> The writers of metaphysics reckon up two other causes besides the efficient and the material, namely the ESSENCE, which some call the formal cause, and the END, or final cause; both of which are nevertheless efficient causes. (*EW*, I, 123)

Hobbes' reduction of formal and final causality to material and efficient causality means that action, even as a possibility of aliveness, is a condition of matter in motion. Hobbes, however, does not hint that he is a hylozoist; on the contrary, life for him is an emergent quality of complex sensate individuals. That mere matter and motion are not *per se* alive seems to have an explanatory gap for the eventual emergence of life from it.

But matter in motion is not life as Hegel understood it—of a rational principle or *Geist* organizing reality. Though efficient causality can describe the norms of materially complex individuals, that is, functional purpose, the question remains, when purpose is missing from the material processes that are the ground of these norms (which is the case in Hobbes), of how value exists beyond the conditional. Perhaps it is Hobbes' point that it does not; he seems comfortable with God's answer to Job that His unquestionable and unexplainable power is the source of the good. Contrariwise, Bramhall inclines to Plato's argument in the *Euthyphro* that the good is recognized by the divine. Hobbes' choice seems to be between a fideist piety and an inability to explain value on ultimate grounds.

The classic presentation of seeking value beyond mere physical explanations is found in Plato's *Phaedo* when Socrates points out that he is in jail not because his body is in a certain physical condition but because he has made certain decisions. To reduce Socrates' decisions to matter in motion is to make of it a bare fact of reality without purpose. Though Hobbes would also consider Socrates' decisions as arising from his desires, Plato would accuse Hobbes of contradicting himself by ultimately reducing those decisions to matter in motion. Hegel, I believe, does not consider Hobbes to have a conception of life, on the grounds that the brute fact of existence, even when expressed as the functioning of a physical system (but without mind), does not have life. And pleasure, as an end in itself, Hegel discounts as even capable of having a meaning, much less of generating value, since it is, as Plato puts it in the *Philebus*, "formless and cannot give form."

Hobbes' notion of life and value is, on the contrary, determined by objects providing pleasure and pain, calculated in relation to the desires: "whatever is the object of any man's Appetite or Desire; that is what he calls Good: And the object of his Hate, and Aversion, Evil: And of his contempt, Vile and Inconsiderable." (*Lev.*, Ch. 6) Of course, the reduction of good to desire does not deny the emergence of a public good through the civil laws. The civil laws provide a safe, though constrained, condition for a man; instrumentally, they foster the primary desire, which is to exist, and, as well, the hope of prospering. The civil laws are demanded or necessary just because all the desires of a man can scarcely be fulfilled. A man cannot have felicity when competing for objects with other individuals whose desire structure is the same as his (though the actual objects of their desires may be different from his). So experience shows a man that he cannot obtain all that he desires, and his pleasures are therefore conditional or limited. Hobbes writes:

> The greatest good, or as it is called, felicity and the final end, cannot be obtained in the present life. For if the end be final, there would be nothing to long for, nothing to desire, whence it follows not only that nothing would itself be a good from that time on, but also that man would not even feel. For all sense is conjoined with some appetite or aversion; and not to feel is not to live. (*De Homine,* XI, 15)

Let us briefly return to Plotinus. Though Plotinus finds the desires or the "duress of human nature and the needs of individual existence" important, it is interesting to compare him to Hobbes on actions oriented by desire:

> When, on the contrary, the agent falls in love with what is good in those actions, and, cheated by the mere track or trace of the Authentic Good, makes them his own, then, in his pursuit of the lower good, he is the victim of magic. For all dalliance with what wears the mask of the authentic, all attraction towards the mere semblance, tells of a mind misled by the spell of forces pulling towards unreality. Contemplation alone stands untouched by magic; no man self-gathered falls to a spell; for he is one, and that unity is all that he perceives, so that his reason is not beguiled but holds due course, fashioning its own career and accomplishing its task. In the other way of life, it is not the essential man that gives the impulse, it is not reason; the unreasoning also acts as a principle, and finds

> its premises in emotion. (IV, 4:44)
> The essential man is beyond harm. (IV, 43:43)

For Plotinus and the classical tradition, much if not all of our existence as animals takes external circumstance as the medium to express our humanness.[3] But our continued existence is not the fundamental value. Action, then, in the fullest sense, is the establishment of our rationally unconditioned essence in this conditional medium. It may be said that acting self-consciously is a thinking despite the constraints of the world: that thinking is the action, and the rearranging of the world is the shadow of action. The accusation against Hobbes' viewpoint is that he takes the shadow for the only action. Hobbes' outward design never loses its conditionality; for him that is evidenced in just this: a man wishes to supersede any particular desire as it is satisfied. A moving finger of finitude, the unity of the individual is in this way not in-and-for itself. The aliveness of self-awareness is reduced to the matter-of-factness of desire where wants, by being met or not, by providing pleasure and pain, in their degrees, are the very organization of individuality.

Since the fundamental principle of matter in motion does not have, so to speak, an inside, it does not have essential value; thus, Hobbes' value is always self-oriented and perspectival. Its bedrock, from which arises a rational perspective, is in maintaining the organization of complex individuals. This argument seems to present an amphibolous division. On the one hand, we can say "man is the measure"—his continuance and pleasure set the agenda. On the other hand, since a man is reduced to matter and motion, we can, without denying the necessity of the former, relate to it with pessimism.

> Whatever accidents or qualities or senses make us think there be in the world, they are not there, but are seeming and apparitions only: the things that are in the world about us, are those motions by which these seemings are caused. (*EW*, I, 102; *EW*, IV, chap. 1, 10)

PART II:
Political Science

CHAPTER SEVEN

Unsociable Man and His Virtues

For Hobbes the State is certainly purposive and functional. It arises out of the desperate need to leave a condition of war—what Hobbes with some rhetorical flourish calls "the condition of nature." The State or Commonwealth is established both by contract and by force, and these elements never leave the political sphere. In Hobbes' *fabula,* coming out of the condition of nature human beings agree to create a sovereign, an organizing body who will do what is necessary maintain and enrich the commonwealth—legislate, judge, and compel the recalcitrant to be obedient. Indeed, even those who disagree about the composition of the sovereign at the commonwealth's initiation are compelled to accept it. And, of course, Hobbes also recognizes conquest as a means to enlarge the commonwealth.

The reason that men need the State in the first place is substantially related to why they must be compelled by it: usually they don't have a "right reasonable" view of their own interest in maintaining the commonwealth. In particular, human beings have a natural tendency to that pride which makes them choose their own momentary and narrow interest over the interest of the State as expressed by the sovereign's will in the civil laws.

In this chapter, I will discuss Hobbes' opposition to the classical position about purposiveness, particularly of man as purposively fit by nature to enter civil society. But first I will briefly review the classical line in Plato and Aristotle. In subsequent chapters, I will deal with the concept of equity, which is the fulcrum between nature and the artifice of the civil law; the idea of obedience; and finally, Hobbes' position in relation to Greek political thought.

In turning to the views of Plato and Aristotle, one notices, as in Plotinus, a different spirit animating their thought about the human condition. It strikes us as noble and dignified in a way that Hobbes' doctrine, based on force and selfishness, is not. Though the State, as they themselves recognize, involves considering frail mankind in general, their thought looks toward human self-development and discipline. Here is a quote from Aristotle's *Eudemian Ethics* which can be contrasted to Hobbes' view that a man's worth is his price:

> He who thinks that one ought to possess the virtues for the sake of external goods does fine things only by accident. (*E.E.*, 1249a, 15-17)

For Plato and Aristotle, one of the various meanings of *arete*, virtue, is excellence of the standard for the character of a thing—for instance, the capacity of a knife to cut, or of a horse to run. It connotes a power to accomplish something. Usually, though not necessarily, such a consideration is approached in terms of class membership. So, an individual thing is judged in relation to its capacity to measure up to the ideal capacity of the kind of thing to which it belongs. Since, at least for natural entities, there has been a presumption of a rational and appropriate order of kinds, the realization in an entity of the capacity or power of its kind has been taken positively, reinforced by the notion that nature is rational and good in its operative structure. To call a man virtuous is not simply to say he can do something; it is to say that he can do what a man has been fitted by nature to do; especially, a virtuous man has commendatory moral characteristics. Yet, over a century before Hobbes wrote, Machiavelli could speak of Cesare Borgia's *virtu*, thereby proposing a sense of power not obviously related to moral excellence. Machiavelli not only implies the position that a man can be virtuous without moral qualities, but he implicitly challenges the rationality of nature, at least its moral effect. This agrees with the widely-held sophist position of considering morality to be conventional, and even opposed to or a perversion of human nature.

The raw antagonism over this question is shown by Plato in the *Protagoras* and also in the conflict between Thrasymachus and Socrates in the *Republic*. In the *Protagoras* the character of nature and, *pari passu*, of human nature, are organized by two questions: (1) whether virtue can be taught; and (2) whether, despite appearances (and a convenient preliminary plurality) there are many human virtues or simply a single human virtue. It has been extremely difficult for modern students to grasp the point and the provocation of the *Protagoras* discussion, but I wish to suggest the following trace of it. First, I believe Plato saw the historical Socrates' "moral revolution" as a stage in liberating man from provincialism without embracing the sophists' relativism. Socrates opposed the cultural mentality of viewing virtues as properties of social types, e.g., that courage is a quality only of the soldier. He opened "courage" to be considered as a certain capacity of human beings which is sometimes to be found in women, children, slaves, etc. Thus he focused attention on the nature of the natural kind, human beings, rather than upon a more limited social group rooted in conventional or historical circumstance.

From this the crucial question arises: "What is the nature of man?" Plato's high-road to answering this seems well beyond the historical Socrates, and proposes a further distance from provincialism by separating the always conditional circumstances of any concrete individual from the purpose of the species' sense of human fulfillment. The maneuvering that calculates conditions on the basis of circumstance is prudence based on experience, whereas from the classical point of view, full-blown rationality identifies a person with the very ordering principle of reality, if not reality itself. From the latter elevated speculation, which seeks intrinsic value rather than the experientially useful, the virtues are either a power merely related to a preliminary and not fully rational concern with conditionality; or, on the other hand, the virtues are aspects of the highest rationality, so that any rational action is timeless (a doctrine we have already discussed in Plotinus and which we find in Kant's ethics as well). Here all the virtues are unified; rationality or wisdom has the properties of courage, temperance and justice. Yet, even in Plato, if the virtues are treated from a less demanding perspective, it is possible to consider virtue, in some sense, to be taught by the society as a whole. If so, society properly instructs the child by precept and example. But if the virtues are treated as aspects of unified rationality, they are elevated beyond the calculation of circumstance. This makes virtue, especially for the Platonists, beyond political experience and its element of contingent practical wisdom or prudence; it cannot be taught by social methods alone. Instead, the Platonists see it to arise through contemplation of timeless things, which they considered the maturest human act, one which purifies the dross of contingency and brings one to one's true nature. Here one knows the good by a sort of knowing in which one cannot have weakness of the will, for it is beyond pleasure and pain. In the *Protagoras* Plato suggests this to be the solution to the problem of *akrasia* or weakness of the will. The tension between man as embodied—and so, perhaps, as never being able to reach the preferred and unified sense of knowing—and man whose destiny and trajectory is toward the higher "divine" knowledge is signalled by Socrates' change of position with Protagoras on whether virtue can be taught or not.

Yet so elevated a possibility of virtue is beyond the conversational possibilities of the marketplace, and in the *Protagoras* Socrates can only ironically and humorously convince his hearers, the sophists, to demand a method to calculate human good. Men generally, I take it, can be convinced of the need for prudence and the rational calculation for achieving a maximum of pleasure, but the divine wisdom is beyond them. They need a doctrine of weakness of the will just because in calculating with pleasures they operate with the order of finite possibilities to satisfy one or another aspect of their lives rather than being in themselves unified with the goal and ground of the contingent.

Whether this interpretation of Plato is an unerringly correct one is here perhaps not so important. Leaving aside the question of whether there even is a single correct interpretation of Plato, I stress Plato's elevated approach to the virtues in terms of the nature and destiny of the soul. This perspective leaves aside or shuns the more usual consideration of squarely locating the virtues in the more familiar socio-political context.

Aristotle, who is explicitly critical of the general usefulness of Plato's approach, considers the virtues in the more usual context. By taking human nature from a bio-social perspective, Aristotle has the virtues fulfill our biological existence through political life. In Aristotle's doctrine men are political by nature; this is necessary to his analysis that human virtue or excellence—human nature—cannot be fulfilled outside the political. The Platonic high-road of the philosopher who is self-sufficient and can thereby live outside a political community, is not engaged. Aristotle's "great-souled man" has aristocratic rather than divine qualities;[2] he is not a contemplator, but rather an actor who can adjust his various relationships with his environment in a socially-educated grasp of all the dimensions of the particularity of each action. Charity, for example, is the virtue of standing in the right relationship to giving. If one has this virtue, one gives with pleasure, appropriate to one's resources and in apt consideration of the receiver's situation, as well as the right manner. Obviously much social knowledge is necessary of one's social context; virtue projects into the concrete social situation the apt generic biological value, and receives as well a context from it. To be put in Robinson Crusoe's situation before the arrival of Friday, where friendship which includes giving is not possible, is thereby to have one's humanity lessened by lacking the opportunity to fulfill a bio-social need.

Like Plato, Aristotle thinks nature offers a normative standard; but unlike Plato, he stresses the rationality of prudence, so that the standard for excellence is the appropriate function of the bio-social organization of the species in a particular situation. For man, then, both he and his instruments are evaluated in reference to mankind's generic structure. This avoids taking a standard from the usual condition of individuals. The nature of an oak is not realized by most trees in an oak forest; and for one reason or another—poor seed, sunlight, earth, water supply—most trees miss the mark of fulfilling their ideal capacity. Only rarely, and now and again, does a tree fulfill it. So also with human beings. Aristotle, from this perspective, can provide a strong rationale for categories like brutality or perversity, which mark some degree of breakdown or non-fulfillment of an individual measured against the idea of species fulfillment. From the same normative perspective, Aristotle considers the political, since the condition for proper functioning relates to the political arrangements. Aristotle finds that conventions or instruments generally created for human purposes are not, in principle, opposed to nature; on the contrary, convention can be an instrument of the normative functioning of being a human being. It all depends on the purpose. A particular convention can either help or harm the fulfillment of man as a *zoon politikon,* but misuse or perversion is equally possible of their instruments as it is of men themselves. Further, Aristotle's viewpoint allows political convention to be a material condition by which the rational order or ideal form of our humanity is concretized. The inevitable element of circumstance and the arbitrariness of convention are just what Plato of the "upper path" seems to connect to the arbitrariness of pleasure in the sophists' view of virtue. Aristotle, however, emphasizes pleasure as the property of a socio-biologically healthy life.

It is quite clear that at the basis of key issues between Plato and Aristotle are metaphysical issues which not only make for absolute differences but also for differences of emphasis and focus. Nevertheless, certain agreed-upon considerations emerge about the nature of virtue. Most important, neither takes virtue as essentially arbitrary or relative, as many sophists did. And both consider virtue in terms of a teleological explanation, making plausible their doctrine that the cosmos is rational and that human rationality coordinates with cosmic rationality to bring man to his appropriate good. This cosmic rationality suggests a purposive *divine* element in nature which can be used as a standard for judging human behavior even in the political arena.

The classical discussion of virtue was certainly in Hobbes' mind. His general preference for Plato rather than for Aristotle, as he understood them, and his disagreement with both on important matters, especially on the nature of virtue, clarifies Hobbes' position. In *De Cive*, Hobbes mentions Plato twice in passing, and once he commends him for his doctrine that memory is knowledge. (XVIII, 4) Among the ten direct and several indirect references to Aristotle's doctrines, Hobbes has many extended discussions in opposition to Aristotle. In *Leviathan*'s chapter "Of Darkness from Vain Philosophy and Fabulous Tradition," Hobbes says Plato was the best philosopher of the Greeks, and cites his loyalty to geometry as the proper method. Of Aristotle he says,

> And I believe that scarce any thing can be more absurdly said in naturall Philosophy, than that which now is called *Aristotle's Metaphysiques;* nor more repugnant to Government, than much of what hee hath said in his *Politiques;* nor more ignorantly, than a part of his *Ethiques*. (*Lev.*, ch. 46)

Hobbes admires Plato's methodological focus. His older contemporary Galileo had developed Plato's suggestion for a mathematical physics against the qualitative physics of the Aristotelians. Hobbes' own claim to be the founder of civil philosophy, as we have seen, rests on using words with a clear, universal meaning and with an orderly connection of definitions. He sees this method to be in concert with that of geometry. Hobbes stresses this kinship by finding man himself constructs, or is the cause of, both civil philosophy and geometry, whereas, as we have discussed, physics is less knowable because it results from hypotheses about effects:

> Civil philosophy is demonstrable for we make the commonwealth ourselves. But because natural bodies are known not from construction, but seek it from effects, thus lies no demonstration of what the causes be we seek but only what they may be. (*EW*, VII, 184)

From this viewpoint, Hobbes must have been disturbed by Aristotle's introductory remark in the *Nicomachean Ethics* that Plato had erred in approaching the ethical-political from a mathematical viewpoint; according to Aristotle, the subject cannot sustain such a degree of rigor and organization.[3] Even more abhorrent than the prudential emphasis of Aristotle's biosocial approach was the wise anecdote, chap-book approach. In fact, in the dedicatory preface of the *De Cive*, Hobbes begins by relating a story about Cato the Roman, only to move away from a popularly held prejudice in favor arguing from such historically revered anecdotes (as was the style of Machiavelli). Platonically, he stresses universal method based on "certain definite appellations" or philosophy as wisdom rather than a mere prudence or "sudden acuteness" that impresses "Giddy People." At the same time, he implicitly disputes Aristotle's division of reason into theoretical, practical, and productive, which puts geometry in the first part of reason and human matters in the second.

> But I have been long since of this opinion. That there was never yet any more-than-vulgar-prudence that had the luck of being acceptable to the Giddy People; but either it hath not been understood, or else having been so, hath been levell'd and cryed downe. The more eminent Actions and Apothegms both of the Greeks and Romans have been indebted for their Eulogies not so much to the *Reason*, as to the *Greatness* of them, and very many times to that

> prosperous usurpation (with which our Histories doe so mutually upbraid each other) which as a conquering Torrent carryes all before it, as well publick Agents as publick Actions, in the streame of Time. Wisdome properly so call'd is nothing else but this, *The perfect knowledge of the Truth in all matters whatsoever.* Which being derived from the Registers and Records of *Things*, and that as 'twere through the Conduit of certain definite Appellations, cannot possibly be the work of a suddaine Acuteness, but of a well-ballanc'd Reason, which by the *Compendium* of a work, we call *Philosophy*. (*De Cive*, Dedicatory, 3-4)

Platonic inspiration is undoubtedly important. But, as well, it must be granted how difficult it sometimes is to identify the specific doctrines of Plato. In the *Seventh Epistle* (if it is genuine) Plato even claims, rather too ingenuously, that he has no doctrines. Even in regard to major doctrines, one can surely be uncertain of what Hobbes understood Plato's to be. Nevertheless, Hobbes' rejection of Aristotle, aside from important and specifically enumerated disagreements, is problematic. Aristotle still seems to consider himself a Platonist (presumably on doctrinal grounds), and for Hobbes sometimes Aristotle stands for scholastic philosophy.

Aside from moving in the waters between the Scylla and Charybdis of Plato and Aristotle interpretations on the one side and Hobbes' on the other, it is striking how much Hobbes and Aristotle obviously have in common.[4] For one: unlike Plato's "upper path" view of human destiny, both take human possibilities more ordinarily. Aristotle, like Hobbes and unlike Plato, writes from the perspective of a need for political life for all men. And like Hobbes, Aristotle emphasizes—or rather, includes—the role of convention. In particular, Aristotle finds convention, in principle, necessary in extending the sphere of human nature into the political. Further, unlike Plato, both emphasize pleasure as basic to human decisions; for both, (political) decisions are properly made in terms of the intimate relation in choice of desire and reason. Hobbes does oppose both Plato and Aristotle by espousing the principle that all men are fundamentally equal. Yet even here, despite his view that there are slaves by nature,[5] Aristotle also has a broad equality among his citizens by way of his biological perspective. Indeed, Hobbes noticed this when accusing him of a prejudice toward democracy.

Also, Hobbes seemingly opposes Plato's politics of the lie, albeit the "golden lie." Avoiding paternalism, he is closer to Aristotle, who as a constitutionalist[6] upholds, with less equivocation, the principle of law. Here, however, Aristotle is criticized by Hobbes for separating the authority of the legal order from the particular sovereign of the moment (as he does as well by finding universal or natural law authoritative).[7] Of course, at the basis of this disagreement is the authoritative efficacy of the spirit or culture of a nation.[8] Like the common lawyers whom Hobbes opposed at length in his *A Dialogue between a Philosopher and a Student of the English Common Law,* Aristotle gives weight to political culture, while Hobbes, the legal positivist who favors the mathematically clear and sharp definition, finds it unauthoritative. But if this issue is indicative of the opposition between Hobbes and Aristotle on the cultural condition of politics,[9] both nevertheless have a keen eye for the conditionality of human action, and both see the good in terms of concrete circumstances—"For the nature of good and evil follows from the nature of circumstances." (*D.H.,* XI, 4) This means that both approach the political order in terms of the temporal. This is unlike Plato, who, though he was perceptive enough about such matters, has a consummate critique of human matters from his view of the divine destiny of man.

The issue of political authority leads to the question of the nature and capacity of man. *De Cive,* as a scientific treatise on politics, immediately addresses the problem of human nature. To approach the nature of politics from the side of universal propositions about the governing principles of human nature seems to commit Hobbes to consider politics as not completely convention; indeed, if the universality of human nature is brought forward into politics, political theory also demands universal propositions.[10] This involves a normative consideration, that is, it involves an "ideal" description of proper functioning. Hobbes, for example, shows this when he normatively asserts that the major purpose of *any* State is peace. He claims on the ground of human nature that a right reasonable person wishes peace, for he does not have the power, as God does, to secure all his desires. Hobbes often notes that he who wishes the end must take the means necessary to that end: wishing peace, Hobbes argues, citizens are committed to obedience to the sovereign as the rational means.

One notices here, as in all functional norms, a kind of ideality.[11] What happens to be a State, an historical State, may more or less function aptly or "healthily"—the normative ideal provides the standard for such judgments. It is a crucial peculiarity of Hobbes, unlike Plato and especially Aristotle, that he is loath to bring his normative analysis of the State into play in an appropriate or political judgment of a citizen in relation to his particular State. Of course, Hobbes wrote judgmentally about particular political circumstances, e.g., the history of the English Civil War in his *Behemoth*. However, in accordance with his "harsh" view of man's natural disposition, Hobbes mistrusts the stability and honesty, and thus the political efficacy, of such a judgment; formally, he precludes subjects from *acting against* their sovereign by judging the civil laws to be flawed. (Except for technical legal reasons, such judgments are formally outside the political order; they are the fact of the sovereign's will. The sovereign's will is a condition of nature—though it's strange to use the word "nature" to refer to an artificially created body. This is especially obvious when the sovereign is more than one person.) Hobbes, in sum, gives no legitimacy to revolution, no matter how "ill" the State; and so the classical classifications of the tyrant or the tyrannical city are not considered proper definitions by him. Contrariwise, despite also having peace as a fundamental purpose of the State, Plato and Aristotle would use that norm to judge States and men. The tyrant is at war with himself, as Plato emphasized in *The Republic*,[12] and the tyrannical State cannot achieve peace because its rule is arbitrary and opposed to the ideal or healthy order of being a State. (These are matters to which I will return in subsequent chapters.) What, therefore, did Hobbes see in human nature that led him not to allow for normative analysis of his particular State by the citizen and, consequently, not to allow revolution?

Despite the differences between Plato and Aristotle, there is an important principle upon which they agree and against which Hobbes formulates his position that men are not social by nature. This is the principle of teleology. In Greek, the word has an association with "complete" or "perfect" (*teleios*) and "end" or "purpose" (*telos*). This etymology explicitly suggests the classical doctrine that the world or *kosmos* is rational, that is, that the interrelation of natural individuals is guided and coordinated, with the consequence that each can be understood and evaluated from its internal inclination to fulfill the character of its ideal or species. Aristotle provides a political instance of this approach when he says, "The impulse (*horme*) to such a community as the polis is in everyone by nature"[13] as "part of the cosmic order."[14]

In Greek, the rationality of individuals, natural and artificial, is captured by the word "*arete*", which means the virtue or excellence of a thing from the viewpoint of its functioning or work (*energeia*). The linking of *teleios*, *telos*, and *arete* in classical doctrine leads to an evaluation of the factors (*aitia*) of the external conditions in which the work or action takes place and of the adequacy of the subject.[15] As mentioned, a crisp sense of breakdown or perversity is thereby had; in Latin, "*pervertere*" means a turning to the wrong way, to destroy, to corrupt.

Let us consider how this classical approach fosters an ontological understanding of truth, against which Hobbes champions a nominalist epistemology, and how classical ontology tends toward political elitism, against which Hobbes champions a radical egalitarianism. The classical viewpoint intertwines the concepts of the true and the good, a state of affairs and its normative quality, by comparing actual individuals to their species ideal. Consequently, a particular individual can be true or truer than other particular individuals of its kind; and, perhaps, certain things can be truer than other things by a comparison to the idea or species to which each belongs (e.g., a man is truer than a worm, a tragedy is truer than an aphorism). In considering man intramurally, the classical orientation marches all but inevitably toward political elitism, which is hinged on the first (and sometimes on both) of the following propositions: (1) some men are better fitted by nature to impose their wills on other men; and (2) each man is best fitted by nature for some specific political activity and condition. Plato's *Republic* vigorously champions both propositions; Aristotle emphasizes the first in distinguishing men as natural masters or natural slaves on the basis of the capacity to deliberate. Further, the polis, as the highest form of political government, is natural—a natural goal—but it is not open to those who are slaves by nature; and for Aristotle this includes the majority of non-Greeks.[16]

Hobbes is not an elitist. In consideration of their mortality, their vulnerability to (violent) death, Hobbes emphasizes the radical equality of men. Also, though their intellectual capacities differ to a degree, that difference is not crucial: each person will sooner or later grasp through experience the political policy leading to peace, which is the policy best able to secure everyone's interest. Each individual, excepting the mad and the feeble-minded, will discover the best policy for his particular circumstances by his own experience. As opposed to Plato's philosopher-king, therefore, anyone can be sovereign according to Hobbes, and impose his will on others through the civil law. It is merely a person's position in the State that makes a significant difference.

This striking difference in political orientation, and Hobbes' turn to conventionalism, relates to Hobbes' separation of truth from goodness. Fundamentally, the good is related to desire, though assessments of the circumstances for obtaining desires and the competition among desires bring Hobbes somewhat back towards classical ways of framing arguments between apparent and real goods. The true is emphasized, as we have seen, along nominalist lines. Recall his saying that: "The words 'true', 'truth', and 'true proposition' have the same force. For truth consists in what is said and not a thing." (*EW*, I, 3, 7) To elaborate, Hobbes adds a decidedly political note: "these alone are the principles of demonstration, namely, truths established by the decision of speakers and hearers, and therefore indemonstrable." (*EW*, 3, 9) It is the politics of agreement, of creating truth through ingenuity, that signals Hobbes' opposition to the classical doctrine of the essential character of things by nature. Hobbes does not sever ontology and epistemology—recall the argument against Heidegger's accusations—, but he loosens their connection. In particular, he leaves room for making truth through the performative utterances[17] of the sovereign, rather than through merely discovering it.

Hobbes conceives of the commonwealth as an artifice based on agreement. The agreement creates a basis for public judgments that organize or "make for hedges" for the social order. Moreover, the agreement creates the sovereign. The sovereign's will or desires create the civil laws, and these are therefore just. The civil law is always assumed to be equitable. By its consideration of the purpose of the civil artifice in protecting men from their natural vulnerability, it is in concert with natural justice or the theorems of nature; granted human nature, its considerations are the considerations that bring peace. In this we see that Hobbes effectively puts forth the artificial character of the State without denying that its basis is in human nature. Nevertheless, his view of human nature has some different characteristics from that of classical psychology: (1) It is the same in all men and at all times in its basic structure—so that by introspection, one can understand not only oneself but all men. Differences result from circumstance and education, but these are not epistemically fundamental. (2) Human nature is not coordinated fundamentally with the rest of nature so that, as in classical psychology, a healthy-minded person is in harmony with the rest of nature. On the contrary, the natural situation of competition and unobtainable desires is modified with difficulty, pain, and inner protest. Circumstances do not allow the general attainment of every individual's total satisfaction, so that satisfaction loses its value. In Hobbes reason is calculative in the negotiation of what one ought to be content with for the sake of security and prosperity, rather than liberating and emotionally transforming.

For Aristotle, on the other hand, the State is natural, despite its conventional elements, for it fulfills man's nature by the processes and conditions of society. It is natural despite Aristotle's occasional reference to the statesman as craftsman (*demiourgos*) and his likening of politics to a craft (*techne*).[18] While Plato's philosopher is self-sufficient (*autarkes*), Aristotle's person cannot obtain happiness without the State.[19] It is the necessary condition for emotional maturity.

Leo Strauss, dealing with these considerations, provides some interesting, if debatable, political conclusions:

> The tradition which Hobbes opposes assumed that man cannot reach the perfection of his nature except in and through civil society and, therefore, that civil society is prior to the individual. It was this assumption which led to the view that the primary moral fact is duty and not rights. One could not assert the primacy of natural rights without asserting that the individual is in every respect prior to civil society: all rights of civil society or of the sovereign are derivative from rights which originally belonged to the individual. The individual as such, the individual regardless of his qualities—and not merely, as Aristotle contended, the man who surpasses humanity—had to be conceived as essentially complete independently of society.[20]

The methodological inclination to the individual as being the original focus marks Hobbes' understanding of teleology. But it is clear that here as well, the Hobbesian individual is not the individual of the essentialist classical tradition:

> The writers of metaphysics reckon up two other causes besides the *efficient* and the *material,* namely the ESSENCE which some call the *formal cause,* and the END, or *final cause,* both of which are nevertheless efficient causes.
>
> ... When it is said that the essence of a thing is the cause thereof, as to be rational is the cause of man, it is not intelligible; for it is all one, as it were said, to be a man is the cause of man; which is not well said.

Though Hobbes allows for an analysis in terms of final causes for human products and other matters related to willing and sensing, this analysis is provisional: "A final cause has no place but in such things as have sense and will; and this also I shall prove hereafter to be an efficient cause." (*EW,* IV, 274) It is not clear that Hobbes made good on his reductivist promise, but certainly purpose has an important place in his political considerations. He says the purpose of the State is to achieve peace, or rather its benefits, which are security and prosperity. Equal in importance to the opposition to classical essentialism for Hobbes' understanding of teleology is his related notion that the cause of action is the external object; it moves the individual. This, as we have seen, opposes the classical priority of an inner principle as the rational motivation for development toward the ideality of the individual's species. In regard to living creatures, Hobbes emphasizes desire and locates satisfaction in circumstance. Compare the following:

> Nothing taketh beginning from itself, but from the action of some other immediate agent without itself. . . Therefore, when first a man hath an appetite or will to something, the cause of his will, is not the will itself, but something not in his own disposing. (*EW,* IV, 274)
>
> [A final cause] as far as man can understand it, is exactly

the same as an efficient cause; from something pleasant arises the thought of enjoying it; from the thought arises the notion of the path to secure it; and from the notion of the path arises the progression towards the object of desire. In this series of effects the object, or goal, is the agent, because the act of the object that is the goal is the efficient cause of our movement towards the goal. (*Anti-White*, XXVII, 2)

The transfer of efficient causality or agency from subject to object, especially in the case of man, takes the teeth out of the classical notion of teleology. The world as a coordinated community of objects where each has the dignity of the striving for fulfillment appropriate to its sort of thing is replaced by fixed individuals whose actuality is the added effect of all the external forces upon them. In the first quototation below, Manfred Reidel, for one, sharply notes the difference between Hobbes' view and the traditional view. In the second passage, Peters and Tajfel consider the reductionist aspect as something particularly modern.

Die fundamentale Relation von Ursache und Wirkung als mechanischem Bewegzusammenhang von Koerper erklaert sich aus der Stellung des Traegheitsgesetzes in Hobbes' Naturphilosophie. Sein Formulierung—Alles, was sich bewegt, is nicht nur bewegt worden, sondern wird auch immer weiter bewegt sein—is zwar unvollstaendig (weil von der Ruhe hier konsipiert), setzt aber voraus, dass es keine "innere" Ursache der Bewegung und damit keinen Kausalzusammenhang im traditionellen Sinne geben kann.[21]

There are many candidates to the title of "father of modern psychology." But the claims of Thomas Hobbes can be pressed very strongly in that he was not only the first to suggest that human beings are machines, but also the first to attempt a systematic explanation of all human actions in terms of the same principles as were used to explain the behaviour of inanimate bodies.[22]

Let us look at Hobbes at work. In the second paragraph of *De Cive*, Hobbes complains against "error proceeding from our too slight contemplation of human nature." His context is that "Man is a Creature born fit for society: the Greeks called him *zoon politikon* and on this foundation they built up the Doctrine of Civil Society." So, without mentioning Aristotle, with whom this position is most closely associated,[23] Hobbes presents as "certainly false" the famous and favorably received doctrine that man is a political animal by nature.[24]

Hobbes' estimate of human nature in regard to political action is "All Society therefore is either for Gain, or for Glory; not so much for the love of our fellowes, as for the love of our Selves." (*Ci*, I, 2) So in speaking against the doctrine that men are naturally fit for society, he argues,

> For if by nature one Man should Love another (that is) as Man, there could be no reason be return'd why every Man should not equally Love every Man, as being equally Man, or why he should rather frequent those whose Society affords him Honour or Profit. We therefore do not seek Society for its own sake, but that we may receive some Honour or Profit from it. (*ibid.*)

Considering his argument from the standpoint of the general structure of classical teleological arguments, Hobbes seems to miss the point. For it seems proper to say of a tree, for example, that by nature it needs water for its existence, and indeed the roots of the tree "selfishly" reach toward ground water; but the tree "loves" itself, so to speak, and not the water. It may similarly be argued that even granted love of self and the seeking of profit or honor, men are still social by nature. Even Hobbes admits that honor needs society and profit is greatly secured by it. So even if we grant such characteristics as the bedrock of human nature, it seems to be properly argued that men are brought into society by them. In this version of the teleological approach, the end and not the means is emphasized. This version, however, may fall away from the strictly classical teleological argument, which idealizes both end and means.

Let us consider a second version, which exploits the species-fulfillment factor of the classical teleological argument. On this consideration, one need not love all men if one loves man, since most men do not fulfill their humanity. If men are unworthy by their behavior, they may be *actually* unworthy of love. The species-fulfillment factor shows the classical teleological argument does not result from a generalization of inductively gathered experiential facts. It always interprets facts in relation to an ideal structure.[25] Hobbes' own view of science accepts this character. In fashioning his science of politics, for example, his formal assumption is that the civil laws are equitable as the means for peace. Here, as in a classical teleological argument, both means and ends are idealized. Yet he certainly admits that in experience many actual civil laws are not equitable and actually oppose peace.

Exploiting the species-fulfillment factor, a teleological argument need not deny that most men have socially negative characteristics. These characteristics are considered unnatural or perverse from the viewpoint of the ideal that is fulfilled (though rarely) in some actual person. If Hobbes is saying that all men have negative social characteristics, and that there is no potential for these to ever be absent from any person, then this argument cannot proceed; however, it could if he admits such an ideal possibility.

The two versions of the teleological argument exploit different factors of the classical viewpoint. One assumes Hobbes' "harsh" view of human nature and works by exploiting the means-end factor; the other denies that the "harsh" view is important to the argument, and exploits instead the factor of idealizing appropriate species functioning. Here numbers do not count. Both versions assume factors in the classical teleological framework, and they fall aside if Hobbes rejects or greatly modifies the classical considerations. And he does. Even when he appears to proceed along the classical lines, as in his formal discussion of *Leviathan,* one must proceed with caution.

The following passage from *De Homine* helps to introduce certain important considerations:

> Whence it is to be understood that they, who consider men by themselves as though they existed outside of civil society, can have no moral science, because they lack any certain standard against which virtue and vice can be judged and defined. (*H.*, XIII, 8)

We have already seen that for Hobbes what is defined—a step necessary to science—is based on agreement. And it is not only that agreement is unstable outside of civil society, but that then there is no authority, no sovereign, to impose judgment about what is reasonable in the particular circumstances at hand. There is no certain standard, because the object is practical and to act involves concrete particulars. One thing that Hobbes is certainly clear about, and which leads to needing the sovereign as guide, is that one's self-interest obscures one's judgment. But there is still a puzzle in the meaning of the above passage: granted that science is a matter of definitions, why should moral science—unlike, say, mathematics—need a social context?

Is it simply that there are no moral considerations when man is outside the social context, and that we would not come upon morality if we saw him so? But the passage speaks in seemingly epistemic terms about the *certainty* of moral things. So though in a condition of nature there would be moral considerations *in foro interno,* there would be no way to bridge the gap between knowing that murder is wrong (which in itself involves the imaginative projection of a commonwealth that makes civil laws governing killing) and knowing what murder actually is. The latter is only made certain by the civil law. Its particularity is the public will of the sovereign. If the laws of nature or "theorems of nature" (as Hobbes reminds us they are better called) are considered a science, this generality misses the particularity of the domain that *interests* us when acting *in foro externo*. This involves a new individual: the artificial political individual. Obviously, the particular characteristics of commonwealth-as-artifice provide "good" with a meaning, unlike the grand certainties of a metaphysical argument such as Descartes' ontological argument. The small certainty of Hobbes has range and validity limited to each particular commonwealth. It is only the formal need of commonwealth that there be a criterion of certainly; there is no material need for having particular civil laws, in the sense of ones that *must* result from the particular public will of a living sovereign.

One commonwealth cannot therefore be compared to another commonwealth in terms of the relative justice of their laws, at least not with certainty. For natural justice does not achieve certainty. It is not rationality but authority—the definer—that provides certainty. The authority of the civil laws depends on the sovereign's will, not on his wisdom. The same principle is involved in the case of judging an individual from a viewpont outside of a particular civil society. In such an instance, one person relates to another person as one State to another State; there is no authority to make judgments certain. For man considered outside civil society, the source of value is in desire, but there is no (political) ruling of the desires of others. This is precisely the profound condition of war.

Value is contained in individuality: "what a man takes to be good is good" is Hobbes' radical and very unclassical doctrine. (It is a doctrine of the sophists, but I do not call that "classical," reserving the latter term for Plato, Aristotle, and their epigones.) Hobbes' teleological arguments are concerned only with the desires or passions of particular men, though the fact that there is a general structure of the passions allows for his political theory. It is the object of desire that locates this general structure particularly and circumstantially, just as the civil laws locate—"are co-extensive and equal to"—the laws of nature. The individuality of a particular man is held together naturally by a need to survive. This, as a boundary condition, makes suicide similar to treason; in each case the structure of individuality is opposed. Plato also considered the State to be an individual, but it must be noted that for him the internal faculties of it work together, and reason rather than desire rules. Further, the wholeness or harmony of the individual exemplifies the rationality that orders all of nature and makes it a whole, a *kosmos*.

The first sentence of *De Cive* reads, "the faculties of Human nature may be reduc'd unto four kinds: Bodily Strength, Experience, Reason, Passion" (or, more or less, desire). From the classical teleological view, these four should have a functional and purposive interrelationship. Thus for Plato the just State was just a version of the just man writ large, and this just man was considered to have the faculties of human nature in a proper functional balance. Hobbes' position, I have argued, is that ultimately all nature is reducible to matter in motion, where there is no good or bad. Values arise in nature only by the complex arrangement of matter in creatures of desire. The complex organization presents the political possibility of value. Man's complexity indeed involves functional systems dependent on faculties like reason and experience. These instruct human desires as to what is both obtainable and—considering the competing desires within each person and the factor of chance—what is possibly best. But what is obtainable and what is prudentially best are different matters from the bare fact of desire or wanting. Wanting provides the very energy for employing the instrumentality of experience, reason, and ingenuity. These are necessary for a person's choices of his real rather than his apparent interest; but "real" is organized by an additional principle. It is related to the prime determination of sustaining one's existence (and wealth); and with this fulcrum, the faculties are not valuable in themselves but simply instrumental in relating desires to conditions. Consequently, real and apparent for Hobbes, unlike for Plato, are a discrimination which depends necessarily on the circumstances of each individual.

Even at this point, a teleological argument seems possible. For even though good is a perspective arising from the desires, are not men ruled by conditions open to a teleological explanation for obtaining these desires, let alone a proper functioning, which seems implicit in the distinction between real good and apparent good? Can one not speak of the sum of those conditions leading men to civil society as "nature" and thereby warrant the proposition that men are by nature fit for society?[26] Hobbes himself argues that our real good (that is, *usually* or by rational policy, our maximum chances for survival and prosperity) is to enter civil society.

Hobbes believes experience and reason lead to the conclusion that the uncivil condition, where glory-seeking and greedy people contend for many of the same objects of desire, results in chaos. This demands the giving up of one's apparent interest or good, one's "right to all things," for the real goods of self-preservation and prosperity in civil society. The laws of nature or moral laws create dispositions necessary for civil society. But to follow these maxims doesn't warrant Hobbes' view that man is fit by nature for civil society. His main reason for this untraditional conclusion, despite the fact that he argues for choosing civil society, seems to be that though prudential knowledge can instruct as to the probable bad future consequences of some present action, it cannot restrain most men from often doing the greedy (and vainglorious) act.[27] He writes, ". . . men cannot put off this same irrational appetite, whereby they greedily prefer the present good (to which, by strict consequence, many unfore-seen evills do adhere) before the future." (*Ci.*, III, 32) In a later work, he puts it as follows:

> Therefore, although the real good must be sought in the long term, which is the job of reason, appetite seizeth upon a present good without foreseeing the greater evils that necessarily attach to it. Therefore appetite perturbs and impedes the operation of reason; whence it is rightly called a *perturbation*. (*H.*, XII, 1)

Perhaps influenced by his Christian milieu, which emphasized the doctrine of original sin, Hobbes implies that no man, not even the philosopher, can be completely loyal to right reason. Yet even if *some few* men can be, nevertheless this isn't a decisive political factor, since the power to harm is equally available to all men. Therefore, the basic problem is to protect oneself against the potentially harmful or antisocial character of most, if not of all, men.

In opposition to the Socratic "superpolitical" position that one should not fear death and ought not to have it determine one's action,[28] Hobbes finds fear of death and of harm to be the major and necessary instrument of political order. Thus a "perturbation of mind," a passion, is enlisted to create society and to fight against the inclination of men to take the more apparent good.

Plato also considered the political power of fear when he recounted Glaucon's challenge to Socrates with the story of Gyges' ring. For Hobbes, if men had the ring of Gyges, a device to protect them from retaliation, they would indulge their desires and do harmful things to others. Socrates and Hobbes' friend Godolphin are exceptions, for most men would, like Gyges, harm others; therefore, they have to be restrained. Being enough equal to each other to kill one another, men are *forced*, against the basic fact of human nature, to create an artificial device for restraining each other: civil society. Plato's Socrates, whose life is evidence that he would not use the ring of Gyges, is a rare man and not the standard for Hobbes. One cannot contemplate Socrates saying, as Hobbes does, "For it is not as the Stoics say, that he who is wise is rich; but, rather, it must be said that he who is rich is wise." (*H.*, XI, 8) Hobbes sides here with Simonides, who is supposed to have said that "he who is rich is wise" to the tyrant Hiero's wife.

Hobbes does not approach politics from the qualitative side of ensuring that the majority of men are ruled by those few who are not unsteady in their self-control and reason. The philosopher-kings of Plato's *Republic*—those whom the Stoics would later call the *kosmopolitoi*, or citizens of nature— are not to be counted on. Paternalistically, the philosopher-kings use such devices as telling lies and rigging lotteries. Hobbes' device is an "Artificial Animal," as he calls the State, and its laws are what he calls "an artificiall *Reason.*" (*Lev.*, "Introduction") Unlike the philosopher-king, the sovereign rules the citizens not by his wisdom, cunning, and lies, adjusting eternal truth for the circumstantial benefit of failed men; Hobbes' sovereign rules men by his power.[29] The sovereign does not have to lie. His power establishes him as the source of political truth by way of the civil laws. There is, however, perhaps something of a "Golden Lie" in Hobbes' proposing the metaphor of the sovereign as a kind of God in relation to the citizens. It bolsters the formal assumption, against experience, that the civil laws of particular States are equitable, not on the basis of wisdom, but on authority based on power.

In one of Hobbes' animadversions against man as fit by nature for civil society, he mentions Aristotle by name and challenges the inclusion of ants, bees, etc., as political animals.[30] His main point of opposition to Aristotle is interesting. Though he admits that these non-human creatures direct their individual actions to the common end of their groups, he says that "the consent of these brutall creatures is naturall, that of men by compact onely, (that is to say) artificiall; it is therefore no matter of wonder if somewhat more [fear of punishment] be needfull for men to the end they may live in peace." (*Ci.*, V, 5) Again, and clearly, the artificial is contrasted to the natural on the basis of the contractual determinations of civil society.

In the English translation (London, 1651) of the *De Cive* (Paris, 1642), there is an annotation addressing what he, Hobbes, meant by "born fit." It is no doubt written in response to Hobbes' critics (though it is unclear by whom it was added). It considers the claim in Aristotle's *Politics* that because human children require much nurturing, the family is the first form of civil society and the basis of an enlarged civil society. Some inroad seems to have been made against Hobbes' earlier presentation with the logical alternative of *either* the condition of nature *or* civil society. Nevertheless, I think, a certain sort of civil society exists in the natural family since, both in and out of the Hobbesian State, adults substantially act for the preservation and prosperity of their children. Thereby the logical alternation that Hobbes often presses is obscured. Indeed, the annotation responds to the pointed criticism that if parents and children are in the natural condition, there is no moral objection to their killing one another. The reply to this seems to go against the logical alternation by considering the child as not in a condition of nature because the child is under the command of the person who has nourished or protected him or her. This is a strange exception indeed. The *in foro interno* and *in foro externo* distinction that halts the natural law of gratitude, etc., in the war of all against all is not in place, but seems to be smuggled in by having the family a sort of kingdom by acquisition. Interestingly, to justify patrimonial sovereignty—which he sometimes calls natural sovereignty—Hobbes allows that the place children have in the family is not "by right" but by "natural indulgence." (*Ci.*, II, 4, 9)

Hobbes tries to recover the logical ground by admitting that men are gregarious but maintaining that "civil societies are not meer Meetings, but Bonds, to the making whereof, Faith and Compacts are necessary." This annotation reiterates the text but seems to beg the question of whether the family forms by nature a polity by accomplishing the purpose of civil society: preservation and prosperity. I think it does. Indeed, the couple that remains together, despite Hobbes, by this continuance seems to have a tacit contract even in the state of nature. Thus their family existence is misleadingly called "a mere Meeting."[31]

But even if there is no contract involved in the family,[32] if preservation and profit are the end of political association, then why not consider the contract only one means to that end? Obviously, the family achieves that for children. Hobbes may well insist that numbers are crucial. The family or the extended family of a clan or tribe may not be the sort of political association that he is interested in, because there are other considerations about danger and prosperity with which the smaller units cannot deal. Even if the protection and goods that parents give to their children are qualified by the vulnerability of the condition of nature, this is a different matter from whether human beings are fit by nature for civil society. The concept of fitness for human society seems to be properly established by the fulfillment of its purposes in the sort of civil society that exists for the family in the condition of nature.

Further, it seems wrong to argue that fitness by nature hinges on the child's capacity. Consider these words by Hobbes:

> Manifest therefore it is, that all men, because they are born in Infancy, are born unapt for Society. Many also (perhaps most men) either through defect of mind or want of education remain unfit during the whole course of their lives; yet have Infants, as well as those of riper years, an humane nature; wherefore Man is made fit for Society not by Nature, but by Education: furthermore, although Man were born in such a condition as to desire it, it follows not, that he were born fit to enter into it; for it is one thing to desire, another to be in the capacity fit for what we desire. (*Ci.*, I, Annotation "Born Fit")

This comment takes "born fit" in a literal sense. For Plato and Aristotle, the condition of infants is, of course, temporally prior but not conceptually prior; rather, it is the perfected condition of maturity that is conceptually prior.[33] It is therefore from the behavior of the parent to the child that the case of social *by nature* is to be made. In any case, it is hard to believe that the "Annotation" doesn't stoop to unfair rhetoric by implying that a consideration of the child's limited capacity exhausts what one might mean by "born fit." That we all were infants cannot be denied, but to say that our existence as infants defines human nature seems to be a genetic fallacy. Indeed, the incapacity of infants to survive on their own points to a natural friendship of parents (and other adults) to children. Plato, Aristotle, and modern psychologists concur in the further matter that this care creates the emotional pattern for adulthood which, if various and sometimes faulty, nevertheless continues a need for caring relationship. After all, despite the Cains among men, expressions like "my friend is like a brother to me" point to what Plato and Hegel elaborate. The desire to care for the child and family relations generally both imply that friendship in its various forms is a natural value. For Aristotle, both the family and the tribal life that Hobbes admits exist in a condition of nature are as well naturally extended (*apoika katu phusis*) into the polis. By nature, the polis exists in these first communities in a potential manner.[34]

Since Hobbes denies such a developmental natural history for man, he treats virtue along contingent lines in terms of each attainment of desire. Reason or calculation, bodily strength and experience, are instruments of desire. The desire for survival is the strongest desire, since existence is the necessary condition for any other desire. Therefore, Hobbes can write that justice and charity are the primary virtues in civil society, but in the condition of nature or war the great virtues are "the two daughters of War, Deceipt and Violence: that is in plaine terms a meer brutal rapacity." (*Ci.*, "Dedicatory," 2) And in the body of the text of *De Cive* he continues:

> for every man is desirous of what is good for him and shuns what is evil, but chiefly the chiefest of natural evils, which is death; and this he doth, by a certain impulsion of nature, no lesse than that whereby a Stone moves downward: It is therefore neither against the dictates of true reason for a man to use all his endeavours to preserve and defend his Body, and the Members thereof from death and sorrowes. (*Ci.*, I, 7)

Experience shows that deceit and violence—human brutality generally—are virtues when no other recourse is available in a condition which is harmful (which is indeed the way Hobbes paints the terrors of the condition of nature). Against Hobbes, classical writers would say that such a disordered and inimical condition cannot afford virtues at all and that its disfunctionality is obvious. That is to say, it cannot appropriately be considered as a healthy description of human nature. While emphasizing our real good to be the condition of civil society, Hobbes refuses to take this line. For him experience shows, despite utopian hopes to the contrary, that one is sometimes in a state of war, and this fact about the vagaries of circumstances means the capacities involved in it also have to be considered virtues. Preservation of the individual is the non-negotiable factor for Hobbes in a way that it is not for Plato and Aristotle. For Hobbes the avoidance of one's own death (especially emphasized in the early writings) is so natural that he compares it to the naturalness of a rock moving downwards. In the name of consistency, it seems that Hobbes must thereby discount as irrational such actions as the sacrifice of one's life for a friend or a parent's willingness to sacrifice his or her life for its child.

It strikes me that Hobbes' comparison of man's avoidance of his death with the naturalness of a rock moving downwards can fitly summarize the analysis given in this chapter. On the one hand the simile—and, indeed, the necessity for Hobbes of human nature having an unchanging core structure—suggests the aptness of classical teleological arguments for his position, bringing him closer to traditional natural law theorists. Yet Hobbes rejects this: his view of a basic structure of human nature is not transferable to the classical notion of essence. The reason is that desire is the motor of action. The doctrine of essences, taken from the classical teleological viewpoint, involves development or the rationalization of form, which becomes the standard for the worth of the action of things. Following a sophistic tradition, desire need not be justified. It negotiates with the world and with circumstances by acting from one desire rather than from another; but if one has felicity (as God does and man does not), then one will act on all one's desires. It is man's powerlessness that restrains him, and that is what drives him—against his nature, so to speak—into civil society, an ingenious artificial condition. This, for Hobbes, is not a rationalization of the development of the form that is appropriate to man, as it is for Aristotle. Rather, it is a device whereby he imitates supreme power by creating a "mortal god" with all its "discommodious" limitations.

Hobbes, then, agrees with the sophists on two points: first, that desire is the basis of value and action; and second, that *the objects* of desire are different among different men. To these propositions it is appropriate to add a third general point of agreement, *viz.*, that conventions are important in organizing this diversity of the objects of desire into an orderly social condition. But for the sophists the variance of the objects of desire is not considered as expressing a universal structure of desire. Hobbes thinks they do. Since, however, he takes that structure to be potentially antisocial, he takes issue with Aristotle's doctrine of man as naturally fit for society. Nevertheless, because he has this *universal* (though debatable) natural characterization of man, Hobbes is able to relate the conventions of society to a firm anchor. Thereby, he achieves distance from those sophists who espouse an extreme anomic relativism. At the same time, he conceptually shows that the incentive to enter civil society is a functional relation between the natural structure and the ensuing conventions of the State. This is somewhat in the direction of Aristotle. Also, Hobbes' view of dispositions and manners from the perspective of the need for creating and stabilizing the State opposes simply giving any desire positive value without the conditional contexts of preservation and prosperity. So again in Hobbes, the conventional discriminates what is to be considered virtue and vice, even though, on the abstract basis of the source of value, all desires *per se* are good.

Hobbes' rational man chooses civil society. It is a means that is necessary to the end of continued existence. By creating the commonwealth, he opens himself to a sphere of obligations where his desires are (formally) ruled by the State's artifacted agency and materially overawed by the sword he and his fellow citizens have given to it. It may be questioned whether Hobbes has provided a formal justification for evaluating the State which has superseded the material and natural evaluations of each man. Perhaps there might be another means for survival and prosperity—say, the ring of Gyges—that might succeed all the better. Hobbes is silent about that; instead, he emphasizes that experience makes Leviathan the only plausible means.

Yet if this is so, then doesn't the State as a necessary means become rather naturalized, as in Aristotle? And if it isn't so, if ingenuity makes another artifice with greater power to the individual than Leviathan, it would seem the sophistic argument of Thrasymachus has won out. It may be granted that in the human condition the desire for felicity is not achievable, because one cannot conceive all human desires as fulfillable. But since desire is the principle of evaluation, then surely it is both logically possible, and evidenced by experience as well, that ingenuity and deviousness can preserve one's life, bring prosperity, and otherwise favor one's desires. If the classical understanding of teleology is undercut, the basis of obedience to the law results from a failure of the ingenuity to yield a better instrument than the commonwealth.

CHAPTER EIGHT

Equity as Justice and Charity in Hobbes

> "In the one, [that Man to Man is a kind of God] there's some analogie of similitude with the Deity, to wit, Justice and Charity, the twin-sisters of peace."
>
> *De Cive*, Dedicatory, 2

Hobbes' view of man, if it were a sculpture, would surely be called monumental and crude. Its monumentality is in considering man *in general* in relation to a State of *any kind whatsoever*. Its crudeness, as well as its powerful form, is in having this great construction built up from a very few premises; and, as well, in Hobbes' constant understatement and suspicion of noble inclination as a factor of political action. For him, the utopian and noble aspirations of social or religious idealism fancifully mislead, for they are made from hope rather than from experience—experience, here, not about particular men, but of men generally. First, the low and broad premise of man as gregarious but not social by nature captures the fundamental fact that men often disagree about, as well as contend for, what they consider good. A second premise is that the need for men to live together demands a check on their inclinations, through vainglory and greed, to war and violence. A third premise is that experience teaches men that their most fundamental desires—first, preservation, and then, prosperity—are only attainable by the preservation of the State. Aside from the fortuitous, this preservation is caused by the obedience of the citizens to the sovereign's equitable laws.

In Hobbes one finds no utopian hope to provide for the particular needs of men or to untangle the knot of disagreement about the good. Instead, his sovereign's sword does the proper work of the political condition by making the civil law to be taken as the criterion of the just—as establishing the mine and thine. In such a context, it is of great interest to understand how, after not depending on noble motives, Hobbes treats the virtues and relates them to politics. Consider Hobbes' own words:

> What is to be understood about men insofar as they are men, is not applicable insofar as they are citizens; for those who are outside of a state are not obliged to follow another's opinion, while those in a state are obliged by covenants. Whence it is to be understood that they, who consider men by themselves and as though they existed outside of civil society, can have no moral science, because they lack any certain standard against which virtue and vice can be judged and defined. Therefore, a common standard for virtues and vices does not appear except in civil life; this standard cannot, for this reason, be other than the laws of each and every state; for natural law when the state is constituted, becomes part of the civil law, and that which we can truly measure by civil laws, which is different in different states, is justice and equity. That moral virtue which we measure purely by the natural laws is only charity. Furthermore, all moral virtue is contained in these two. For all the virtues are contained in justice and charity. (*H.*, XII, 8, 9)

With the above rich text in mind, I will briefly assert the elements of Hobbes' political theory in order to elaborate on duty and charity in the practice of the sovereign.

The foundation of the State arose, historically or by implication, in the covenant to obey the sovereign. The author of the civil domain is the sovereign. The citizen, by delivering up his natural rights, must act in accordance with the sovereign's creation of civil laws.

The sovereign, as the source of the civil laws, is not bound by obedience. In this, the sovereign, unlike the citizen, is in a condition of nature. Yet, he is in an altered circumstantial relation to the condition of commonwealth. Unlike men in a condition of nature, where each is at war with everyone else, the sovereign, as an unendangered person (and, literally, an individual when the sovereign is a king), can have more than the intention of equity, *in foro interno;* he can also act on this intention *in foro externo.*

Indeed, it is prudent for him to do so. His reputation possessions, and dominion over others depends on the welfare, prosperity, and even the cultivation of his State. (*Lev.*, XIX, 4) It is rational for him to increase the happiness of the citizens, for much unhappiness creates sedition and even revolution. And though revolution is not formally allowable, since the sovereign's authority cannot be questioned, it is nevertheless a possibility which is increased by the sovereign's human failings: the lack of the virtues of prudence, temperance, and courage. Duty and rational self-interest converge.

The sovereign's capacity to exercise charity arises from his freedom—his being in a state of nature in relation to civil society. For Hobbes, as the passage quoted above shows, charity is the moral virtue containing all the moral virtues of man as man. He defines a lack of charity as "a mind insensible to another's evils." (*H.*, XIII, 9) The sovereign, however, needs not to consider the good or evil of each particular man, but the good of the commonwealth as a whole. His duty is to the whole, for the good of the commonwealth provides the sole secure context for each citizen achieving his private good. "For just as every citizen hath his own private good, so hath the state its own public good." *(ibid.)* The sovereign's charity to his subjects is coextensive with his duty; as in God's rule, his justice and charity are one, seen under different aspects. Though duty and charity are seemingly opposed notions, since duty involves obligation and charity involves a free giving, the sovereign's political actions can be considered to express either, and thus both. For though it is his duty to act for the good of the commonwealth, his being in a state of nature—and, therefore, free from obedience to any human authority—also makes this fulfillment of duty charitable.

In this sense, striving for equity, a law of nature for Hobbes, can be considered an expression of the sovereign's charity. But equity is also an expression of justice or even characteristic of it. Indeed, Hobbes presumes it, as a principle of legal interpretation: the sovereign's laws are always to be considered equitable. Consequently, judges, as delegates of the sovereign who receive all their authority solely as his representatives, must interpret his will with this presumption. But Hobbes seems to go further when saying, "The things that make a good Judge, or good Interpreter of the Lawes, are first, *A right understanding* of the principal Law of Nature called *Equity:* which depends not on the reading of other men's Writings, but on the goodness of a man's own natural Reason." (*Lev.*, XXVI, 28)

Hobbes, therefore, uses "equity" both in terms of the political condition (the sovereign's laws or artificial reason) and in terms of a natural condition (each individual's natural reason). And since, for some purposes, he opposes a state of nature to the artificial civil condition, it is easy to be confused when, remembering the above, one reads, "Moreover, that moral virtue, which can be truly measured by civil laws, which is different in different states, is justice and equity; that moral virtue which we measure purely by the natural laws is only charity." (*H.*, XIII, 9) Against the massive evidence of Hobbes' writings, it would be inappropriate to suggest that any man who is a good reasoner could discover a natural justice which opposes the civil laws. But, it is only when the connection of the laws of nature and the civil law is seen that the temptation to accuse Hobbes of contradiction vanishes. Indeed, Hobbes is at his most ingenuous with the central problem of the nexus between the moral and the political.

In this chapter I hope to clarify this matter by examining

the relation of natural law to civil law. As a preliminary, it will help to keep in mind the fact that the sovereign is involved both in the state of nature and also in the creation of the civil law. Recall that in a state of nature each individual has a view of what is his good. The desires a man has in the state of nature, i.e., before he binds his will by promises, are limited only by his capacity to fulfill his wishes. But in the state of nature, desires arising from man's biological condition cannot be fulfilled, or cannot easily be fulfilled, since often there is a scarcity of objects of satisfaction and a competition for them. Introspection and experience, in addition, give evidence that human beings tend to be vainglorious and to seek ascendancy over their fellow men. Now, the sovereign is in a condition of nature in the civil condition, whereas the others in the State are not; indeed, they have covenanted or promised obedience to him in order to obtain the advantages of security. Since they must, they thereby take his will (to speak only of kingly sovereignty, for the sake of simplicity) as the public good, ensuring this by providing him with the power of arms to compel obedience. They also, thereby, provide the sovereign with the capacity to have any man's wife or property. To the extent that he does not avail himself of these opportunities, he practices charity or equity. For in a state of nature, a man's will is only limited by his capacity to achieve his desire. Since men are fundamentally equal for Hobbes, the sovereign's advantage over his subjects is a result of their trust. Without betraying this trust, the sovereign already has much. He has the benefits of domination and glory: "he is the font of all honors." One supposes that this might be enough to satisfy his vanity. His human, all-too-human tendency for ascendancy has been fulfilled.

Further, unlike the condition when all are in a condition of nature, the sovereign can act for the sake of peace. He can practice equity by following the laws he creates. These are, after all, for the sake of what he considers to be good for men generally. In this way his equity is both charity and justice. Consider Hobbes' words:

> Now all the duties of Rulers are contained in this one sentence: *The safety of the people is the supreme Law:* for although they who among men obtain the chiefest Dominion, cannot be subject to the Lawes properly so called, that is to say to the will of men, because to be chief, and subject, are contradictories; yet it is their *duty* in all things, as much as possible they can, to yield obedience unto right reason, which is the naturall, morall, and divine Law: But because dominions were constituted for Peace's sake, and Peace was sought for safeties sake, he, who being placed in authority, shall use his power otherwise then to the safety of the people, will act against the reasons of Peace, that is to say, against the Lawes of nature; Now as the safety of the People dictates a Law by which Princes know their *duty,* themselves a benefit; for the power of the Citizens, is the power of the City, that is to say, his that bears the chief Rule in any state. (*Ci.,* XIII, 2)

> They therefore who had undertaken the administration of power in such a kinde of government, would sinne against the Law of nature (because against their trust who hath committed that power unto them) if they should not study, as much as by good Laws abundantly, not only with the good things belonging to life, but also with those that advance to delectation. (*Ci.,* XIII, 4)

It takes a careful reading of Hobbes to see the plausibility of his remark that "The Law of Nature, and the Civil Law, contain each other, and are of equal extent." (*Lev.,* II, 26:4) For it to be plausible, it would have to be shown that those passages which speak about the Law of Nature are not in opposition to those that speak about the Civil Law. Now, just as it was shown that equity in the sense of justice and equity in the sense of charity are compatible, and even intimately related, so Hobbes proposes a similar compatibility—and, if anything, a stronger necessity—to this relation. Indeed, only if this is plausible is Hobbes' political teaching convincing. I will show problems do arise here. Let us proceed directly by recalling Hobbes' definitions:

> A LAW OF NATURE is a Precept, or generall Rule, found out by Reason, by which a man is forbidden to do that, which is destructive of his life or taketh away the means of preserving the same and to omit, that, by which he thinketh it may be best preserved. (*Lev.*, XIV, 14)

To this Hobbes adds the "Fundamentall Law of Nature; which is, *to seek Peace, and to follow it.*" (*ibid.*) Thus, he says:

> And consequently it is a precept, or generall rule of Reason, *That every man, ought to endeavour Peace, as farre as he has hopes of attaining it; and when he cannot obtain it, that he may seek, and use, all helps, and advantages of Warre.* (*ibid.*)

Turning to the civil law, Hobbes provides this definition:

> CIVILL LAW, is to every subject, those Rules, Word, Writing, or other sufficient Sign of the Will, to make use of, for the Distinction of Right, and Wrong; that is to say, of what is contrary, and what is not contrary to the Rule. (*Lev.*, XXVI, I)

In text after text, Hobbes speaks of the Natural Laws as universal and the civil laws as the laws of particular States and as differing from one State to another. How, then, can that which is always one and that which differs from State to State, and even differs in a particular State from time to time, be equal in extent, the former contained in the latter?

It is proper to notice that Hobbes gives the definition of

natural law in the part of the *Leviathan* dealing with man and the definition of civil law in that dealing with commonwealth. Now the premise is that man is always and everywhere equal in a radical natural sense; this is a crucial premise. That is to say, with the exception of infants, imbeciles and madmen, differences of intelligence or of objects of desire do not alter a person's capacity to perceive his need for peace. However, another crucial premise is that in each particular commonwealth, the commonwealth alone provides peace. As the prudential basis for enjoying various objects of desire or goods in safety, peace is the supreme, rational desire: "the condition of Warre remaineth, contrary to the Law of Nature." (*Lev.*, XV) Consequently, all the laws of nature preserve the life of a man by leading to peace in some manner, where commonwealth provides the context, with its civil laws providing the particular arrangement for peace. For this reason Hobbes says:

> The Lawes of Nature are Immutable and Eternal; For Injustice, Ingratitude, Arrogance, Pride, Inequity, Acception of persons, and the rest can never be made lawfull. For it can never be that Warre shall preserve life, and Peace destroy it. (*ibid.*)

From what perspective can nature and convention be considered so that the former contains the latter? Let us begin by emphasizing that, for Hobbes, the civil law is not just any convention. It arises from the deepest need of man's nature to secure peace. Its purpose is to fulfill what human nature demands, and in this sense, keeping in mind Hobbes' opposition to man as born fit for society, it fulfills nature. In the State, however, the legal decision is the sovereign's will: by it he creates or artifacts public or universal civil arrangements. Considering the natural basis of this conventional demand, he writes, "the principles of politics depend on knowledge of the motion of minds, and the knowledge of the motion of minds from the knowledge of sense experiences and of cognitions."

(*EW*, I, 7, 7) This arrives at the fact that the appetites of men and the motions of their minds are such that they will wage war against each other unless restrained. This fact can be known by the exprience of each and every person who examines his own mind. Thereby, unlike the natural law theorist of the Thomistic sort, Hobbes doesn't organize a system of natural moral definitions as a standard or ideal to test the civil laws of a particular State. Instead, the civil laws are a kind of definition. They all have the purpose of securing peace by means of providing rules. Despite their outward diversity, all have the efficient causality of moving one from chaos or war to the peace of the civil condition. The laws of nature are therefore not laws in the proper sense:

> For the lawes of Nature, which consists in Equity, Justice, Gratitude, and other morall Virtues on these depending, in the condition of meer Nature are not properly Lawes, but qualities that dispose men to peace and obedience. (*Lev.*, XXVI, 8)

The peace to which the laws of nature dispose men is opposed by their selfish inclinations; and, without the civil condition—the sovereign's civil laws and his power to enforce them—the laws of nature are ineffective. As uncovenanted, they do not bind action. It is not reasonable that they should, Hobbes argues, for in the condition of war, self-preservation cannot be secured by their means. So the laws of nature are fulfilled in the rational condition of the State, which both defines the just and, by its power to punish, restrains antisocial behavior. So the above quotation continues:

> When a Common-wealth is once settled then are they [the laws of nature] actually Lawes, and not before; as being then the commands of the Common-wealth; and therefore also Civill Lawes; For it is the Soveraign Power that

obliges men to obey them. For in the differences of private men, to declare, what is Equity, what is Justice, and what is morall Vertue, and to make them binding, there is need of the Ordinances of Soveraign Power, and Punishments to be ordained for such as shall break them; which Ordinances are therefore part of the Civill Law. The Law of Nature therefore is part of the Civill Law in all Common-wealths of the world. Reciprocally also, the Civil Law is part of the Dictates of Nature. (*ibid.*)

It is because the law of nature intends peace and the civil law concretely brings peace that, I think, Hobbes can say they contain each other and are of equal extent. But this means that the civil laws of each particular State, no matter how they differ from those of other States, are equally for the sake of peace. And even if a State's civil law is in formal opposition to that of another State—one saying "Do X" and another, "Don't do X"—, both are equally just. It is just like a man doing X in one circumstance and not doing X in another, and yet being just in each instance.

But again, how so? Though Hobbes began, experientially, with something we can plausibly accept as a fact—namely, that human nature needs restraint and guidance—has he ended with something one can hardly accept as a fact: that the civil laws of all States intend and foster peace and justice? Doesn't experience deny this? Are not some laws, to use his term, inequitable and, as such, only formally but not materially serving peace?

The clue to Hobbes' response is in the sovereign standing in the formal relation to the citizen as "God to man." This means his equity cannot be questioned, and its results are a grace or charity—for to have a State is to leave the condition of war, where each is equal to each in his right, but none are under the universality of law. Yet, Hobbes' answer must go beyond merely repeating that laws are necessary. Since the authoritative judgment of equity in public matters has been given by them to the sovereign, the citizens cannot act as if it had not been given. This would be in contradiction to their own will and, in effect, a broken promise. The desire for the State, i.e., the desired end, involves obedience as the means to it. But isn't this a case of the emperor's clothes? Doesn't one sometimes see the exercise of nakedly iniquitous power by sovereigns? And are not some laws made for the sake of inequity rather than equity? For instance, only to have a tax on bread or salt has a false universality, for the burden is on the poor.

Hobbes' developed answer does consider the duty of the sovereign to be equitable, and so he implicitly distinguishes between good and bad laws in principle. However, for the subject there is no formal mechanism to make such a decision about the equity of the law or to question the will of the sovereign, since the State was instituted just to have a sovereign who makes rules. Thus obedience to the sovereign has a presumption of the equity of his rules, without always having a commonsense view of that equity. This is a great tension—a tension heightened by the fact that most of the laws of nature seem simple enough. Consequently, civil laws against things like murder and theft are not only to be present, in whatever particular detail the sovereign wills, but broadly judged in terms of their effectiveness.

Hobbes' approach is twofold. First, considered from the situation of the sovereign, the exercise of wickedness—that is, of acting not in accordance with peace or the laws of nature when he can safely act in accordance with them—is counterproductive. Inequity is against peace; and the peace of the State, I stress again, not only fulfills the duty of the sovereign, but is in his material interest. Therefore, a policy or a disposition to inequity is harmful to the sovereign. So, though tyranny is not in Hobbes' political vocabulary (for power legitimates), nevertheless I think Hobbes holds that the vicious character of the ruler brings harm to himself and to the State. (cf. *Lev.*, XXX, 4) Of course, this is only an argument to restrain wickedness; but, as such, it implies the fact that a wicked sovereign does occur. I will elaborate on the problem of tyranny in the next chapter. Second, though in the scientific exposition of the nature of a State the citizen is formally committed to obedience, in extreme cases, where it is obvious that much war has entered the gates, it implies that it is prudent to return to a condition of nature by rebelling against the sovereign. Whatever the cause—wickedness or some other incapacity—he would not be fulfilling his civil function. Therefore Hobbes says, "Negligent government of Princes [is naturally punished] with Rebellion" (*Lev.*, XXXI) In brief, then, the material possibility of revolution acts as a deterrent against any outrageous incapacity on the part of the sovereign, though Hobbes tends to be silent about this and it is never formally justified. It is not that all States are equitable; it is that they have to be assumed to be such, and when this assumption becomes impossible to hold, the State cannot endure long. The moral basis of politics is both in this assumption of the coextensiveness of the natural laws with the civil laws and, materially, it is enlightened self-interest. The moral secures the political both for sovereign and citizen, for the moral is a disposition to acts of peace which is the end of civil society and its benefit. This implies that Hobbes considered the coordination of natural law and civil law a task to be accomplished in each commonwealth.

* * *

It is the State, with its awesome power, to which Hobbes gave the name Leviathan. His intention was to remind his readers of the *Book of Job,* where almighty God teaches the upright Gentile, a man of righteous *inclination,* to be truly righteous in obeying Him with understanding. If the imagination is not sufficient to see God and reason is not sufficient to grasp his purposes, Job's pride can be sufficiently humbled even by God's creation, by Leviathan. As the power and authority of God is displayed to Job, Hobbes asks his reader to consider a similar relationship between the State (or more precisely, the sovereign) and the citizen.

Though many of his contemporaries doubted either the authenticity or the probity of Hobbes' religious scruples, Hobbes cunningly chose the persuasiveness of a biblical metaphor in speaking to his countrymen in the mid-seventeenth century. The secular, academic audience, which is, for the most part, Hobbes' audience now, can appreciate the ingenuity of the metaphor more easily than its boldness and persuasive power. Our age offers answers to Job. Hobbes attracts and repels a consciousness that has lost the ideology, as well as much of the habit, of obedience to supreme power. Yet ours is a consciousness which, like Hobbes' own, locates creative social arrangement in man. Hobbes entices this aspect of the modern consciousness with his notion of the radical equality of men, which implies that any man or group of men can be sovereign. Other conditions being equal, if acting on rational self-interest Hobbes' sovereign causes the civil condition, which is peace, by creating rules of public behavior through the civil laws. The simple excuse for disobedience to the civil law is when the citizen's disobedience does not oppose the purpose for which the State was created: "When therefore our refusall to obey frustrates the End for which the Soveraignty was ordained; then there is no Liberty to refuse; otherwise there is." (*Lev.*, XXI, 15) Except for this, Hobbes differs from our age in seeming to ask for obedience to the civil law without quibble, whether the quibble originates in momentary self-interest, religious orientation, or what is usually considered moral scruple.

In our own time many still living have the memory of Auschwitz as a testimonial to the results of obedience conjoined to State power. (And it is small consolation that a postwar Germany gives money to its Auschwitz victims as a kind of carrion comfort; it seems to modern man that God replaced Job's dead children with others.)

But you and I ought not to be hostages to images. Hobbes himself knew well the power of images to terrify when he presented a condition of nature where the order of civil law was replaced by the conflicting individual wills of men. The brutal image he created in words was to restrain his reader from the brutality that occurs when the governmental authority is not in effect. Yet though Hobbes' condition of nature is a possibility and Auschwitz is certainly a fact, as mere images they simply frighten the child in us. And though sometimes the child in us ought to be frightened, as adults we must seek a rational sorting out of such images; nightmares also need interpretation. One must avoid the dizzying distraction of shining one image against another so that neither can help us to clarify experience. Fancy needs such a context of restraining argument, and experience must be made useful by a plausible ordering based on a rational determination of the human condition.

* * *

For the sake of bringing men to right reason and to equity, Hobbes offers a minimalist theory of law.[1] Its goal is the peace, security, and prosperity of the commonwealth rather than the optimum moral development of individual persons. Hobbes is not in agreement with Plato and the Platonic tradition concerning the ontology of the good; nor would he agree, for example, with the spirit of Socrates' advice to Glaucon to choose the "upward path." Nevertheless, Hobbes' view of the law is not just simply opposed to a Platonic or other more "elevated" and sanguine view of the human condition, in the sense that his view can be broadly accepted by anyone who grants the defensive proposition that self-interest of a crude and commonsensical sort is paramount, and which considers punishment a major aspect of decision-making in governing a large number of persons. It is especially these—the party of Gyges—which must be restrained.

Even if Hobbes' theory provides a rational view of the legal sphere, isn't it still open to the objection that it justifies great moral evil through its emphasis on obedience to the law? Hobbes is not completely satisfactory on this point. For him, as we have seen, it is the sovereign's rational self-interest to protect the State from internal and external enemies, to promote art and commerce and, generally, to establish peace and prosperity. Therefore there is, *in theory,* a relatively minor lack of congruence between the individual or individuals that compose the sovereign and the goals which create the State. Indeed, Hobbes considered this the important political doctrine to teach his countrymen. He stresses that "education and discipline" can remedy man's non-social inclination. Yet teachers do not always have good pupils; a doctrine that informs of true interest can still be at odds with the concrete fact that many do not learn their true interest or do not act on it. (And, of course, there is always the real possibility that mankind is simply madder than Hobbes estimated).

Though one may accept the need of obedience to the State as a fact of life, I propose some reasonable modifications of Hobbes. The following fundamental rights which I find arising from the nature of the State pushed Hobbes a bit toward Locke and Kant in some ways, but they don't overthrow the Hobbesian approach. I would argue for an elaboration of Hobbes which would include the following: (a) The freedom of the individual to openly critique the political sphere for its policies, laws, procedures, and actions. Hobbes would call this counsel, but would not always allow it. Censorship is a rational possibility, and Hobbes, in the divisive atmosphere of his time, even encourages it. Indeed, experience shows that with the benefits of free discussion arise the dangers of demagoguery. (b) The freedom of the individual to leave the State without harassment.

I take these to be boundary conditions of the individual's relationship to the State. It is indeed a condition for the State's existence that it must be obeyed whether one agrees with its directives or not, so long as those directives do not contradict the very basis of peace and security for which the State was created. Yet if action is limited, intellectual opposition is not. It is the very knowledge of self-interest—which Hobbes grants, and which is implicit in creating the State—that I consider a persistent aspect of the will of the citizen in relationship to the State. This interest is exercised not merely by obeying civil laws, but also by a freedom to educate the State, as Kant emphasized.

Further, speaking to the second point, a boundary condition of our obedience-relation to the State is the right to leave it. One is bound to obey the civil laws as long as one is a member of the State, but one is not bound to be a member of the State.

A person has a right to decide the primary condition for the expression of his will: namely, how it is represented. I do not mean the citizen can pick and choose among the civil laws in terms of obedience—one cannot be true to Hobbes and assert that—but a citizen can choose to be part of the State or not. Fundamental decisions of this sort are basic to the very capacity to become a citizen in the first place. I take this as a sort of *ur*-decision—reminiscent of Kelsen's *urgrund*—and in continuous operation in the citizen-State relationship.

I am aware that the freedom of dissociation, as well as the freedom of speech, has certain practical limits, and Hobbes saw these clearly. The State can refuse to allow a citizen to leave because he would pose a freedom to its peace and security if he were elsewhere. Hobbes no doubt wished to avoid obscuring the logical line of his position, and the additions do create some complexities. Though much benefit of doubt must be given to the sovereign (thereby going in the direction of Hobbes' demands), nevertheless it is to be emphasized that these fundamental principles follow from the initial possibility of being a citizen. I retain them not for the sake of questioning the particular decisions of the sovereign, but for clarifying the sovereign's duties and providing a determination for judging whether the State is functioning correctly. As such, they exert an ideological leverage that I consider to be materially helpful.

The State's task is to preserve the citizen. From the standpoint of conscience, its actions are not always moral, its laws are not always fair, despite Hobbes' hypothetical of the sovereign's equity. But this is the price one pays for the existence of the State and arises from living with imperfect men. Yet I offer three distancing procedures. One is the educative one of free speech. The second is the disassociative one of leaving the State. The third concerns the situation in which the State has broken with its rational function to provide peace and security. In this case the State is merely a *state apparatus* rather than a genuine State. When one judges oneself to be in a condition of nature, there is a natural right to take arms against this state apparatus. This last is not a right of civil life; rather, as Hobbes observed, it opposes civil life. But such opposition may occur for the sake of creating a State to replace a grossly inequitable state apparatus.

This approach to the legal sphere provides a way to briefly show the character of the Nurnberg trials from both a legal and a political perspective; and in turn the Nurnberg trials afford a good historical example to test and illustrate my views.

The Nazi German State or, better, the Nazi state apparatus, violated the fundamental basis of the State. Its aggression was not only against other sovereign States, but against the boundary of its own being as a State. It deprived a substantial number of its citizens of peace and security, freedom of speech and religion, and the capacity to emigrate. By doing this, it dissolved its authority as a State, and stood as a brute force in relation to all men, including those Germans it did not yet deprive of their rights. Its moral nefariousness attacked the minimum conditions for having a sovereign. The Nazi civil laws, which were opposed in essence to political order and the rule of law, constituted an apparatus for brutality, and were in contradiction to the purposes of their own foundation. While having the appearance of being in place, the civil laws did not meet the test of leading to peace and security. They were obviously inequitable.

Yet since a minimalist theory bases juridical authority on the sovereign, the Nurnberg Trials have no legal foundation. "Crimes against humanity" have no legal justification. Though punishment of Nazis is morally appropriate, at least on the basis of dissuading others from acts of brutality, the agencies of coercion, the Allies, acted merely with the naked power of the victor. Without the authority of a sovereign—made obvious by there being here an *ex post facto* legal condition—there can be morally apt decisions about culpability, but there can be no valid legal punishment. In the Nurnberg trials, punishment was justified on moral sentiment backed by coercive power. Ironically, the tool to deal morally with the Nazi state apparatus—and a tool for moral propaganda—was the Allies' judicial apparatus.

The minimalist position inspired by Hobbes makes the legal sphere autonomous, but it understands the law to be grounded in politics, with all its limitations. Nevertheless, it expresses a moral intention: a State need not be perfect in our eyes to demand our obedience. Yet, the fundamental boundaries marking the civil condition also provide both a prudential and (in a broad sense) a scientific understanding of when a State opposes peace and security. It is no light matter to disobey the State; but there is no obligatory ground for obeying an apparatus whose appearance of being a State is belied by its obvious and exceedingly brutish disregard of the purposive ground of the civil condition.

CHAPTER NINE

Hobbes on the Character and Use of Civil Law

For orientation, one can speak in a general sense of three political postures. They are amelioration, revolution, and salvation. Without seeking further refinement of the member types in each of these constellations, I consider Hobbes' political frame of reference to be that of amelioration because of his legal doctrine.

The hortative Hobbes appears in all his social and political writings, even in the "Introduction" to his Thucydides translation, his earliest published work. The Athenian historian's observations about the fragility of human nature, with its greed and its tendency to mad and vainglorious adventurism, freed of restraint and driven to brutality in a condition of war, are offered by Hobbes to his countrymen as a warning. In his own protreptic voice, the "Dedication" to the *Elements of Law* states, "and it would be an incomparable benefit to commonwealth, if every man held the opinions concerning law and policy here delivered." The "Dedication" to *De Cive*, by implication, refers to his country's turbulence: "I have been very wary in the whole tenour of my discourse, not to meddle with the civil laws of any particular nation whatever: that is to say, I have avoided coming ashore, which those times have so infested both with shelves and tempests." To this, the "Preface to the Reader" adds that the work has been written primarily for "the establishment of peace, and by one whose just grief for the present calamities of his country may very charitably be allowed some liberty."

The therapeutic agenda of the *Leviathan* is also explicit. As a professed purpose, Hobbes wishes to influence the universities, which, in turn, form the minds of the ministers who instruct the common people in religion. His country's current status doesn't seem far from his mind. At the end of the second part of "Of Commonwealth," he notes that one of the "natural punishments [which] must be naturally consequent to the breach of the laws of nature" is the consequential chain of "negligent government of princes, with rebellion; and rebellion, with slaughter." Hobbes thereupon offers the *Leviathan* to a vigilant king as political amelioration. He is confident that he has provided "a science of natural justice [which] is the only science necessary for sovereigns and their principal ministers." Taking seriously Plato's view of philosophy's therapeutic responsibility to political life, Hobbes says:

> neither Plato, nor any other philosopher hitherto, hath put in order, and sufficiently, or probably proved all the theorems of moral doctrine, that men may learn thereby, both how to govern and how to obey; I recover some hope, that one time or other, this writing of mine, may fall into the hands of a sovereign, who will consider it himself. . . and by the exercise of entire sovereignty, in protecting the public teaching of it, convert this truth of speculation, into the utility of practice. (*ibid.*)

This intention to ameliorate has a focus: it is the civil law, for Hobbes, which is the proper instrument of political sanity. The Archimedian point on which it rests is outside the natural world, in the sense that it belongs to man's capacity to create artifices. By his own ingenuity, by creating a State (and thereby, necessarily, a legal system) man lifts himself out of the dangerous and miserable natural condition of war. Hobbes' legal philosophy cannot be separated from his political philosophy. It is by considering the origin of the State, more important in its logical than in its historical character, that the duties and obligations of ruler and subject can be charted. The public word of the sovereign or civil law is to express equitable rule, and it is to receive promised obedience. His elaboration of these two aspects of civil law is, putting technicalities about effective operation aside, equivalent to Hobbes' legal philosophy.

For Hobbes, the law is not evolutionary. It does, or should, reflect social conditions, just because its goal of providing order and welfare must necessarily consider circumstance. Also, it provides the *certain* measure of its own social condition; it measures, whereby it creates or constructs. There is a natural measure as well, arising from the need to leave the natural condition of war and to maintain the peace of commonwealth. Its clear boundary condition is the preservation of the individual. This is not a moral factor for Hobbes, but rather the necessary condition for morality. Yet the preservation of the individual has its best chance through peace, and this is the goal of the State. Those laws of nature which make for peace do not, however, measure the civil law, as they would in the natural law tradition; but they are made concrete by the civil law. The basic failures of his political and legal doctrines—or, at least, the theoretical tensions to be found in them—come from his conceptual separation of nature and artifice, on the one hand, and his seeing them as necessary and intertwined in the description of the civil condition, on the other. In any case, Hobbes' legal philosophy reflects his particular sort of ameliorative humanism: one that conceives man to create his own best condition.

I will present the details of Hobbes' philosophy of law by primarily discussing *Leviathan,* Chapter XXVI, "Of Civil Lawes," and the piece, written late in life by him and published posthumously, entitled *Dialogue Between a Philosopher and a Student of the Common Laws of England.* This close account of Hobbes' legal philosophy will supplement the discussion of the previous chapter, with its focus on the political position of the sovereign.

To focus matters, let us consider the definition that Hobbes provides of civil law in *Leviathan*. The definition is preceded by two points about scope. The first deals with the enterprise itself. He says that he is not concerned with the particular or actual laws of States. He wishes to show the character of law, "as have done Plato, Aristotle, and Cicero." The second point concretely offers his understanding of the law. He says law has the following elements: (1) it is a command; (2) it is by someone who has been given authority to command; (3) it is addressed to someone who is expected to obey the command; and (4) that person is expected to obey the command because he has previously accepted the authority of the person commanding.

Hobbes' orientation is the command theory of law—that is, a version of legal positivism. To show the character of that positivism, let us briefly note some comparisons with H.L.A. Hart.[1] Hart, unlike Hobbes, considers laws primarily to be rules and norms which rely on habits of obedience rather than on threats. Hart's positivism is therefore more powerfully moved by sociological considerations than the positivism of Hobbes. From Hobbes' viewpoint, the more sociological a legal theory is, the less it is scientific. He believes the civil laws are indeed embedded in circumstance, but that a legal *theory* defines concepts universally and necessary. Like Hart, Hobbes sees that normally laws based only on threats cannot succeed. But unlike Hart, he argues that since the need for law arose from man's contentious self-interest, its essence is threat. On the basis of self-interest as a universal character of man, Hobbes' legal philosophy is without concern for a particular nation's legal tradition, whether it be the common law or the character of the citizen's habitual responses to civil law.[2]

It is to be emphasized, then, that Hobbes' command theory has its ground in a vision of man—not this or that man, but man generally, which is the execution of the task of the political theorist. It is this meta-legal aspect, to use Warrender's phrase, upon which Hobbes bases his demand for the use of civil law to control aggressive, anti-social inclinations. Both the use and the character of civil law will soon become clearer as we now turn to examine Hobbes' definition of civil law. He says:

> Civill Law, is to every Subject, those Rules, which the Common-wealth hath Commanded him, by Word, Writing, or other sufficient Sign of the Will, to make use of, for the Distinction of Right, and Wrong; that is to say, of what is contrary, and what is not contrary to the Rule. (*Lev., XXVI, 312*)

First, who is a subject of a commonwealth and what is a subject's condition? A subject is one who has consented—that is, has contracted, either overtly or tacitly—to obey the sovereign in all matters with the exception of killing or physically harming himself or of accusing himself of a crime. (*Lev., XXI, 269*) The principles in this are important: (a) one must be capable of consent to be a subject; as Hobbes puts it, "there being no obligation on any man, which ariseth not from some act of his own." (*ibid.,* 268) Consequently, children, fools, and madmen are not properly to be considered subjects, but rather as wards of the commonwealth. (b) The obedience of a contractor is an act of will: "in the act of our submission, consisteth both our obligation, and our liberty." (*ibid.*) This involves the ability to transfer to another what is ours to dispose of, our liberty, so that we are obliged to obey him. The sovereign thereby impersonates our will, having been given authority to create the civil laws or political rules that bind us concretely. Also, because he is not a party to the contract, his will is not bound by it; the subjects have therefore bound their wills so as not to impede the will of the sovereign. (c) The important correlate to this is that the greatest liberty of subjects depends on the silence of the civil law. (*ibid.,* 271) (d) There are boundary conditions to the subject's transfer of liberty and the authorization of the sovereign. Hobbes presumes that no sane man acts without an intention of benefiting himself; one enters into the condition of civil society for the primary sake of preserving one's life, to preserve oneself from other harms, and to prosper. A subject certainly does not oblige himself, *per impossibile*, to give up his life or the means to preserve his life.

Hobbes emphasizes, "the end of the institution of sovereignty [is] the peace of the subjects within themselves, and their defense against a common enemy. (*ibid.*, 268) From which he considers "the obligation a man may sometimes have, upon the command of the sovereign, to execute any dangerous, or dishonourable office, dependeth not on the words of our submission; but on the intention; which is to be understood by the end thereof. When therefore a refusal to obey, frustrates the end for which the sovereignty was ordained; then there is no liberty to refuse: otherwise there is." (*ibid.*, 269) This opens a possibility for disobedience on the basis of the citizen's judgment, which may clash with allegiance to the sovereign's authority. At any rate, from the viewpoint of capacity rather than intention, a correlate of the above is the assertion, in Hobbes' words, that (e) "The obligation of the subjects to the sovereign is understood to last as long, and no longer, than the power lasteth, by which he is able to protect them." (*ibid.*, 272)

Just a word here. The giving of consent can be taken more strictly than Hobbes apparently takes it. The Platonic tradition takes the state of being childish, foolish or mad to be to some degree characteristic of most men, and therefore proposes the elitist politics of the philosopher-king. In arguing for this the Platonic tradition distinguishes, as does Bramhall in his discussion with Hobbes, between a rational will and other sorts of will. Hobbes does not make such a distinction. He believes experience and prudential calculation will bring all men to peace. A Platonic emendation of Hobbes would move him too much in a paternalist direction, whereas the liberal reading of (d) would move him too far from his conservatism. If the subject's judgments of self-benefit and danger are given much allowance as proper causes for disobedience, this would clash with Hobbes' emphasis on men's great difficulty in judging equitably. He believes that men generally are too much pulled by vain or esurient emotions that demand immediate gratification, especially where their own interests are involved, and that lacking prudence, they seek their narrow self-interest. A too-liberal interpretation, therefore, destroys the place Hobbes has reserved for the sovereign's equity and the reason for finding a certain standard in the civil law. It would undercut his opposition to civil disobedience by emphasizing "rights" rather than "duties."

The above principles were generated by the subject's contracted obligation to obedience; the command of the sovereign provides others. The relation between the subject and the sovereign is obviously close. To borrow from Descartes, the sovereign's relation to the commonwealth is more intimate than that of a captain to his ship. The particular and natural human being (or beings), as the artificial person who represents the commonwealth, may and will, of course, be changed, but a State cannot exist without a sovereign, a public individual to create the laws and to enforce obedience to them. The primary principle of sovereignty is a logical one about command, *viz.*, (a) "the sovereign is the sole legislator." (*Lev.*, XXVI, 313) Closely related to this is (b) "The sovereign of a commonwealth, be it an assembly, or one man, is not subject to the civil law." (*ibid.*)

The primary principles of sovereignty are grounded in the need to control the passions which lead to inequity. In the state of nature, where there is no such control, each man pursues his interests to the general danger of others. Since, for Hobbes, human nature does not change in the civil condition, one implicit task of government is educational, *viz.*, to show that, in general but overwhelmingly, the interest of the individual is best served by preserving the State. As the fundamental means for this, self-interest (let alone gratitutde and honoring promises) demands obedience to the civil law.

It may be a wise policy on the part of the sovereign to educate, but the explicit task of government is to command. Its task is to create laws and to enforce obedience to them, even when the lesson of self-interest is not learned. In Hobbes' own words, "the laws of nature (as justice, equity, modesty, mercy, and, in sum, doing to others as they would be done to them), of themselves, without the terror of some power to cause them to be observed are contrary to our natural passions that carry us to partiality, pride, revenge, and the like. And covenants without the sword, are but words, and of no strength to secure a man at all." (*Lev.* XVII, 223)

But along with the threat of sanctions as the material condition to compel obedience, the logical condition of creating rules must be met. For the coherence of the logic of authority, the State needs a single sovereign; in actual fact, without a sole legislator conflict can hardly be avoided. Of course, it is possible, and practically necessary, to split responsibility for aspects of governance. But if that split involves indefeasible authority and not the provisional or institutional delegation of power by a single sovereign, then, Hobbes asks, who among these multiple sovereigns will limit the others' power? If one says it should be a constitution, then who will interpret the constitution? Hobbes' point is that such an interpeter, logically, would be the sovereign. Because of the logical need to be the sole maker of law, the sovereign must be outside the civil law, or in a condition of nature.

This engenders a further principle: (c) the sovereign or legislator is also the sole or final interpreter or judge of the law. So Hobbes says, "All laws, written, and unwritten, have need of interpretation. . . the knowledge of [the law's] final causes is in the legislator. To him therefore there cannot be a knot in the law, insoluble; either by finding out the ends, to undo it by; or else by making what ends he will, as Alexander did with his sword in the Gordian knot, by the legislative power, which no other interpreter can do." (*ibid.*, 322) The unity of the legislative, judicial and executive powers of the State avoids the chaos of judicial legislation competing with the legislative acts of government. It consolidates State power logically and materially.

Fundamentally, this contains Hobbes' argument against Coke's[3] response to James I: "quod Rex non debet esse sub homine sed sub Deo et Lege" (12 *Coke Reports,* 63) or, as Coke (and indeed all the Chief Judges) affirmed in plain English three years later, in 1610: "the King hath no prerogative but that which the law of the land allows" (12 *Coke Reports,* 74). For Coke, and later for Hale[4] in his opposition to Hobbes' *Dialog* there is a favoring of the supremacy of the common law.

Cleverly using Coke's own words against him, Hobbes approvingly quotes the statement: "no man out of his own private reason ought to be wiser than the law, which is the perfection of reason." (1 *Coke Commentaries,* 97b) The common lawyer's taking of custom or previous legislation to be the supreme legal authority, like recourse to a constitution, opposes Hobbes' doctrine of the sovereign's sole power to make the law and, consequently, to judge its intention. A more apt and general statement of (c), therefore, is that the will of the sovereign is both united and supreme for the sake of rationalizing authority. This is the *urgrund* of the legal system. Kelsen captures Hobbes' understanding when he says, "The basic norm is not created in a legal procedure by a law-creating organ. It is not—as a positive legal norm is—valid because it is created in a certain way by a legal act, but it is valid because it is presupposed to be valid; and it is presupposed to be valid because without this presupposition no human act could be interpreted as legal, especially as a norm-creating act."[5]

If the sovereign's will is the basic norm, Hobbes' argument against the common law follows: "it is not length of time that maketh the authority, but the will of the sovereign." (*Lev.*, 313). Thus, in those instances where custom or previous legislation are not opposed, "the will of the sovereign is signified by his silence... length of time shall bring no prejudice to his right." (*ibid.*) Further, a particular judgment, like other municipal actions by delegates of the sovereign, is valid "because he [the judge] giveth it by authority of the sovereign, whereby it becomes the sovereign's sentence." (*ibid.*, 323) These considerations delineate the sovereign's power to command. The sovereign's obligations are best treated by considering the character of his intent in making civil laws: the aspect of Hobbes' definition of civil law which distinguishes right and wrong.

Before turning to this important and complicated aspect of the civil law, let us briefly consider the technical matter of the communication of the sovereign's command. The definition refers to the sovereign's command to the subject as taking place "by word, writing, or other sufficient sign of the will." Hobbes holds that the civil laws must be promulgated, must be clear, and must not be opposed one to another. The principle is that the sovereign must adequately communicate his will "because a man knows not otherwise how to obey." (*ibid.*, 312) By this, and only by this, a legal argument can be made against the sovereign, that is, a law can be challenged as poorly made or as not sufficiently promulgated. Consequently, (a) the civil laws must be adequately available to the subject, and (b) "the law can never be against reason" (*ibid.*, 316), that is, in opposition to itself. It must have what Aristotle called *meta logou*, but it does not need an extra-legal normativity, the *kata ton orthon logon*. (*Ethics*, 1144b26-7)

Yet, because Hobbes believes the law is hostage to interpretation, this factor erodes some of the importance of, and demand for, adequate communication. The gap that is opened thereby is one of the "incommodious" aspects of politics. To some extent, Hobbes closes the gap by having the judge assume that the law is equitable, that is, that the intention or will of the sovereign is always for equity. Thereby, in what seems a rather liberal inclination, the letter of the law is made less important than equity. To understand the artificial reason of the law, the judge's natural reason, seeking equity, must be brought to the task, Hobbes says, "So that the incommodity that follows the bare words of the written law, may lead him to the intention of the law, whereby to interpret the intention of the same better." (*ibid.*, 326) Nevertheless, in order to maintain the sovereign's sole prerogative of judging what is and is not equitable, the sovereign can overrule his delegate, his appointed judge. Here we see Hobbes conservatively balancing the liberal move of having the judge as interpreter of equity. Hobbes, in this regard, adds that "no incommodity can warrant a sentence against the law. For every judge of right and wrong is not the judge of what is commodious, or incommodious to the commonwealth." (*ibid.*, 327) The crispest way to put the matter is that, from the viewpoint of the judge, the sovereign's understanding of equity has the force of a definition, while from the viewpoint of the sovereign, it has the force of a moral obligation and a prudential aspiration. Practically, however, the judge's natural understanding of equity is given much discretion till the sovereign speaks against the judge's interpretation. It is characteristic of Hobbes' philosophy of law to balance liberal and conservative tendencies. One must therefore avoid the temptation selectively to read him as "essentially" either a liberal or a conservative. He must be understood in terms of the balance—that is, as Hobbes.

Now let us turn to the final aspect of the definition of civil law in *Leviathan* XXVI: civil law as the maker of the distinction between right and wrong. Here we must indeed directly engage the question of equity. There is an obvious tension between, on the one hand, the formal assumption that the sovereign, fulfilling his obligation to the commonwealth, creates equitable laws, and, on the other hand, the evaluation by any man of the actual or material equity of a particular law. Of understanding equity, which Hobbes puts first for a good judge or interpreter of laws, he says after all that it depends "on the goodness of a man's own natural reason." (*ibid.*, 328)

As already mentioned, the theoretical emplacement of right and wrong rests on the proposition that "The law of nature, and the civil law, contain each other, and are of equal extent." (*ibid.*, 314) Equity, as a law of nature, is a disposition to peace. As such, Hobbes points out, "in the condition of mere nature [they] are not properly laws." (*ibid.*) The transformation of the condition of nature into the civil condition depends precisely on creating a sovereign to make right and wrong by means of the civil law. It follows from this that the concreteness of the civil law is necessary for the disposition to peace, "*in foro interno,*" to achieve its goal, to become "*in foro externo.*"[6]

But what is the standard for the sovereign? On the one hand, taking Hobbes' sovereign as a mortal God, we are tempted to accept the proposition that the sovereign's will is the certain standard of moral action. However, because the sovereign is also a man (or men) who comes to his position by also escaping from the dangers of the state of nature, he is obliged, by the natural law of gratitude (and other natural laws, which Hobbes sums up as charity) to direct his will, as best he can, for the sake of peace. The State, that had made him a mortal God by not "binding fast" his will while his subjects are so bound, imposes a moral obligation upon him. Moral obligations do exist for the sovereign, though he is in a state of nature. Yet—and I emphasize this—how the sovereign is to fulfill this obligation is uncertain. He, unlike his subjects, who are organized by his legal or public will, has no certain definitions to guide him in his duty; he has only his conscience.[7] The morality of the law, therefore, cannot be formally questioned by the citizen, though its equity is a moral obligation for the sovereign.[8]

In sum, the fundamental moral principle is that right and wrong is measured by what makes for peace. But, more narrowly and sometimes against the facts, the basic principle of the legal order assumes that the sovereign always intends peace; and, further, his decisions cannot be opposed. Experience disputes that the sovereign always intends peace. Yet, according to Hobbes, there is no alternative but to have a sovereign who has the overawing power to create rules and enforce obedience. Hobbes must persuade on two fronts; he must persuade that it is both in the self-interest of sovereign and of subject to seek peace. I therefore read *Leviathan* as Hobbes' attempt to ameliorate the thinking of the one who commands and of the ones who obey in order for the commonwealth to better fulfill its universal purpose: peace.

In *Dialogue between a Philosopher and a Student of the Common Laws of England,* which is taken to be Hobbes' last work on the subject, the tension between actual legal command and the purpose of political command is again considered.[9] The proof texts are: (a) "It is not wisdom, but authority that makes a law" (*Dial.*, 55) and (b) "God made kings for the people, and not people for kings" (*Dial.*, 61).

Before commenting on the contents of the *Dialogue*, there are two matters which should be mentioned in relation to its presentation of Hobbes' views. By evidence of internal reference, it was written late—in the form we have it, not till at least 1662. It was published posthumously in 1681. Joseph Cropsey, in the introduction to his edition, cites the evidence from Aubrey and from Hobbes' publisher, Crooke, to provide some background on the *Dialogue* and its authenticity as Hobbes' work. Of this authenticity there is little doubt, and Hale had indeed responded to it as Hobbes' while Hobbes was still alive. The background, however, is a hazard for interpretation. The *Dialogue* takes up the controversy between Bacon and Coke that took place about 1615. This allows the possibility that any differences between its doctrine and Chapter XXVI of *Leviathan* is due less to a change in Hobbes' own position than to an attempt to defend Bacon. A second hazard for interpretation is the dialogue form. It can always be contended that the views expressed by the Philosopher in the *Dialogue* are not precisely Hobbes' own (though it is obvious that they are at least broadly those of Hobbes). As in Plato's dialogues where, because of the form, there is room for both Socratic and Platonic irony, the *Dialogue* has the complexity of an indirect voice.

Though these matters cast a shadow of interpretive doubt on any change or supposed change of view found in the *Dialogue*, it is nevertheless worth considering. For one, it is the work of Hobbes. Also, concretely, it casts itself into direct struggle with its major competitor in terms of legal theory: the common law. In this, one can again see Hobbes as a spokesman for political amelioration. Besides opposing the weakening of the authority of the sovereign by common law, he opposes, as in the *Leviathan*, the weakening of the sovereign's authority through sectarian religious doctrines, defending Erastianism. With these preparatory remarks, we turn to the *Dialogue,* whose theoretical stance will be considered, leaving unengaged its detailed discussions of particular laws of England of the time.

The *Dialogue* opens with the Philosopher correcting the Student about law being less rational than such studies as mathematics. This, I take it, is related to Hobbes' claim in *De Cive* to have established a science of politics (which includes law), and so to rank with Euclid and Galileo as an inventor of a science.

But the *Dialogue* is not a scientific treatise. Cropsey wonders why the *Dialogue* has no (direct) reference to the state of nature. I hypothesize that this is because the analytic or resolutive method which is discussed in *De Corpore* as part of a scientific investigation is replaced in the *Dialogue* by experience and learning as the basis for the discussion. Like Hobbes' other dialogue, *Behemoth,* which deals with England's civil war, this dialogue also seems conceived to engage the historical domain, and only tacitly to presume the better argument of Hobbes' scientific writings.

It is from this historically concrete vantage point that a strategic attack can be made against the common lawyers. They claim that the common law is authoritative on the basis of the conservative principle that many generations have made and accepted it. It is a limited argument, despite its seemingly plausible response to motive of individual self-interest. More important, it does not provide a justification for the reasonability of the common law. Hobbes, of course, emphasizes that self-interest distorts judgment, but the temporal endurance of a law is no insurance against its not reflecting the self-interest of a class, even through many generations. Indeed, Hobbes, in *Behemoth,* stresses the politics of class. Further, what is a reasonable and equitable law depends upon its ability to foster peace in concrete historical circumstances.[10]

But the question of how reason stands in relation to the law must be further considered, since this is crucial in the confrontation between Hobbes and the common lawyers. The *Dialogue*'s Philosopher calls "true, evident, and undeniable" the following words of Coke: "Equity is a certain perfect reason that interprets and amends the written law, itself being unwritten, and consisting in nothing else than right reason". (*Dial.,* 54) Ingenuously (I take it), the Philosopher claims to be confused about the implication of his antagonist's words, saying, "I find my own reason at a stand [concerning the quote I certainly accept]; for it frustrates all the laws in the world: for upon this ground any man, of any law whatsoever may say it is against reason, and thereupon make pretence for his disobedience." (*ibid.*)

The Student, asked to clarify this matter, provides the meaning of reason for the common lawyer; this, in turn, is rejected by the Philosopher as "partly obscure and partly untrue." What is taken as obscure is the Student's use of the phrase "legal reason." It and the phrase "artificial reason" are absurd speech, for the Philosopher takes reason to be always natural. By this rhetorical assertion, he opposes the common lawyer's specialist claim to be the sole (or at least, the most adequate) interpreter of law, a claim embedded in the legal maxim of *stare decisis,* or the authority of precedent. The Philosopher's opposition is made yet more forcefully by what he finds untrue, *viz.,* "This legal reason is *summa ratio;* and therefore, if all the reason that is dispersed into so many several heads were united into one, yet could he not make such a law as the Law of England is, because by so many successions of ages it hath been fined and refined by an infinite number of grave and learned men." (*Dial.,* 55) The Philosopher's response is that it is not anyone else but the King of England who makes the law: in a word, "It is no wisdom but authority that makes a law." (*ibid.*) Thereby, the Philosopher contends that the correct interpretation of "equity being right reason" is not Coke's, but rather is the doctrine of the *Leviathan.*

That Hobbes considers his philosophic or scientific view of the political condition more appropriate, at least as far as method, than the common lawyers' learned understanding of the legal life of England, is signaled at the initiation of "On Sovereign Power." Responding to the Lawyer's statement that all human law is peace and justice, the Philosopher asks what justice is. Since it is assumed that authority can provide peace, the question about the nature of justice probes the relationship between the two. The Lawyer's answer, as the Philosopher points out, is Aristotle's: "Justice is giving to every man his own." (*Dial.,* 58) By this, Hobbes emphasizes that understanding the law depends on a philosophic or scientific method rather than on a study of the particular laws of a State, such as the laws of England. The Philosopher puts this rhetorically, but with much force: "See you lawyers how much you are beholding to a philosopher, and 'tis but reason, for the more general and noble science, and law of the all the world is true philosophy, of which the common law of England is very little part." (*ibid.*)

It is to be recalled that equity is equated by Coke with perfect reason in the law, and the Philosopher had emphatically agreed with this. Perfect reason in the law is necessary to perfect knowledge or wisdom; recall Hobbes' words from the "Dedicatory" of *De Cive, viz.*, "Wisdom properly so called is nothing else than this, the perfect knowledge of the truth in all matters whatsoever." Hobbes, the philosopher, seems to know at least the perfect truth of politics, for how otherwise can he have established it as a science? Therefore he is fit in this sense to be sovereign. And, as reason is natural, even when creating the artifice of law, he is fit by nature to be a sovereign. But if the truth known by Hobbes is that authority and not wisdom is supreme, then authority does not rest on truth. It does not rest on artifice, either, but on the threat against one's welfare: on power. This is the position of the sophists, and so also is Hobbes' doctrine that man is the measure of political facts, since he creates these conventions.

Truth is indeed dependent on reason; but what moves a man, and is the authority or author of his actions, is not reason but passion—yet another sophist doctrine. The State arose from the passion for self-preservation; this is not a moral matter. The ground of distributive justice is the equality by nature of each man to preserve his life; which, in turn, instrumentally, necessitates a sovereign's authority. This conclusion, with its central assumption of moral agnosticism, is presented in the "Preface" of *De Cive:*

> by most firm reasons to demonstrate that there are no authentical doctrines concerning right and wrong, good and evil, besides the constituted laws in each realm and government; and that the question of whether any future action should prove just or unjust, good or ill, is to be demanded of none but those to whom the supreme hath committed the interpretation of his laws. (*De Cive,* 98)

Such moral agnosticism—or the separation of truth and morality—means that what Hobbes seems to give to philosophy is the theoretical, and not the practical, superiority. From

Hobbes' sophism, we can reflect on H.L.A. Hart's understanding of legal positivism, i.e., "that simple contention that it is in no sense a necessary truth that laws reproduce or satisfy certain demands of morality."[11] For Hobbes, unlike for Hart, there are no "certain demands of morality." The civil law is certain in a way morality cannot be, because the former is artificial.

Also, for Hobbes the nominalist, truth is artificial in being a matter of language and not of things. The sovereign makes the law in terms of a conventional certainty of defining legal concepts, e.g., murder, marriage, property. Indeed, Hart himself argues that legal concepts are *sui generis*, i.e., they cannot be logically equivalent to non-legal concepts.[12]

Because of this constructive aspect of the law and the uncertainty of moral actions outside of the law, Hobbes may further argue that it is misleading to consider the relationship of law to morality as involving the measure of each particular law against a moral postulate (as Hart suggests). The commonwealth, through the civil laws, allows morality to exist *in foro externo*. So it seems, under the moral obligation to keep the civil contract, that the citizen must rather take the law (as Hobbes once said about religion) as a bitter pill not to be chewed, but to be swallowed whole. Yet, seeking his usual balance between theory and circumstance, Hobbes does allow disobedience to the sovereign when very great and obvious actions are demanded against peace, that is, against the necessary condition for morality.

Hobbes does not teach kings to be philosophers. But his protreptic does teach them that their self-interest and their duty—the establishment of peace—are roughly equivalent. Equity, therefore, ought to guide the making of civil laws and hence their construction of social truths.

From this viewpoint, the will of the sovereign as the personifier of the people cannot be constrained in acting in its self-interest; that would impede the very condition in which authority or power can be effectively exercised to secure peace. Hobbes makes this point deftly. The Lawyer brings to the Philosopher's attention statutes where the King has obliged himself to never levy money without the consent of Parliament. The Lawyer's *apercu* follows the Philosopher's praise of philosophy in preference to the study of statutes, and it illustrates his point. For the Philosopher provides the proper understanding that, despite the words of the King, a sovereign cannot so part with his authority. Such statutes are in opposition to the will of the people, by which the State is instituted—a point that the acute Rousseau seems to have learned from Hobbes.

This appears paradoxical. The sovereign is given all political authority, which depends on his maintaining power to be politically effective, but he is obliged by the reasons of peace; so, the Philosopher says, "God made Kings for the people and not people for the King... Shall the King, who is to answer to God Almighty for the safety of the people, and to that end is intrusted with the power to levy and dispose of the souldiery, be disabled to perform his office by virtue of these acts of Parliament which you have cited? If this be reason, 'tis reason also that the people be abandoned, or left at liberty to kill one another, even to the last man; if it be not reason, then you have granted it is not law." (*Dial.*, 61) The rationality of the law is therefore not simply the coherence of statutes, which indeed the lawyer can handle, but the coherence of the statutes in terms of the very *raison d'etre* of the State. This is what Hobbes' legal philosophy teaches, and to disagree with him must involve engaging him on the deeper level of philosophy: by challenging his sophist positions.

It is appropriate to ask Hobbes why he has not contradicted himself when he grants all political authority to the sovereign.[13] By his own wisdom, as a philosopher, he finds that the King of England has no authority to abrogate his own power when he has been a negligent sovereign. Can the Philosopher find other acts of this sort, where the statute is not properly a law because it contradicts the *reason d'etre* of commonwealth? Perhaps there are many such acts, and if so, despite words to the contrary, is it not the Philosopher, or he who uses right reason about political things, who is the final interpreter of the laws, and therefore the real sovereign? Has he not then given to himself, and not to the unphilosophical sovereign, the reason to properly understand the law which he denied to the common lawyers? But then, it might be said that the sovereign still has the sword, and that this is the ultimate basis of authority. But if the sovereign does not have the understanding of the law that the philosopher has, and because of that he is less capable—perhaps sometimes even incapable—of securing peace, does the the philosopher not have a good reason (isn't it a moral ground?) to try to take the sword from his hand?

CHAPTER TEN

Hobbes and Xenophon's *Tyrannicus*

I.

It is remarkable that Hobbes has no substantial discussion of tyrants or of tyranny. This seeming lack stands against the classical tradition of political discussion originating in Socrates. Socrates' two young literary "friends," Plato and Xenophon, each found the topic of tyranny crucial. At the end of Book VIII and in Book IX in the *Republic,* Plato finds that, although they are envied by the *hoi polloi,* tyrants have the least pleasure and lead the worst lives. In this they are the very opposite of the philosopher-king, the best ruler. The government of tyrants, like their lives, is unbalanced and unstable as a result of brutally unenlightened self-interest. Xenophon's *Hiero or Tyrannicus* broadly agrees with this view.

Hobbes not only does not discuss the tyrant, but has no conceptual need to do so. This suggests the following: (1) he has no need to treat forms of government in terms of degrees of excellence, as Plato and Aristotle explicitly did and as Xenophon implicitly did. (2) Hobbes' political psychology, unlike that of our classical Greek authors, does not need to engage forms of excellence. These two matters are related.

The task is to explain why Hobbes did not have these two needs in constructing his political science. Further, by confronting Hobbes with the Socratics, the usefulness of Hobbes' politics is tested by worthy opponents. Though I will refer to Plato's discussion of tyranny in the *Republic*, I have chosen Xenophon's work[1] for the leitmotiv. Xenophon is currently a much underrated political thinker. He may not be greater than Plato, but in many ways he is more attractive, just because Plato's thinking spills into nearly overwhelming metaphysical issues. Another reason is a circumstantial one. Xenophon's dialogue has received a thorough expository reading from Leo Strauss; this prompted a response by the distinguished Hegelian Alexander Kojeve, to which Strauss in turn replied. This contemporary confrontation of a defender of classical and especially Socratic political wisdom with a defender of the historical development of political forms raises another issue which tests the endurance of Hobbes' politics. This issue can be put as the question: (3) Why does Hobbes have no *theoretical* need for an historical or a sociological view of politics? Hobbes' position is attackable on two fronts. From the Socratic orientation, the focus of the assault is his denying the relative excellence of political forms. From the Hegelian orientation, the focus of the assault is Hobbes' not engaging the historical development of political forms (which brings to mind Hobbes' disregard of the factor of national identity).

In Chapter XIX of the *Leviathan*, Hobbes says:

> The difference of commonwealths consists in the difference of the sovereign, or the person representative of all and every one of the multitude. . . . When the representative is one man, then is the commonwealth a monarchy: when an assembly of all that will come together, then it is a democracy, or popular commonwealth: when an assembly of a part only, then it is called an aristocracy. Other kinds of commonwealth there can be none: for either one, or more, or all must have the sovereign power (which I have shown to be indivisible) entire. There be other names of government, in the histories and books of policy: as *tyranny* and *oligarchy:* but these are the same form misliked.

Some paragraphs later, Hobbes continues: "The difference between these three kinds of commonwealth, consists not in the difference of power; but in the difference of convenience, or aptitude to produce peace, and security of the people; for which end they were instituted." Because of convenience he prefers monarchy, since the king "bears in his own natural person." Hobbes argues that "where the public and private interests are most closely united, there the public is most closely advanced. Now in monarchy, the private interest is the same as the public.... Whereas in a democracy or aristocracy, the public prosperity confers not so much to private fortune as one that is corrupt..." Hobbes continues at some length to discuss the general conveniences of monarch and its special inconvenience for succession, but in the words cited we have the essence of his position.

Let us enter into Hobbes' thinking by examining more closely the maxim that the three kinds of government do not consist in the difference of power but in differences of convenience. There is a logical sharpness to the *quantitative* exhaustion of possibilities in one, some, or all of the forms of government (with the ensuing argument against the logical possibility of mixed or mingled forms). But noteworthily, Hobbes treats the civil condition as the *qualitative* opposite of the state of nature. By this either/or, one is in the condition of peace and the other in the condition of war. From the formal consideration of this created or artificial entity, the commonwealth—no matter the form of governance—has no difference in power. Conceptually, in essence, commonwealth creates society—that is, obligations by means of the will of the sovereign, especially civil law. Contracted or "bound in his will," the subject is equally committed to obey the law whatever the composition of the sovereign. Power is taken, then, in terms of the authorization of command. Convenience, on the other hands, deals with the material circumstances of processing that authorization, e.g., with such considerations as the usual jockeying for advantage within aristocratic elites and demagoguery in democracies.

II.

The *Hiero or Tyrannicus* presents a conversation on the nature of tyranny. The participants in the conversation are the tyrant Hiero and the poet Simonides. Simonides had a reputation for being a wise man, but the reputation was not entirely untarnished. He had a reputation for greed,[2] and it is not clear whether he was wise or only clever. Plato indicates the latter, especially in the *Protagoras*.[3] In Xenophon's dialogue, however, Hiero addresses him as being a wise man. For the Socratics, the wise man is admired for himself, in his own happiness, rather than for his usefulness, though wisdom allows him to be very useful. Simonides offers to be useful to Hiero in making him a better tyrant. Hiero is unhappy—or at least claims to be unhappy—because of the burdens of being a tyrant. He especially fears being murdered; and, as a circumstance of tyranny, he despises being surrounded with ignoble men, particularly greedy ones. Hiero cannot have "noble" friendships. Simonides advises Hiero how to ameliorate the circumstances which have produced his fear and isolation, and argues that if he is a better tyrant, he will also be a happier man.

Simonides may wish to be useful because he is greedy (if indeed he is greedy). On the other hand, he may try to appear to be useful because he wants to replace Hiero as tyrant, which would be another form of greed. Indeed, at the start of the discussion he says that all men envy the tyrant, and this implies that he himself does, too. This seems to startle Hiero; in fact, its boldness may have forced Hiero to try to dissuade Simonides from envying him. Why the advice is given is not clear to Hiero, nor to the reader. Why then is the dialogue interesting and useful in understanding politics? Why do we confront Hobbes with it?

The answer is that it contains the assumptions of Socratic politics, which are quite different from those of Hobbes. The contrast between the two is illuminating. Consider: at the outset Simonides asks Hiero about tyranny, just as in the *Republic* Socrates asks Cephalus about old age. In each case the condition seems to lie outside the questioner's experience. What indeed is essentially outside of the wise man's experience, however, is not so clear. And what if Simonides is a tyrant in disposition but has never had a tyranny? What does experience of the outer condition add? In any case, the Socratic ploy is that such a question presumes that knowledge is important to what is central to the existential position of the person questioned. The general is asked about courage, the lover about love, the tyrant about tyranny. The denouement of the ploy is that though he who is questioned ought to know, and needs to know, he doesn't, and therefore must listen to the wise man. This, in a sense, is to agree to be ruled by him.

Hobbes starts from a radical democratic position which, at least in appearance, is opposed to this intellectual elitism. For Hobbes, the deepest desire or natural value is self-preservation, and he argues that in the rough equality of the state of nature, no person, whatever his strengths, is without danger either to his life or to his welfare. The rough knowledge of what is in one's self-interest is open to all; in civil society, he says, "What makes the sovereign is not wisdom but authority." (*D.*, 55) The sovereign need not be a philosopher-king. Yet, as we discussed it at the end of the last chapter, perhaps by a "hidden agenda" that brings him closer to the Socratics, Hobbes advises a prudent king to heed his *Leviathan* and *to be ruled by the results of Hobbes' own introspection.* Though very useful, understanding oneself and thereby Everyman's human nature is very difficult and rarely accomplished.[4]

Another Socratic assumption is that one's passions are either checked by reason or transformed by reason. Hobbes would agree to the passions' being checked by reason if one means by that that deliberation brings forward images of the possible outcomes of action which are opposed by images arising from another passion. Generally speaking, this is the battle in the mind between fear and hope. The Socratics, however, give reason in its most excellent sense a motivating character. It provides vision (*theoria*). This isn't Hobbes' understanding of the matter. To him reason is merely calculation and essentially an instrument of desire. Simonides' rational advice to Hiero is not only for the sake of his accomplishing his desires to mitigate fear and to find friendship, but to create a situation which makes him more like a king than a tyrant. It changes *who he is*. The psychological as well as policy changes that Hiero must make for the royal condition transform his being into a more rational one and harmonize his inner emotional life with a natural structure in outer circumstances. It gives him a new vision which reorients his desires.

In the *Apology*, Socrates says that nothing can harm a good man in this life or the next. Harm, in the essential sense, comes not from circumstances but—as Socrates says in the *Crito*—from a mutilation of one's inner self, a degradation of rational vision. Thereby, Socrates teaches that one is not to fear death but rather the chaos of desires when they are not controlled by us and are unhinged from their rational, natural structure. Hobbes, on the other hand, bases his politics on the fear of death, especially violent death. His political strategy is to organize human desires by playing one off against another, enlisting the most powerful one, fear of death, to socialize man. He does this by inventing contexts[5] which foster peace rather than war; but he connects virtue to circumstances rather than to excellence. Thus, where invention fails or is not available, brutality, deceit, and so on, become virtues (*Ci.*, I) if they help one to avoid death.

Hiero or Tyrannicus shows a different approach to desire. It discusses Hiero's unhappiness in the rather crass terms of the denial of pleaures. The Socratic posture is that as a tyrant, Hiero cannot be approached on any other level. The tyrant, despite his cleverness and great abilities, is so disoriented that he is at a distance from the best pleasures open to man. Simonides talks about food and sex—basic pleasures, indeed. The very advantages which the tyrant has in obtaining pleasures is a temptation to unnatural excess and refinement, so it is somewhat ironical that Hiero himself becomes a spokesman for moderation. That he must (and therefore assumptively, can) bring moderation, or the natural, to combat these temptations is the first step in reorganizing himself to be truly royal. The second step involves his longing for a kind of love and friendship that is not bought but freely given in terms of respect. This is a more refined pleasure than food and sex; however, it is excluded by the pleasure the tyrant has in his self-assertive power, for this surrounds him with sycophants. Indeed, he even fears the honest person—ironically, the only one whose love Hiero says he wants. The soul of the tyrant is chaotic. Hiero wants groveling. It is a mark of his hubristic power; but to get that, he must lose the honor of genuine respect. The desire to be respected for his own self rather than because of the other's fears and schemings cannot be fulfilled through Hiero's present behavior. Aristotle puts it like this: "The tyrant should win the notables through companionship and the multitude by flattery. For then, of necessity, his rule will be happier, because it will be over better men whose spirits are not crushed; over men to whom he himself is not the object of hatred, and of whom he is not afraid. His power, too, will be more lasting. His disposition will be virtuous, or at least half-virtuous: and he will not be wicked, but half-wicked only."[6]

In instructing Hiero in political moderation, Simonides asks him to act in an honorable manner to earn respect for himself. The political changes create for him as a person an opportunity to "return" to the more natural. Nature, as Plato points out in the *Republic,* is not, as in Hobbes, the total state of affairs in the world, but rather the rational organization of a concrete particular that exemplifies its excellence of form and purpose. If the compassionate philosopher-king is the most natural ruler, at least the honor-loving king goes in the right direction. Xenophon and Aristotle, both more conservative in their political proposals than Plato, emphasize the latter. Aristotle writes, "Whereas a tyrant has no regard or any public interest, except as conductive to his private ends, his aim being pleasure, the aim of a king is honor."[7]

Honor, which Simonides instructs Hiero to obtain, is a substantial movement toward the natural, but it cannot actually provide Hiero with what Simonides promises in the last words of the dialogue: "And if you do all these things, know well, that of all the things among you, you will acquire the noblest and most blessed possession; for being happy, you will not be envied."[8] (*T*, 20) Simonides' meaning is not clear, and perhaps it cannot be clearly put if it would deal therapeutically with a tyrant's psychology. Does Simonides think that engaging in politics, even when properly done, is most natural or excellent for man, and therefore provides man's highest possible happiness? Or does it provide a "decent" happiness, though not the highest possible one? Further, would political rule ever be unenvied? Plato's philosopher-kings may escape envy because they undergo great hardships and seeming deprivations for the sake of inferior men; while the latter see their rulers' hardships, they may not be able to appreciate their pleasures. But would Hiero, if he followed Simonides' advice, advance towards an "ordinary" and honorable citizen serving kingship? Perhaps Simonides is flattering Hiero or treating him as a child whose situation doesn't allow the full truth to be told. Socratics are fond of the politics of the lie, though they may be benevolent, paternalistic, "golden" lies. In any case, Simonides never advises Hiero to give up his mercenaries, which suggests that his situation will never be quite that of a king. Again Aristotle sharply makes the point: "The salvation of a tyranny is to make it more like the rule of a king. But one thing that the tyrant must carefully preserve: he must keep enough power to rule over his subjects, whether they like him or not, for if he once gives up his power he gives up his tyranny. But though power must be retained as the foundation, in all else the tyrant should act or appear to act in the character of a king."[9]

For Hobbes, as mentioned, a tyranny is a kingship misliked. But what does it mean for Hobbes to have one's sovereign liked? Perhaps very little, since he emphasizes that the sword is necessary for the king's authority. But then, like Xenophon, Aristotle, and Machiavelli, Hobbes does not think that appearances count for nothing; and also such "mental" relations as friendship, habitual obedience, and education are sources of power. At the heart of the matter is the fact that Hobbes has a different psychology from that of the Socratics. This goes beyond matters of significant details, and, in fact, it may to some extent explain them, i.e., Hobbes' emphasis on prosperity rather than friendship. In Hobbes' "science of politics" there is no place for Simonides' advice which, in Strauss' summary, is considered to be cruder than similar advice from Aristotle: "The correction of tyranny consists in nothing else than the transformation of the unjust or vicious tyrant who is more or less unhappy into a virtuous tyrant who is happy." (*T,* 70) Self-interest, with emphasis on preservation and prosperity, are chosen by Hobbes as fundamental, because he is interested in constructing a politics for men generally, one that would even be workable, as Kant put it, "for a race of intelligent devils."[10] Hobbes appreciates honor and friendship, but does not trust it as the basis of political rule. (It seems indicative of Hobbes' attitude that although he praises his dead friend Sidney Godolphin for honor and friendship, he actually dedicates the *Leviathan* to the living brother from whom he might still gain something.) And though there is a natural justice in the laws of nature, since men are partial to their own interest, it is only in the State that justice receives its certainty. Hobbes' sophistic principle is that not nature but rather artifice or convention provides the certain standard for political justice. Of course, in a complex way Hobbes does consider the artificial as an extension of the natural; but that basis is the asserted universal desires for preservation and prosperity. Those desires orient the other desires, assuming one is not mad. This brings Hobbes' understanding of moderation and his treatment of "being liked" into focus. Hiero is too childish. For the Socratics, this in a man is madness, whereas in a child it is simply diminished sanity. On one occasion in which he sounds uncharacteristically Socratic, Hobbes even speaks of the tyrant as "a child grown powerful."

Sanity, as a mature self-image, is the criterion for having the sovereign follow the laws of nature or equity. If, for Hobbes, the central purpose of rule is not that of being loved—Hiero's problem—but that of following the laws of nature, why does Hobbes not make the traditional distinction between a king and a tyrant on that basis? The tyrant would be childish and the honor-loving king mature, or much more mature; the incompetent or negligent ruler would also miss the mark. And if peace is proper to man's welfare, shouldn't Hobbes have distinguished between the royal disposition of peace and the tyrannical and childish one of war? This might have shown that one man was fit for proper rule and another not, instead of suggesting, as Hobbes stated position does, that the Socratic distinction is merely rhetorical. Of course, if Hobbes had made that his position, he would have had to take into account those psychological qualities which Plato discussed as leading to the various forms of the good or bad State. As it is, his attempt to have a science of politics confines itself to dealing with only those psychological characteristics which necessitate having a State at all. He seems to consider other psychological factors as matters to be dealt with by cunning and prudence and not by science, despite their material importance.

III.

In Diels-Kranz[11] can be found an aphoristic fragment from Alkaimon of Croton which reads as follows: "Men perish because they cannot join the beginning to the end." Whatever Alkaimon may have meant by this, the words can certainly apply to Kojeve's understanding of Hegel's wise man. Kojeve says of Hegel, "he was convinced of the circularity of his System."[12] (*I*, 291) This is the circularity that the "Gestalt des Geistes" (Pattern of Mind) presents at the end of history. As Koveje says, "Wisdom is not realized till Hegel at the end of history." (*ibid.*, 288) The Sage has this knowledge, and his own life expresses it. This is an absolute knowledge whose mark is that it can answer any question properly in terms of its System, which captures the concrete historical pattern in its mature completion. Kojeve says, "The real aspect of the circularity of Wisdom is the 'circular' existence of the Sage. In the absolute knowledge of the Sage each question has its proper answer; but it does not overreach the completeness of questions and answers which form the organization of the System. Likewise, in his existence, the Sage establishes his identity in himself and is complete in that identity, a completeness which is established because of a unification with others. And it is shut out in himself what is missing in the completeness of others in society." (*ibid.*) Thus Kojeve on Hegel—though it is not the place here to discuss whether this is the "true" Hegel.

Not Simonides, not Xenophon, not Socrates—not anyone else till Hegel is there really a wise man for Kojeve. Until Hegel, the answers men gave to political questions were not complete, and their own lives were fragmented in the respect that their relationships to other persons in the State were incomplete. Consequently, Kojeve calls Simonides an intellectual and a utopian: "a typical 'intellectual' who critizes the real world in which he lives from the standpoint of an 'ideal' constructed in the universe of discourse." (*T*, 145) His cleverness cannot—as no man's can—anticipate the maturity of History before the rational maturity of History has established itself concretely. Kojeve calls this "the totality of time beyond which no particular man could pass, nor could Man as such." (*ibid.*) Therefore the talk of Simonides is simply chatter; his ameliorative advice to Hiero does not touch Hiero's "current business." Indeed, Kojeve adds, "current business may take more years than belong to the tyrant himself. And who can say whether some of this business may not require centuries of effort to complete." (*ibid.*, 145) In other words, the appropriate discussion of politics comes with the completion of political forms. Then it is merely, as in Hegel's System, a description of how the mature present reality (or the "virtual reality" of the bourgeois State) was necessitated by less mature political forms, including tyranny. Kojeve says, "it can be assumed that history, at the opportune moment, will take it upon itself to put an end to the indefinite continuation of the 'philosophical discussion' of a problem that it [history] has virtually solved." (*ibid.*, 179)

Kojeve thereby challenges Strauss' belief in classical political wisdom. Strauss, in his original essay on Hobbes' *Dialogue*, had said, "I never believed that my mind was moving in a larger 'circle of ideas' than Xenophon's mind" (*T*, 25) This is a challenge by Kojeve to the Socratics about the importance of human nature for considering political action. For all the important differences between them—say, between Plato and

Aristotle—, the Socratics were united in believing that nature provides a *telos* toward excellence which, though it generally involves social conditions, is not bound by them. Becoming wise, especially for Plato, psychologically overcomes the limits of the State: the wise man indeed is an *idiota,* one who can live outside the State by his own natural discipline. Such a person overcomes the limits of time by not being essentially molded by circumstance. To use the metaphor Spinoza used for truth, he shines for himself and into the darkness. Strauss believes that Xenophon, and certainly Plato, can teach about the misformation of political things that occur in history, because a wise man, as fulfilling human nature, understands healthy or excellent politics. He does so because he understands healthy or excellent men.

Strauss' reply to Kojeve disputes the doctrine of historical determination leading to the Hegelian State, saying "its orientation leaves aside the particular differences between individual men." The Hegelian wise man, one recalls, is in and for the State in such a way that his own life is not separated from the others in the State. Consequently, his personal ability to answer all political questions is of minor importance. The organization of the State answers all questions in actuality, not in words; and the wise man, by his words, has no excellence aside from the State's homogenous and corporate reality. Against this, Strauss says, "But if the final state is to satisfy the deepest longings of the human soul, every human being must be capable of becoming wise. The most relevant differences among human beings must have practically disappeared. We understand now why Kojeve is so anxious to refute the classical view according to which only a minority of men are capable of the quest for wisdom. If the classics are right, only a few men would be truly happy in the universal and homogenous state, and hence only a few men will find their satisfaction in and through it." (*Restatement,* 225)

Hobbes is in somewhat of a middle position. Like the Socratics, his politics is based on human nature or psychology as permanent, though of course the important psychological structures are not considered by him in terms of excellence (and thereby favoring the intellectual elite or wise). But Hobbes is more like Hegel than the Socratics in emphasizing a science of politics. Its systematic character is not dependent on prudence or witty "quick insight." Indeed, Hobbes says, as Kojeve says of Hegel, that the wise man knows everything (cf. *Ci.*, "Dedication). The "system" of Hobbes is constructive, taking a basic assumption about human nature and showing its implications. This has a mathematical thrust, and it is perhaps not surprising that Hobbes says Plato, with his love of geometry, is the best of the ancient philosophers. Hegel, of course, favors Aristotle, for his system describes the rationality in historical forms; and he has the sensitivity of the biologist who cannot anticipate the living "program" of the organism. Further, Hobbes takes the commonwealth as the sharing of interests of individuals who authorized it by their natural will. The State represents them; it does not transform them, so their discreteness is assured. Hegel's homogenous State, on the other hand, subdues the individual or person and provides for the hegemony of social psychology over individual psychology. This integrates the individual mind into a corporate *Geist*. It thereby prepares the way for nationalism and disavows the boundaries of Hobbes' individual self-interest. The citizen of the Hegelian State has no real appeal when the State orders his punishment or sends him to war. When the Hobbesian State threatens a citizen with death, however, the citizen is put into a position resembling the state of nature vis-a-vis the State. Even the legitimacy of the State sending the citizen to war is a problem.

Hegel—or rather, Kojeve—finds the wisdom of Xenophon "precious" or "of a typical intellectual," because it assumes the solving of political problems by a wise man who, by being psychologically excellent, can transform the "business of history." For Hobbes, the objection is different. Though he can be sympathetic to Socratic dialectic as a form of instruction, he believes it does not offer an explanation of the essential nature of the State. That, Hobbes thinks, can only come by extrapolating from the asocial desires of Everyman. For Hobbes, therefore, Socratic dialogue offers some material or prudential insight, but not a scientific understanding of the form of commonwealth. The true form, he thinks, has different quantitative possibilities for governance, but unlike the Socratics, he thinks it has no different forms of excellence. Men make it themselves, and its purpose is not a matter of degree. It is the need of most, if not all, men to cooperate in guarding themselves against one another. This is the political oxymoron Hobbes explains.

AFTERWORD

Hobbes, Kant and Hegel as Political Theorists

Hobbes and Hegel are clearly good candidates for being the most influential political philosophers in the Western tradition in the modern period, that is, from the seventeenth century to our time. Locke, Hume and Marx are surely important, and it is clear that as direct purveyors of political ideas to large numbers of human beings they, along with Rousseau, are most influential. Yet, despite their own originality and stature as thinkers, leaving Rousseau aside, they are epigones. The fundamental political gestalt of Locke is found in Hobbes[1]; Marx is very influenced by Hegel, as he openly admitted. The classification of Rousseau is more difficult. That he was influenced by Hobbes and in turn greatly influenced Kant is well-known. Yet I find Kant, who is generally underrated as a political thinker, is not an epigone, because he considered political theory from the revolutionary intellectual standpoint for which he is famous. So I have chosen these three—Hobbes, Kant, and Hegel—as the paradigmatic thinkers of modern Western political thinking.

Yet, I am not interested in simply classifying, nor am I interested in discussing Hobbes, Kant, and Hegel merely because of their influence on others. Both of these interests necessarily have elements of the rhetorical and historical which intrude upon and obscure the centrality of the political problem that makes these paradigmatic thinkers philosophically seminal and illuminating. I recognize that what I call the central political problem also has such elements in it, but here the historical element is how the modern West defines the political-cultural struggle in its widest sense. I see this as the problem of the relation of the individual to the State. A second, but related, problem is the relation between States.

Since our thinkers are modern philosophers, and their breadth and richness is philosophical, they pursue the individual/State relation in terms of conception of nature and of human nature which has to be made convincing by arguments about how to investigate such topics. I have especially chosen these thinkers because their positions provide three distinct possibilities for the relation of the individual to the State. And when the view of Hobbes is juxtaposed with that of Kant and Hegel, it makes clearer his place within the political debate of modern Western political theory.

As I have mentioned, the depth and range of a philosophical discussion of politics is built on arguments of method which present the value of political life in the economy of human values. This, of course, must arise from a view of the capacity and character of human nature. This complexity tends to validate the normative nomenclature of the phrase "systematic theory" for the philosophical enterprise. At any rate, how a philosopher considers the concepts that make distinct his argument—concepts such as unity, completeness, and rationality—is intimately related to empirical considerations of his position. These together, the woof and warp of a position, must in a full estimate be considered. In a thorough study of Hobbes, Kant, and Hegel, much attention would properly be given to these.

It is not without difficulty to follow the theoretical threads between each philosopher's position on international relations and the individual/State relation, and it becomes even more complicated when Hegel, and to a lesser degree Kant, work with an individual/nation relation as well. This makes for alternate interpretations and detours within each theorist's broad pattern. Nevertheless, this connection between the internal and external relations of the State moves through all the important questions of political theory, from the necessity of the State for the individual's preservation to the question of whether the State provides not merely life but a valuable identity as well. This latter question involves both what an individual can be alone or for himself, what he can be within and by organizations composed of many men, and, indeed, how he stands to all men. Since the answers that our philosophers provide are grounded in their understanding of the limits of the State and of human nature, thereby they presume that narrower studies of political relations are about tactics, and that only a philosophy of man allows political strategy in the optimum sense.

Within the confines of this brief Afterword, it is not possible to adequately discuss the systematic theory of our three major philosophers, but I would like to suggest some contours and conclusions on the principle of clarity and distinctness. For clarity, I will present the philosophers' view of the relation of the individual to the State; for distinctness, to better see the implication of their views of the State, I will consider the State as an individual in relation to other States. Thus the State will be considered in itself and in its relation to other political entities, i.e., in both in its internal and external relations. So I turn to a short characterization of Hobbes, Kant, and Hegel on the individual/State relation and then to their views on international relations. Without a presumption of preference in the order, I would like to alter the chronological order and put Hegel after Hobbes, the better to show their opposition; then will come Kant, who, in a general way, holds a middle position.

(1) HOBBES: The State is composed of individuals whose interests, security and prosperity are in a general way very much furthered by the State, but, though circumstances are better, human nature is not transformed by civil society.
(1a) States are in a condition of nature or war with one another. This condition remains even when there is no armed struggle, and even when there are treaties and international laws—laws improperly so called in this anarchic condition, for these are merely instruments of the struggle for domination.

(2) HEGEL: The State, in its mature form, provides the individual with an essential or spiritual identity: he is absorbed and transformed in, for, and through the State. Human nature is only properly and clearly grounded in such a State.

(2a) Each State has a character or identity which guides its relations to other States, and this is expressed in a demand to be recognized: its honor. When no agreement is reached between States, war settles the matter of identity. Though this exposes the ethical to contingency in the short view, Providence or the "cunning of History" progressively orders the existence of various forms of State as "necessary moments in the Idea of the World Mind"; thereby, States have an organic relation to one another through rational historical development, despite the "butcherblock of History."

(3) KANT: The tension between being absorbed into the State and in maintaining one's individuality is a permanent condition of human nature as it exists at the present time. Consequently, an individual is forced by the struggle of one and the other aspect for dominance.

(3a) A League of Nations is possible to secure "perpetual peace." It would adjust disputes without war, encouraged in this especially by economic interdependence and the increasing financial burden of war. Man recognizes ethical universality, but self-interest impedes both individuals and nations from being ethical, creating a tension between the two. "Speculative history" assumes a final resolution of conflict and the concretizing of the ethical in social, including international, relations, even if this may well involve a change of human nature.

Many scholars consider Machiavelli the initiator of the modern political viewpoint, and they have especially noted how in *The Prince* he advises that all political behavior, including religious behavior, should be oriented toward getting and holding power. Hobbes is also conscious of the need to get and hold power, for he, like Machiavelli, never forgets that fear of harm, and especially of "violent death," is the strongest of natural motivations. Granted the untrustworthiness of men to honor their promises, this means that the State must have the power to compel obedience to its laws, despite the explicit or tacit promise of citizens to obey. Hobbes never ridicules religion or blasphemes, as does the author of *Madragola*, but by means of extensive biblical interpretation Hobbes neutralizes religious opposition to the State by making the sovereign the sole interpreter of doctrine and practice. The individual's relation to God is relegated to what Luther called "verborgene innerlichkeit." This private matter does not relate to the public sphere except under the most extraordinary, and therefore negligible, conditions—those that lead to martyrdom. Beyond this Machiavellian turn, Hobbes as philosophical methodologist has no place for God, or at least the God of traditional religion, despite passages that consider God as First Cause.

Though his readers have frequently questioned Hobbes' sincerity when he speaks of God, nevertheless Hobbes' treatment of God's felicity or perfect contentedness makes an important political point. By saying that God alone has felicity, he expresses the doctrine that desire is the basis of value and that the power to achieve one's desires is the measure of what is good. Therefore the world is good to God, for He desired it and made it, as the Biblical story goes. The pious statement that God can achieve felicity is important. It is somewhat neutralized by Hobbes' real skepticism about knowing God's desires, but it sharpens the point that man cannot achieve his own desires. This human powerlessness demands the condition of the State, which allows the most reasonable or calculable chance at self-preservation and prosperity: man's deepest desires. Unlike God, whose power is adequate to fulfill all His desires (at least according to pious belief or a pious piece of rhetoric), man must maturely and rationally give up some of his desires for the sake of his deepest desires. Yet even here, because he is limited in his ability to calculate, a human being can never be quite certain that circumstance will ensure achieving even those deepest desires: "experience teaches nothing with certainty."

I will now proceed rather schematically with Hobbes' rather utilitarian conception of the relation of the individual to the State. (a) The rhetorical parallel to God's ability and desire to order nature is man's own creation of the State which demands a "mortal god" to provides its laws. (b) Without a State, man, who is vain and gregarious, but not social, is in a condition of nature or war. (c) For there to be cooperation in a stable environment, it is necessary for the "mortal god," the sovereign, to have the material power to compel obedience to his will or civil laws through force or the fear of force. (d) Formally, the will of the sovereign is not questionable. It provides a certain measure for the State's social order, since such an artificial or stipulated measure was seen as necessary at the institution of the State to curb the anti-social acts resulting from the narrow self-orientation of many of the passions. Materially, however, any perception that the sovereign is negligent or mad raises the danger that he will be overthrown, despite the formal prohibition against revolution. Consequently, it is in the interest of the sovereign to attend to the prime directive of his election: the security of the citizens. The sovereign may still be in a state of nature and so legally uncompelled to oppose his own vanity and greed, but for pragmatic reasons he will oppose them, and therefore there will be a broad convergence of the interests of sovereign and subject.

The sum of these brief descriptive remarks is that Hobbes is committed to a naturalistic theory of politics, as opposed to transcendentally grounded ones. Power is centralized and the laws of the State have their decision principle vested in the sovereign. Since there is no independent source of value aside from desires, the will of the sovereign represents public desire. When Hobbes considers the relation of individual States, he finds their desires do not have a public dimension in relation to one another. The public dimension arises only to compel obedience in a particular State. It rationalizes private desires, and more or less adjusts them on the basis of interest. This interest, in turn, rests on the strongest desire of human nature—self-preservation—and on the somewhat less powerful desire for prosperity; together they bring men to the State. (The desire for prosperity is perhaps as strong in men as their vanity, but desires, even vanity, can under certain conditions be channelled for the sake of general welfare; the desire for prosperity is more reliable than vanity because its fulfillment is more obvious and finite.)

The principle of the institution of the State is the fundamentally equal vulnerability of men to harm. The artifice of the State creates inequalities of position and wealth in a condition which is the contrary of the condition of nature or war. The ground beneath this iron dialectic is still the sovereign, who is in a condition of nature and who, as the "font of all honours," reminds the citizen of the still-present untamed equality that generates his civil condition. But States are not equal. In the past generally, as today, large and powerful States may either incorporate weaker States outright or simply control them while allowing them some measure of independence. The equalizing power of atomic weapons, the technology of world economics and communication, and the global ecological danger that exist today, however, make the situation different from that of the seventeenth century; and it may be argued that today self-preservation (and also the prosperity of States) demands world government, on that equality suggested by the terrifying modern phrase "mutually assured destruction."

Hobbes' view of nature, at which he claims to have arrived by introspection and experience, is opposed by Kant's transcendental ethical viewpoint. Kant says that a race of intelligent devils could create Hobbes' State, that is, one based on interest. For Kant, circumstance or a hypothetical principle of interest is not all of what must be discussed in considering man. Kant finds a categorical structure—universal and absolute—in a rational being's ethical capacity, which he links to freedom and not to the causal physical order. In this way Kant accounts for something which experience and the introspective reflection on one's motives for acting—interest politics—do not account for. In linking the very essence of man to ethical transcendence, Kant offers values that are beyond desire and also beyond a State built on desire, i.e., the Hobbesian State. If an ethical state is possible (where ethical is taken in

Kant's proper sense of an internal principle, the acting of the good will out of a respect for ethical demands), then the implication seems to be that politics must have a transnational, cosmopolitan character. Circumstance, which is an important aspect of interest, no longer orients the behavior of States.

One sees that Kant's introduction of an *a priori* ethical character of man involves a new attempt at unity, completeness, and rationality. Kant seeks a systematic explanation of the political condition which introduces positive elements of fulfillment for the sort of person man claims to be or ought to be, rather than merely negative elements dealing with the individual's relative powerlessness to achieve his desires, a powerlessness which compels the creation of the State in Hobbes. Because Kant maintains this positive conception, he is faced with the problem of dealing with what I have called minimal or narrow interest, which is Hobbes' orientation. Kant admits that men generally act on interest; he even admits that because being ethical is to act from a disinterested respect for the universal maxims of the ethical, it may be that no man has ever been ethical in the strictest sense. Thus Kant is in the strange position of presenting a practical philosophy that is hardly practical in the ordinary sense of the word. It is not descriptive of facts, but contemplates an ideality—how man ought to act to reach what is his highest possible conception: an autonomous rational being.

Consequently there seems to be a theoretical derailment in Kant. Hobbes also had a "derailment." It was noticed by his very systematic contemporary, the philosopher Spinoza. In a letter to Jelles (*Epistle 50*), he responded to the question of what the difference was between Hobbes' political theory and his own. Spinoza replied that he, unlike Hobbes, never lost nature, never thought of the State as artificial. This is a very succinct way of pointing out the balancing act that Hobbes had to accomplish between the formal obligation, by contract, of the citizen to follow the will of the sovereign, and the material "natural causality" by which the citizen's own or natural will overthrows "negligent princes." If Hobbes is derailed by a formal condition (which, in fact is often ambiguated, and perhaps to a degree always ambiguated), Kant is derailed by an ideal opposed to the facticity of the world and made useless by it. Spinoza's comment that all philosophers before him were utopian—and we must assume he included his older contemporary Hobbes in this—is matched by Hegel's criticism of Kant as "abstract." The identity of Kant's citizen is schizophrenic. He is caught between what he ought to be and what he is. This is not too dissimilar from the ideality of Hobbes' State, which is built on what might be called "abstract" obligations, but in which circumstances sometimes occur which, despite promises, speak to present interests, and where sovereigns are sometimes mad and/or negligent.

Before elaborating Hegel's response to Kant, it is necessary to elaborate on Kant's own theory, with its struggle to resolve the fissure between the fact of interest in individual psychology and the ethical "ought" of his transcendental, anthropological psychology. First, Kant attempts to close the breach from the negative side, that is, from that of political action in concert with ethical demands, whether or not they are truly ethical in the sense of being done *from* an ethical motive. (Indeed, it can be assumed they are not done from an ethical motive, but rather from prudence). For measuring the justice of the acts of the sovereign, there are universal ethical grounds available to Kant; this is an advantage Hobbes lacks, since he accepts whatever the sovereign does as (formally) just. By the same token, for Kant there are formal or rational grounds to measure the behavior of nations in relation to one another, and thus there is a rational basis for international arbitration. And since an unjust State does not represent the ethical identity of its citizens as persons, there seems, as well, a formal ground for revolution. The formal constraints of Hobbes' theory, of course, allow for no such thing.

Yet Kant himself is quite cautious here. Though he says in *Perpetual Peace* (VIII.373 note) that political wisdom will not suppress a revolution "when it happens naturally," he argues that there is no natural law without positive law, that is, the civil law. This view of the efficacy of natural law as depending on the civil law is also characteristic of Hobbes' position. And, indeed, despite the universal character of ethical law and its measuring of the civil laws of the State from without, Kant, like Hobbes, fears that revolution is a falling back into the condition of nature (*ibid.,* 299) with all its chaos. But like Hobbes, Kant also accepts the fact (*qua* legitimacy) of a new government even if it has arisen from a revolution. Kant's respect for lawfulness brings him to measure the positive or civil law against its deepest ground in the ethical; but Kant is less consistent than Hobbes, just because he has the ethical option based on his universal anthropology. Kant's respect for law inclines him to accept whatever civil laws are in place, but this utility—with "moral sentiment"—is in tension with the rationality of absolute ethical knowledge.

Kant's suggestions for dealing with the schism between the fact of political life and the ethical ought which provides the dignity and freedom of man's rational vision of himself are ultimately prudential. His suggestion of a League of Nations is, after all, grounded in prudence; it is based on a patchwork of economic interest and national vanity. It is Kant's own "interest" proposal for man considered as he is, not as he ought to be. But there is also a second and more positive, if speculative, approach which exists in Kant's thinking, and this approach lies beyond merely prudential suggestions. Daringly, from the leverage of the "ought," he presents a view derived from what he calls "speculative history." Its basic assumption is that nature does nothing in vain. Since man's highest characteristic is the ethical, nature in the course of time works to achieve (to use Hobbes' phrase) *in foro externo* what man recognizes as a demand *in foro interno.* In fact the tension between man trying to achieve his own interests and the demand of civil law prefigures the tension between human nature as it is now and human nature as it must be for a truly ethical order. So Kant writes in *Idea for a Universal History from a Cosmopolitan Viewpoint:* "The means employed by nature to bring all its gifts to unfoldment is antagonism in society, provided that this too will turn into a cause of social order under law."[2] But, beyond this, the point of speculative history is not only to create a condition of law, but an intention to obey the ethical law from the recognition of its own quality. The mechanism nature uses for the latter, which Kant supposes may involve a change of human nature, is not known, whereas the more modest achievement of law-abiding citizens, though not necessarily an ethical one, provides some obscure clues for its achievement. These clues center on how conflict can be resolved within political unity, and are reflected in Kant's suggestions for a League of Nations.

The concreteness of his logic of the historical progress of the forms of political order is offered by Hegel as a conceptual remedy for the "abstractness" of Kant's theory. He argues (and I follow the Kojeve interpretation here) that the development of political maturity is finally achieved in the bourgeois State, where there is an essentially true and actual unity (or virtually true and actual unity) and identity of State and citizen. Of this mature political form Hegel writes: "The State is the actuality of the ethical Idea." (*Philosophy of Right*, 155) On this basis—that the citizen's identity is in and for the State—Hegel resolves the Hobbesian separation of a public and a private will and the Kantian antagonism between private interests and the social order. The inner will of the person is united to a concrete or historical State. The overcoming of the alienation of private will from the public or social will is tantamount to a change of human nature, though Hegel speaks of it more commonly as the fulfillment of human nature. Hegel therefore believes he has properly achieved Kant's intention to oppose Hobbes when Hobbes has the State be based not on grounds of an ethical identity but merely on the grounds of providing security and prosperity. Hegel writes:

> If the State is confused with civil society, and its specific is laid down as the security and protection of property and personal freedom, then interest as such becomes the ultimate end of association, and it follows that membership in the State is optional. But the State's relationship to the individual is quite different. Since the State is *Geist* objectified, it is only as one of its members that the

individual has objectivity, individuality, and ethical life. (*ibid.*, 156)

Hegel thinks he has described in the homogenous bourgeois State the realization of Rousseau's *volonte generale* with an inner vitality of ethical expression emphasized by Kant but not adequately argued by him. The outcome of the necessity, of struggle, which Kant noticed, results in freedom, but not a kind of Kantian freedom separated and estranged from natural necessity. Instead, the struggle is to consummate, in history, the perfecting of the idea of political order. The attractiveness of Hegel's theory is that it purports to have rationalized everything; nothing remains outside the System's vision, and there are no opposing principles that ultimately have not been unified. Yet a number of difficulties arise for international relations that seem to belie this. For one, nations at different stages of political maturity—that is, of a different ethical quality—make the ethics of international relations problematic.

Hegel, like Hobbes and Kant, believes that relations among States are grounded in a recognition of their particular sovereignty or autonomy. Like Kant, Hegel believes that States ought to honor their treaties on ethical grounds; but like Hobbes, he sees that disagreement leads to war when their particular wills cannot be harmonized. Hegel is not always consistent on this matter. He even writes, at one place, that "warfare is the highest law governing the relation of one State to another." (*ibid.*, 214) But if indeed States are on different levels of maturity, then is there not an inherent condition of conflict which persists just because of this? Further, can circumstances always favor the maturer State, even the maturest State? If not, war cannot be the highest law, unless war is the most rational interpreter of ethical quality. That sounds like badly understood Nietzsche (or perhaps the young Nietzsche); at any rate, no man ought to be fool enough to believe it.

The unavailability in Hegel of a temporally horizontal, concrete relation to the ethical—that is, to freedom, for men of different nations—seems a retreat from Kant's cosmopolitan intention. Obviously, Marx intends to mend this conceptual gap by providing a world communal concept to replace the bourgeois State; and such a concept is all the more plausible because of world technological unification, global environmental considerations, and the economic interdependence unique to our era. The rift in Hegel between men of different nations is an ethical alienation which can only be justified if one believes in the ethical value of war and colonization. Against Hegel, it may be argued that most, if not all, the reasons-of-state that oppose the welfare of individuals result from war and from the having of many individual States. But Hegel suffers other difficulties which his epigones inherit, even when (like Marx) they go beyond Hegel and propose world government to overcome the schism implied by Hegel when he said, "The welfare of the State has claims to recognition totally different from the welfare of the individual." (*ibid.*, 215) Apparently, Hegel does not ultimately see a need to separate success and justice. His "butcherblock of history"—that is, war and victory in war—provides the mark or standard for progress: "The history of the world is the world's court of judgment." (*ibid.*, 216) Hegel's theoretic assumption that that the laws of development cannot be anticipated and are only open to description after the fact—the owl of Minerva only flying at dusk—forces him to estimate success so highly. The danger of this principle is not only that it tempts special pleading to perceive in the historical carpet the figure one wants, or the one which justifies one's own nation; more substantially for theory, this principle, by itself, has nothing to offer for an argument based on the rationality of development. It therefore relates to another principle that Hegel offers with it: that the logic of the maturity of the (political) form explains each of its stages completely. But though some may disagree, it does not seem that either Hegel or Marx has described the political order without important matters having been left out. If revisions are continually necessary, their theories are primitive; and not only would they be partially wrong if revisions are necessary, but they would be essentially suspect. I think this is so. I believe we have not yet arrived at a political theory that is unified, complete, and rational.

But if a plausible political science is not yet ours—and perhaps will never be ours—is not Hobbes' institution of the State the most attractive, the most sensible of available proposals? It takes us away not only from ingenious supposition but, more important, from ideology. It offers the meat and potatoes of trying to achieve peace despite our imperfect humanity; it offers, as a minimum, concern for preservation and prosperity, and this is full of common sense. It takes into account the fact that most men, most of the time, are motivated by their own interests. But if there is someone better than most men, then such a person has the condition of peace, established on the basis of those interests, to show his own extraordinary virtues. I think, in the last consideration, it is better to have the Hobbesian canoe than the overrated Titanic, with a hole in its side, if one is heading through the turbulent white-water which tosses men together in the threshings of their desires. As Machiavelli put it, "Men commit the error of not knowing when to limit their hopes."

NOTES

Preface

1. Michael Frede, *Essays in Ancient Philosophy* (Oxford, 1982).
2. Martin A. Bertman, "The Rational Function in Aristotle," *The Thomist* (1973), 769-80.
3. For the use of the words "leviathan" and "behemoth" in the canonical Hebrew scriptures, see Samuel I. Mintz, "Leviathan as Metaphor," *Hobbes Studies*. II, (1989) 3-9.

Chapter One: "Body and Body in Motion"

1. Gary Herbert, *The Unity of Scientific Wisdom* (Vancouver: University of British Columbia Press, 1989), p. 44.
2. Thomas Spragens, *The Politics of Motion: The World of Thomas Hobbes*, (University of Kentucky Press, 1973), Ch. 4.
3. Jeffrey Barnouw, "Hobbes's Psychology of Thought," *History of European Ideas*, Vol. 10, 5 (1989) 519-45.
4. Jeffrey Barnouw, "The Importance of Purpose in Hobbes's Psychology," in *Thomas Hobbes: De la Metaphysique a la Politique*, eds. Bertman and Malherbe (Paris: Vrin, 1989) 47-62.
5. David Johnston, *The Rhetoric of Leviathan* (Princeton University Press, 1986).
6. Frithiof Brandt, *Thomas Hobbes' Mechanical Conception of Nature* (Copenhagen, 1927) p. 327.
7. Gary Herbert, *The Unity of Scientific and Moral Wisdom* (Vancouver: University of British Columbia Press, 1989) p. 34.
8. Martin A. Bertman, *Hobbes: The Natural and Artifacted Good* (Lang, 1981) Ch. VII.

Chapter Two: "The Order of the Sciences"

1. Alan Ryan, *The Philosophy of the Social Sciences* (London, 1970) pp. 102-3.
2. Noel Malcolm, "Hobbes's Science of Politics and his Theory of Politics," in *Hobbes Oggi,* eds. Willms and Alteri (Milano, 1990) pp. 145-57.

Chapter Three: "Nominalism and Protagorean Humanism," with Appendix "On Identity"

1. J.W.N. Watkins, *Hobbes's System of Ideas* (London, 1965).
2. John Herman Randall, Jr., "The School of Padua," *Journal of the History of Ideas,* I (1940) 196.
3. George Berkeley, "Introduction," *Treatise Concerning the Principles of Human Knowledge,* sec. 12.
4. Brandt, *op. cit.,* p. 233 ff.
5. Ernst Cassirer, *The Philosophy of Symbolic Forms,* Vol. I, trans. R. Manheim (New Haven: Yale University Press, 1953) p. 134.
6. Martin A. Bertman, "Regulative and Constitutive Rules in Hobbes," in Van der Bend, *Hobbes* (Amsterdam: Rodolpi, 1981) 3-11.
7. Keith Donnellan, "Reference and Definite Descriptions," *Philosophical Review,* LXXV (1966) 281-304.
8. John Locke, *An Essay Concerning Human Understanding,* Vol. II, ed. Fraser (New York: Dover, 1959).
9. Bertrand Russell, *Logic and Knowledge,* ed. Marsh (London, 1956).
10. Saul Kripke, "Identity and Necessity," in *Identity and Individuation,* eds. Kiefer and Munitz (New York: NYU Press, 1971).
11. Hilary Putnam, "Is Semantics Possible?" in *Language, Belief and Metaphysics,* eds. Kiefer and Munitz (New York: NYU Press, 1970).
12. Baruch Spinoza, *Works,* Vol. I, ed. Elewes (New York: Dover, 1955).
13. Martin A. Bertman, "The Is-Ought Problem in Hobbes," in Walton and Johnson, eds., *Hobbes's Science of Natural Justice* (Hague, 1987) 99-109.
14. Ludwig Wittgenstein, *Philosophical Investigations,* I, 380.
15. Anthony Kenney, "Cartesian Privacy," in *Wittgenstein,* ed. Pitcher (Garden City, 1966).
16. Roderick Chisholm, *"Agency,"* in *Person and Object,* (La Salle, 1976), Ch. 2.
17. Michael Frede, *Essays in Ancient Philosophy,* p. 134.

Chapter Four: "Heidegger on Hobbes' Nominalism"

1. The edition of Hungerland and Vick is preferable to the Molesworth for *Computatio sive logica*. Under that title it is published by Arabis, New York, 1981.
2. All the quotes from Heidegger are provided simply by page number to the English translation of *Die Grundprobleme der Phaenomenologie*, that is, *The Basic Problems of Philosophy*, trans. A. Hofstader (Indiana University Press, 1985).
3. See William Sacksteder, "Hobbes: The Art of the Geometricians," in *Journal of the History of Philosophy*, 18 (1980) pp. 131-147; "Hobbes' *Logistica,*" in *Philosophy Research Archive*, 1982.
4. See Arrigo Pacchi, *Convenzione e Ipotesi, nella formazione della filosofia naturale di Hobbes* (Firenze, 1965); also, Michel Malherbe, "Hobbes et la Fondation de la Philosophie premiere," in *Thomas Hobbes: De la Metaphysique a la Politique*, M.A. Bertman and M. Malherbe, eds. (Paris: Vrin, 1987) pp. 17-32.
5. See Yves-Charles Zarka, *La Decision Metaphysique de Hobbes: Conditions a la Politique* (Paris: PUF, 1987), pp. 255ff.
6. Cf. "For the nature of good and evil follows from the nature of circumstance." *De Homine*, XI, 4.
7. Cf. "But when we reason in words of general signification and fall upon a general inference which is false, though it is commonly called error, it is indeed an ABSURDITY, or senseless speech. For error is but deception, in presuming that something is past, or to come; of which though it were not past or to come, yet there be no impossibility discoverable. But when we make a general assertion, unless it be a true one, the possibility of it is inconceivable." (*Lev.*, pp. 112-3).
8. *Descartes*, Vol. II, eds. Haldane and Ross, (New York: Dover, 1955) pp. 60-78.
9. See Martin A. Bertman, "Kierkegaard: How a Clever Theologian Finds Unhappiness," *Sophia* (1988) 31-41.
10. Jean Berhardt, ed., *Short Tract* (Paris: PUF, 1988) p. 14.
11. Cf. *De Cive*, XVIII, 4; *O.L.*, I, 419; *Lev.*, p. 218.

Chapter Five: "Action and Reference"

1. Machamer and Sakellariadis, "The Unity of Hobbes's Philosophy," in *Hobbes: War Among Nations*, T. Airaksinen and M.A. Bertman, eds. (London: Augsbury, 1989) Ch. 2.
2. Hobbes says: "I believe those that worship no other God but the one they understand are not Christians and that those who think they can demonstrate any attribute of God, something they do not understand, are not Philosophers." *Anti-White*, Ch. 27, p. 326.
3. Of all the medievals, Maimonides is the boldest in asserting the *via negativa*. God's unity precludes that He has any attributes separate from His existence, including relations, e.g., His covenant with His people Israel: "There is no difference whether various attributes refer to His actions or to relations between Him and His works, in fact, these relations exist only through the thoughts of men." *Guide for the Perplexed*, Ch. LIII.
4. Cf. *Anti-White*, Ch. 27, *passim*.

Chapter Six: "Causality and Inner Design Metaphysics"

1. Georg Henrik von Wright, *Explanation and Understanding*, (Ithaca: Cornell University Press, 1954).
2. Gilbert Ryle, *The Concept of Mind*, (London, 1949) 63-4.
3. Martin A. Bertman, "Plato and Hegel on Wisdom," *Idealistic Studies*, (1988) 170-179.

Chapter Seven: "Unsociable Man and His Virtues"

1. Martin A. Bertman, "The Thrasymachus," *Manuscrito* (1988) pp. 1-28.
2. Martin A. Bertman, "Pleasure and the Two Happinesses in Aristotle," *Apeiron*, (1972) 30-36.
3. Cf. *N.E.*, 1094b12ff.; *N.E.*, 1142a12ff.
4. Martin A. Bertman, "Hobbes and Aristotle," *Review of Politics* (1976) 534-44.
5. Cf. *Politics*, 1254b15ff.
6. Cf. *Politics*, 1289a13ff.

7. Cf. *Rhetoric*, 1368a7-10.
8. Cf. *Politics*, 1288b25-40.
9. Cf. *Physics*, 199a9-19.
10. Cf. *Post. An.*, 73b27ff.
11. Cf. *Meta.*, 1031b18-22.
12. Cf. Martin A. Bertman, "Plato on Tyranny, Philosophy, and Pleasure," *Apeiron* (1986) 119-131.
13. Cf. *Politics*, 1253a29-30.
14. Cf. *De Caelo*, 311a15.
15. Cf. *Physics*, 198b1-9; 199b32-33.
16. Cf. *Politics*, 1280a32-34.
17. Martin A. Bertman, "Hobbes on Performatives," *Criteria* (1978) 42-53.
18. *Politics*, II, 12; VII, 4.
19. Cf. *Politics*, 1252b27-30; 1254b34-1253a1; 1253a26-29.
20. Leo Strauss, *The Political Philosophy of Hobbes* (Chicago, 1936).
21. Manfred Reidel, "Kausalitaet u. Finalitaet bei Hobbes' Naturphilosophie," *Kant Studien*, 60 (1969) 425.
22. Peters and Tajfel, "Hobbes and Hull: Metaphysicians of Behaviour," *Journal of the Philosophy of Science*, 8, (1957-8) 152.
23. Cf. *Politics*, 1253a1-2.
24. By emphasizing the internal force of essential causality in Aristotle, some scholars, eg.g., David Keyt, "Three Fundamental Theorems in Aristotle's *Politics*," *Phronesis* 32 (1987) 54-79, have seen the *zoon politikon* doctrine as a muddle. Cf. the wide and narrow uses of it: *Politics*, 1253a1-4, 7-8; 1278b17-21; *N.E.*, 1097b8-11, 1162a17-19; 1169b17ff.; *E.E.*, 1242a22-27; *H.A.*, 487b33-488a14. It is also to be noted that Althusius in *Politica Methodice Digesta* (1603) preceded Hobbes in disputing the *zoon politikon* doctrine.
25. Cf. *Post. An.*, 86a4ff.
26. Cf. *De Anima*, 432b21; *Politics*, 1253a29-35.
27. Arrigo Pacchi, "Hobbes and the Passions," *Topoi* (1987) 111-19.
28. See Martin A. Bertman, "Socrates and Civil Disobedience," *Studium Generale*, (1972).
29. Cf. *Politics*, 1259a14.
30. Cf. *H.A.* 488a7-10; *Politics*, 1152a7-18. Aristotle distinguishes political animals from merely gregarious ones on the basis of work (*to ergon*): "Those of which work become one common thing." In the *Politics*, that men are more political animals than a bee is mentioned.
31. Cf. *Politics*, 1252a24-32.
32. For Aristotle, that which exists by nature cannot be the artifact of reason alone without the impulse to fulfill a natural capacity. *Meta.*, 1032a12; 1065b3-4; 1070s6-9; *N.E.*, 1112a31-33; 1140a14-16; *Rhet.*, 1359a30-32; *Politics*, 1333a22-3; *Physics*, 198a9-10.
33. Cf. *Politics*, 1253a19ff.
34. Cf. *Politics*, 1252b30-31.

Chapter Eight: "Equity as Justice and Charity"

1. Martin A. Bertman, "A Defense of Legal Positivism,' *J. of Value Inquiry* (1983), 219-26.

Chapter Nine: "The Character and Use of Civil Law"

1. H.L.A. Hart, *The Concept of Law* (Oxford: Clarendon Press, 1961).
2. Enid Campbell, "Thomas Hobbes and the Common Law," *Tasmanian Law Review* (1958) 20-45. Also, Paulette Carrive, "Hobbes et les juristes de la Common Law," in *Thomas Hobbes: De la Metaphysique a la Politique*, eds. Martin A. Bertman and Michel Malherbe (Paris: Vrin, 1989) 149-173.
3. Edward Coke, *Justice Vindicated* (London, 1660).
4. Matthew Hale, "Reflections on Mr. Hobbes in his Dialogue on the Law," in *History of English Law*, Vol. V (London: Methuen, 1922-66).
5. Hans Kelsen, *General Theory of Law and the State*, (New York, 1961) p. 45.
6. The point is perhaps made most strongly in *De Homine*, where Hobbes says, "Whence it is to be understood that they, who consider men by themselves as though they existed outside civil society can have no moral science, because they lack any certain standard against which virtue and vice can be judged and defined." (XIII, 8) Hobbes does not say that one cannot have some standard in the state of nature, but that one cannot there have a certain standard.
7. To put the same matter slightly differently, for Hobbes "the condition of war remains contrary to the law of nature" (*Lev.*, XV, 214)... "For it can never be that war shall preserve life, and peace destroy it" (*ibid.*, 215). The commutative justice or fair value of the contract, which creates a State by transfer of one's liberty to the sovereign, though he is not party to the contract, involves giving the sovereign the power of distributive justice or equity. Since Hobbes assumes the inevitable partiality of each man, it is only by having a sovereign that war is averted.
7. Consequently, it is a logical impossibility to question the rulings of the sovereign, since having his rule or laws is the necessary condition for entering the condition of peace. This is captured in the seventeenth law of nature: "And seeing every man is presumed to do all things in order to his own benefit, no man is fit arbitrator in his own cause: and if he were never so fit; yet equity allowing to each party equal benefit. if one:

be admitted to be judge, the other is to be admitted also; and so the controversy, that is, the cause of war, remains, against the law of nature" (*ibid.*, 213).

8. "Now all of the duties of Rulers are contained in this one sentence: The safety of the people is the supreme law: for although they who among men obtain the chiefest dominion, cannot be subject to the laws properly, that is to say to the will of men, because to be chief, and subject, are contradictories; yet it is their duty in all things, as much as is possible they can, to yield obedience unto right reason, which is the natural, moral and divine law: But because dominions were constituted for peace's sake, and peace was sought for safety's sake, he, who being placed in authority, shall use his power otherwise than for the safety of the people, will act against the reasons of peace, that is to say, against the laws of nature." (*De Cive*, XIII, 258).

9. Martin Kriele, "Zwei Konzeptionen des modernen Staates: Hobbes und die Englische Juristen," *Studium Generale* (1969) 839-48.

10. Simone Goyard-Fabre, *Le Droit et la Loi dans la philosophie de Hobbes* (Paris: Klincksieck, 1975).

11. Kelsen, *op. cit.*, p. 181.

12. See G.P. Baker, "Defeasibility and Meaning," in *Law, Morality and Society: Essays in Honour of H.L.A. Hart*, Hacker and Raz, eds. (Oxford: Clarendon Press, 1977) p. 28.

13. John Bowles, *Hobbes and his Critics: A Study in Seventeenth-Century Constitutionalism* (London, 1951).

Chapter Ten: "Hobbes and Xenophon's Tyrannicus"

1. Hobbes' friend during his old age, Aubrey, wrote that Hobbes always kept a book by Xenophon on his reading table.
2. See *Diels-Kranz*, 21. Cf. *N.E.*, 1121a7; *Rhet.*, 1391a8.
3. *Protagoras*, 339b ff.
4. The argument from introspection is weak. Hobbes himself admits that introspection is extremely difficult. It assumes a universal psychological structure which is the basis of the rhetorical point against an elitist and utopian politics.
5. My phrase "inventing contexts" may be somewhat misleading. More precisely, on presenting a *science* of politics, Hobbes describes the condition of nature as one of war, and he contrasts this with civil society, the condition of peace, where the sovereign invents laws which create the conditions ensuring protection and prosperity. Laws here include the edicts that muster resources for the creation of useful civic institutions

and structures, e.g., bridges.
6. *Politics*, 1315a40 ff.
7. *Politics*, 1311a4.
8. The abbreviation "T" is followed by a page number and refers to Xenophon's *On Tyranny* (containing Xenophon's dialogue, Leo Strauss' commentary on the dialogue, Kojeve's essay "Tyranny and Wisdom" and Strauss' response to Kojeve, the "Restatement." All are in English.) Ithaca: Cornell University Press, 1963. Also, I suggest a reading of Strauss' *Xenophon's Socratic Discourse* (Ithaca: Cornell University Press, 1970).
9. *Politics*, 1314a34 ff.
10. Kant, "Uber den gemeinspruch: Das mag in der theorie Richtig sein, taucht aber nicht fur die Praxis," II.
11. Diels-Kranz, "Alkaimon of Croton," 2.
12. The "I" is followed by a page number and refers to *Introduction a la lecture de Hegel* (Paris: Gallimard, 1947). I recommend also Kojeve's *Essai d'une histoire de la Philosophie paienne* (Paris: Gallimard, 1968). The Kojeve essay in the Strauss' *On Tyranny* is "Tyrannie et Sagesse" (Paris: Gallimard, 1954).

Afterword: "Hobbes, Kant and Hegel as Political Theorists"

1. Lewis White Beck, *Early German Philosophy* (Harvard University Press, 1969), p. 243: "Most of the ideas thought characteristic of the 'Age of Locke and Newton' can be found as far back as Hobbes and even Bacon."
2. "Idea for a Universal History from a Cosmopolitan Point of View," in *Kant on History*, ed. and trans. L.W. Beck (Bobbs-Merrill, 1963), p. 12.

INDEX OF PROPER NAMES

Adam 86
Alexander the Great 68, 170
Alkaimon of Croton 192
Anselm 38, 63
Aquinas, St. Thomas 79, 81
Archimedes 164
Aristotle 4, 7, 11, 13, 24-25, 35,
   37, 48, 66 79, 99-100, 113-114,
   117-125, 127, 130, 133, 137,
   139-142, 166, 172, 177, 183,
   189-190, 194-195
Aubrey 174

Bacon, Francis 55, 175
Barnouw, Jeffrey 11-12, 14
Bergson, Henri 80
Berkeley, George 30-31
Borgia, Cesare 114
Bramhall, Bishop 12, 75, 77, 84,
   94, 96, 105, 108, 168
Brandt, Frithiof 5, 14-15, 31

Cain 139
Carnap, Rudolf 39
Cassirer, Ernst 32
Cato the Roman 120
Cephalus 186
Chisholm, Roderick 44
Chomsky, Noam 41
Cicero 166
Coke, Edward 170, 175-177
Crooke (publisher) 174
Cropsey, Joseph 174-175

Derrida, Jacques 48
Descartes, Rene 3-6, 8, 14, 38, 41-42, 49, 60-64, 71, 82, 103, 133, 169
Diels-Kranz 192
Donnellan, Keith 37

Einstein, Albert 40
Epicurus 48, 101
Euclid 99, 175

Frede, Michael 46

Galileo 8, 22, 99, 100, 119, 175
Glaucon 136, 158
Godolphin, Sidney 136, 191
Guanilo 63
Gyges 136, 142, 158

Hale, Matthew 170, 175
Hart, H.L.A. 166, 179
Hegel, G.W.F. 99-101, 107-108, 139, 184, 192-195, 197-200, 205, 207-209
Heidegger, Martin 47-54, 56-57, 62, 64-72, 126
Herbert, Gary 10, 14-15
Hiero 136, 186, 188-191, 193
Hobbes, Thomas
  on action and reference, 73-97; on body and body in motion, 3-16; on causality and inner design metaphysics, 99-110; on character and use of civil law, 163-181; on equity as justice and charity, 145-162; on identity, 43-46; his nominalism and Heidegger, 47-72, and Protagorean humanism, 27-43; on the order of the sciences, 17-25; his political theory compared with that of Kant and Hegel, 197-210, and Xenophon, 183-196; on unsociable man and his virtues, 113-143.
Hume, David 197

Husserl, Edmund 66
James I, King 170
Jelles 204
Job 82, 108, 156, 157
Kant, Immanuel 4, 5, 7, 10, 44, 81-82, 97, 100, 106, 116, 159, 191, 197-200, 203-208
Kelsen, Hans 160, 171
Kenney, Anthony 42
Kierkegaard, Soren 66
Kojeve, Alexander 184, 192-195, 207
Kripke, Saul 39
Kristeller, P.O. 49

La Mettrie 5
Leibniz, Gottfried 14, 32, 47
Locke, John 7, 37, 159, 197
Luther, Martin 48, 201

Machamer 73-74
Machiavelli, Niccolo 114-115, 120, 190, 200-201, 210
Malcolm, Noel 23-24
Marx, Karl 197, 209
Mersenne 3
Milton, John 86
Moliere 36, 39

Newton, Sir Isaac 40
Nietzsche, Friedrich 208

Ockham, William of 5, 48

Parmenides 9, 68
Peters 129
Plato 5, 14, 24, 29, 32, 37, 40, 41, 48-49, 54, 60, 63-66, 100, 102-103, 106, 108, 113-125, 127, 133-134, 136, 139, 141, 158, 164, 166, 168, 175, 183, 184, 186, 189-190, 192-195
Plotinus 48, 100-105, 107, 109-110, 114, 116
Protagoras 5, 28, 41, 42, 48, 49, 55, 116

Putnam, Hilary 39

Reidel, Manfred 129
Rousseau, Jean-Jacques 180, 197, 208
Russell, Bertrand 38, 39
Ryan, Alan 23, 24
Ryle, Gilbert 103

Sacksteder, William 53
Sakellariadis 73, 74
Scott, Sir Walter 36, 38
Simonides 136, 186, 187-191, 193
Socrates 38, 63, 71, 102, 108, 115, 116, 136, 158, 175, 183, 184, 186-188, 190-196
Spinoza, Baruch 40, 80, 83, 194, 204, 205
Spragens, Thomas 11, 14
Stoics, The 46, 136
Strauss, Leo 48, 127, 184, 191, 193, 194

Tajfel 129
Tarski 39
Theseus 45
Thrasymachus 115, 143
Thucydides 163

Warrender 166
Watkins, J.W.N. 14, 20, 29, 32
Wittgenstein, Ludwig 4, 42
Wright, George Hendrik von 99

Xenophon 183, 184, 186, 189, 190, 193-195

Zeno 9